M000289558

THE BURIED
SPITFIRES
OF BURMA

THE BURIED SPITFIRES OF BURMA
A 'FAKE' HISTORY

ANDY BROCKMAN AND TRACY SPAIGHT

First published 2020

The History Press
97 St George's Place, Cheltenham,
Gloucestershire, GL50 3QB
www.thehistorypress.co.uk

British Library Cataloguing in Publication Data.
A catalogue record for this book is available from the British Library.

ISBN 978 0 7509 9385 2

Typesetting and origination by The History Press
Printed and bound in Great Britain by TJ International Ltd.

CONTENTS

A Note About Facts   7

Dramatis Personae   8

Foreword by Al Murray   13

Foreword by Sir Tony Robinson   15

The Fact   17

Part One: The Legend   19

Part Two: CSI Yangon   173

Part Three: Burmese Daze   201

Part Four: A Finding of Fact   251

Part Five: Fake History   303

The Ground Truth   314

Afterword   316

Bibliography   322

Index   332

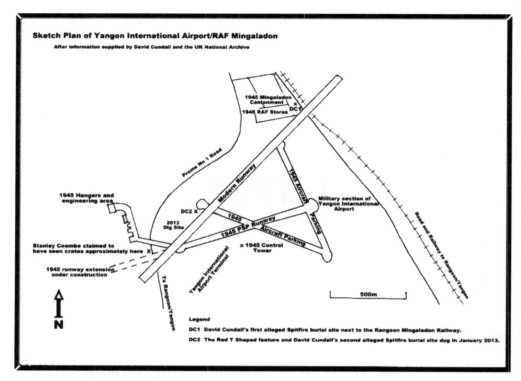

Sketch Plan of Yangon International Airport/RAF Mingaladon

After information supplied by David Cundall and the UK National Archive

1945 Mingaladon Cantonment

1945 RAF Stores

DC1

Prome No 1 Road

Modern Runway

1945 Aircraft Parking

1945 Hangers and engineering area

DC2 X

2013 Dig Site

1945 PSP Runway

1945 Aircraft Parking

Military section of Yangon International Airport

Road and Railway to Rangoon/Yangon

Stanley Coombe claimed to have seen crates approximately here X

x 1945 Control Tower

1945 runway extension under construction

Yangon International Airport Terminal

To Rangoon/Yangon

500m

N

Legend

DC1 David Cundall's first alleged Spitfire burial site next to the Rangoon Mingaladon Railway.

DC2 The Red T Shaped feature and David Cundall's second alleged Spitfire burial site dug in January 2013.

Pilots of 607 Squadron walk to their aircraft on RAF Mingaladon during the monsoon season of 1945. (© IWM)

A NOTE ABOUT FACTS

The Spitfire fighter, designed by aeronautical genius R.J. Mitchell, which first flew on 5 March 1936, is a real aircraft and an international icon.

South East Asia Command and Force 136 of the British Special Operations Executive were real military formations active in the Far East during the Second World War.

Lord Louis Mountbatten, Sir Keith Park, General Aung San and Private Stanley Coombe are real people and held the ranks and positions described in Burma in 1945 and 1946.

Operation Zipper was the planned invasion of Malaya by a multi-national task force spearheaded by the Royal Air Force. Following the dropping of the atomic bombs on Hiroshima and Nagasaki in early August 1945 the operation was scaled down and finally took place under the code name Operation Tiderace.

At the end of the Second World War hundreds of aircraft were declared surplus to requirements in the Far East and were disposed of by the Royal Air Force.

Wargaming.net is a real international computer games company and David Cundall is a real potato farmer from Lincolnshire on the North Sea coast of England.

David Cameron became British Prime Minister in May 2010 and discussed the recovery of buried Spitfires with Myanmar's President Thein Sein during an official visit in April 2012.

All the descriptions of people, events, airfields, aircraft, buildings, documents and interviews contained in the story of the buried Spitfires of Burma are accurate …

… except for those which are not.

DRAMATIS PERSONAE

General Aung San: Founding father of the modern Burmese Army and nation, father of Daw Aung San Suu Kyi.

Aung San Suu Kyi: Leader of the National League for Democracy and Nobel Peace Prize Laureate.

Peter Arnold: Spitfire expert, self-styled 'independent reporter' for the Key Publications Historic Aviation Forum and outspoken supporter of David Cundall.

Dr Adam Booth: British geophysicist working at Yangon in 2004 and 2013.

Anna Bowers: Room 608 Productions, Producer Burma Spitfires documentary film.

Andy Brockman: British archaeologist and historical researcher, lead archaeologist for the 2013 Burma Spitfires project.

Steve Boultbee Brooks: British multi-millionaire property developer, Spitfire enthusiast and, according to Fox News, 'A British version of Donald Trump'.

Martin Brown: British field archaeologist, fieldwork director at Yangon in 2013.

Major Roger Browning RE Rtd: Served at Mingaladon with 657 Mechanical Equipment Company, Indian Engineers, in autumn 1945.

David Cameron: British Prime Minister elected in 2010 and argued by some to be Britain's second worst holder of that office of modern times (at the time of writing).

CBs: United States Army Construction Battalions (phonetically identical to, but not to be confused with, the US Navy Seabees; see Seabees).

Dr Roger Clark: British geophysicist and aviation enthusiast working at Yangon in 2013.

Stanley Coombe: Private, 9th Battalion, Royal Sussex Regiment, later the Berkshire Regiment, served in Burma twice between 1944–47.

Sebastian Cox: First civilian to head the RAF Air Historical Branch, the RAF's in house historians who advise the RAF, the UK Government and the public.

David Cundall: Lincolnshire farmer and Spitfire enthusiast, originator and leader of the Burma Spitfires project.

Fergus Eckersley: British diplomat, Second Secretary, British Embassy Yangon, 2012–13.

Mr W.C. England: Pioneering British aviator and the first man known to have exported an aircraft to Rangoon in a crate.

Flying Tigers: Popular name for the American Volunteer Group (AVG) serving with Chinese forces 1941–42.

The Flying Tigers (1942) and ***The Fighting Seabees*** (1944): popular Hollywood flag wavers starring John Wayne. The plot of neither film involved burying Spitfires.

Michael Hatcher: British-born, Australian-based salvage diver and treasure hunter, worked with David Cundall at Yangon in 2004.

Mathew Hedges: Deputy British Ambassador to Myanmar during the Burma Spitfires expedition.

Lt Thomas Barclay Hennell RNVR: British watercolourist and war artist, killed in Java in November 1945 shortly after completing a series of paintings in Rangoon and on RAF Mingaladon.

Andrew Heyn: British diplomat, Her Majesty's Ambassador to Burma, 2009–13.

Meghan Horvath: Researcher, Room 608 Productions.

Htoo Htoo Zaw: Managing Director Shwe Taung Por group of companies.

Isabel Hunt: Head of Communications, University of Leeds, formerly of the British Home Office.

Walter Henrik Juvelius: Finnish poet, librarian, mystic and interpreter of alleged secret manuscripts, who claimed to have discovered the burial place of King Solomon in Jerusalem.

Fergal Keane: Award-winning BBC journalist and historian of the Second World War in Burma.

Karen: (aka Kayin, Kariang or Yang) A hill people from the east of Myanamar and the Union of Myanmar's third largest ethnic population. Allies of the British during World War two, but left in Limbo after independence, the Karen National Union has engaged in a struggle for independence against the Burman dominated central government since 1949.

Brigadier-General Khin Nyunt: Formerly Intelligence Chief, Prime Minister of Myanmar in 2004 until he was deposed and arrested.

Lieutenant General Ko Ko: Myanmar Home Affairs Minister in 2013, former head of Southern Command.

Victor Kyslyi: Founder and CEO Wargaming.net.

Gavin Longhurst: Senior executive with Wargaming.net and project photographer.

Adam Lusher: British journalist covering the Burma Spitfires project for *The Sunday Telegraph*.

Manny Machado: Civil engineer and excavator operator, Yangon Airport dig site 2013.

Mark Mannucci: Room 608 Productions, award-winning director of the documentary *Buried in Burma*, telling the story of the 2013 Burma Spitfires Project.

Andy Merritt: University of Leeds PhD student geophysicist, Yangon Airport 2013.

RAF Mingaladon (aka Mingladon): Principal Royal Air Force base in Burma, now Yangon International Airport.

Lord Louis Mountbatten (1st Earl Mountbatten of Burma): Member of the British Royal Family, Supreme Allied Commander South East Asia Command (SEAC) 1943–46.

Nay Pyi Taw (City of the Kings): Made capital of Union of Myanmar by the military government in November 2005 as an unwitting tribute to Shelly's poem 'Ozymandias'.

Frazer Nash: Public relations manager for Wargaming.net and the Burma Spitfires project 2012–13 and not a bit like the spin doctors in *Veep* and *The Thick of It*.

Ne Win: Soldier and Head of State in Burma 1962–81, placed under house arrest 2002.

George Orwell (real name Eric Blair): Author of *Burmese Days*, a novel inspired by his service in the Burma Police 1922–27. Afterwards a journalist and novelist who wrote the manual on fake history and fake news in the form of his classic distopian novel *1984*.

Sir Keith Park: Allied Air Force Commander, South East Asia Command 1945–46.

Captain Montagu Brownlow Parker: British war hero and treasure hunter who led the expedition to Temple Mount in Jerusalem based on the evidence of Walter Juvelius.

Jim Pearce: Retired British crop duster pilot and, in the historic warbirds community, a legendary finder, importer and dealer in historic aircraft.

Poe Poe: Buddhist monk associated with the family of Htoo Htoo Zaw.

Andy Saunders: British aviation historian and, in 2013, editor of *Britain at War* magazine.

Rod Scott: Field archaeologist, explosive ordnance disposal officer and historic ammunition specialist, Burma Spitfires project, working at Yangon in 2013.

South East Asia Command (SEAC): the Allied command overseeing the reconquest of Southeast Asia, including Burma, from the Japanese during the Second World War.

Seabees: United State Navy Construction Battalions (phonetically identical to, but not to be confused with, the US Army CBs).

Sergeant Birtles: Trusted side kick to Sir Charles Warren in Jerusalem. The kind of Victorian non-commissioned officers who were the backbone of the British Army, who built the British Empire, and whose experience often bailed out their officers.

Group Captain Maurice Short MBE AFC: RAF engineer and pilot who served at RAF Mingaladon in the Autumn of 1945 and who later heard stories of buried spitfires.

Shwe Taung Por (STP): David Cundall's Burmese business partner for the 2013 excavations.

Shwe Win: Former political prisoner; local translator/fixer in Yangon for Room 608/Wargaming during 2012–13.

State Peace and Development Council (SPDC): The official name of the oppressive Burmese Military Government 1997–2011 and an unintended tribute to George Orwell's 'newspeak'.

Swan Aah Shin: In English 'strong and capable person'; a shadowy organisation of street thugs and ex-prisoners employed by the Burmese military regime to intimidate and arrest monks, protesters and journalists during the 2007 Monks Rebellion.

Tracy Spaight: Director of Special Projects for Wargaming.net.

Nicholas Springate: BBC producer with a long-standing interest in covering events in Burma.

Supermarine Spitfire: RAF fighter and aviation icon designed by R.J. Mitchell and first flown in 1936.

Tatmadaw: The collective name for the four armed services of Myanmar: the Myanmar Army, Navy, Air Force and Police.

Tay Za: According to the US Treasury Department 'an arms dealer and financial henchman of Burma's repressive junta'. David Cundall's agent in Myanmar during the 2004 excavations.

Than Shwe: Dictator, superstitious kleptocrat, and last General standing as Chairman of the Burmese military regime. Oversaw the return to partial democracy retiring to a large fortified compound in 2011.

Thein Sein: President of the Union of Myanmar, inaugurated 30 March 2011.

Daw Tin Ma Latt: 'Auntie Latt', STP Director of Foreign Communications, translator Yangon International Airport dig site.

Tin Naing Tun: Myanmar Director General of Civil Aviation 2012.

Malcolm Weale: Owner Geofizz Ltd; undertook site survey at Yangon Airport 2004.

U Pe Win: STP general manager, Burma Spitfires dig site at Yangon International Airport 2013.

U Soe Thein: Geophysicist, retired Professor of Geology, Dagon University.

Louis-Hugues Vincent: French Dominican monk and archaeologist on the Parker expedition to Jerusalem.

Wargaming.net: global video game developer and publisher.

Sir Charles Warren: Royal Engineer and pioneering archaeologist in Jerusalem.

Gerrard Williams: British TV journalist and filmaker turned conspiracy theorist.

'Willie' Wills: Named by David Cundall as being involved in the burial of the Spitfires and allegedly one of the people whose activities on their behalf governments affect to deny.

Keith Win: Founder of the Myanmar–British Business Association. Business partner of David Cundall (*c.*1997–2000).

Yangon (formerly Rangoon): Capital of Burma under British rule, and focus of civil discontent against the military government; replaced as the national capital by Nay Pyi Taw in 2005.

Ziv Brosh: Former operator with Israeli Special Forces, entrepreneur and Spitfire enthusiast.

And of course, the Union of Myanmar (previously Burma): One of the most beautiful, culturally rich, diverse and troubled nations in Southeast Asia.

Names

Because the place names imposed by the military regime remain controversial, for example Yangon replacing Rangoon, we debated which convention to adopt in this account. Ultimately, to avoid confusion, or perhaps as a messy compromise, we decided to use modern names, such as Myanmar and Yangon, when discussing the events of 1990–2014 and the older names such as Burma and Rangoon when discussing historical events.

All are, of course, translations into English of the original Burmese.

FOREWORD
BY AL MURRAY

I think it's probably not an exaggeration to say that I grew up on the Supermarine Spitfire. Other people had pop music, football team stickers, telly they liked. Whatever, as we didn't say back then. I was into the Spitfire. Fate had decided that my generation – and it always spooks me a little when someone my age doesn't know what I'm talking about on this subject – would be raised on the beautiful elliptical wing and the elegant lines, the rate of climb, the turning circle … look see, there I go. You set me off.

And here's the important thing to explain to the non-believer or Spitfire agnostic – and I see this in fans of other aircraft, like Concorde nutters for instance – the things I'll say about the Spitfire are articles of faith, bound up in truth as much as they are in myth, born of science, industry, legend, art, symmetry, form and function, war, gallantry, brute force and Airfix. Winning a book prize at school I spent the token on a great big book full of pictures of Spitfires. Articles about twin-pitch propellers, pressurised cockpits, indulged my mild distaste for the look (though appreciation of the efficacy) of the clipped wing tips in later Marks, and fed my distaste for the not very Spitfire-like Mark 24, the beauty fading, courtesy of more than a dozen face-lifts trying to keep up with the younger, newer, more glamourous models.

To this day I have still a favourite Mark of the darned thing (I shan't tell you what it is, you'll have to ask me if you see me), and even though I've done all I can to set this love affair aside – perhaps I'm just as much in love with the Spitfire as I ever was, but now I'm older so there's room for other things too. But never Hurricanes. Ugh.

So, like everyone else with a taste for these things – and if I know one thing it is that we are legion, we happy few, we band of brothers (fans) raised on all Spitfire, Mosquito, Merlin engine matters, the often dubious glamour of the Second World War that cast a khaki light over us all in the 1970s and beyond in the UK – I had kept one eye on the buried Spitfires of Burma story. How could I not? The most iconic fighter plane of all stashed away in mint condition? Forgotten but now recovered? Somewhere inaccessible? One eye? Be reasonable! I'd watched this thing like a hawk.

A sceptical hawk, mind; I would scoff to anyone who'd listen that there was no way these Spits were there or existed or for that matter that anyone would have hidden them like this at this point in the war for heavens' sakes! None of it made any sense, did it? Wasn't it obvious this whole thing was aviation fuel sniffing baloney? After all, planes like this wouldn't just be forgotten … and then I would recognise that the reason I was interested wasn't because I thought it was nonsense, something to scoff at with reflexive ease, no, it was because somewhere inside me, lingering, loitering perhaps, was the tiniest hope that it might be true.

Because if it were true wouldn't that be utterly fantastic? A dozen (two dozen? It depended which version of events you read) Spitfires, signed, sealed, delivered, potentially pristine, the aviation equivalent of a herd of perfectly preserved Mammoths locked in the Siberian ice. My mind would entertain the possibility, the tangents – after all, what would twenty or so mint condition Spits do to the price of picking one up on the open market? But the story – and that's all it was at the time – had got me. Could it, would it possibly be true? At the same time I realised this is the same childhood thrill at the notion of maybe seeing a ghost or a UFO even though I firmly didn't (and don't) believe in them: in other words the thrill of the world not being as orderly and predictable in some aspects – say the burying of Spitfires in the Burmese jungle at the end of the Second World War – as you might know it to be.

And in this sense *The Buried Spitfires of Burma: A Fake History* tells the story of how wanting to believe, of how something being too good to be true can be irresistible; as we seem to, collectively, be losing our grip on knowing full well that things that sound like bunkum most likely are. I knew better and it had me wanting it to be true, and lots of people who knew more than me and definitely should have known better, chose to believe. An entertaining tale packing a warning, but also, god wouldn't it have been great if it had been true? Even now, knowing the depths of dim-wittery involved, there's its appeal – the rational drops its guard and in charges fake history, knocking over the truth, and smashing it to the floor. And if you break it, you pay for it.

Al Murray
January 2020

FOREWORD
BY SIR TONY ROBINSON

Archaeology is a heart-warming subject. Bright young men and women discover artefacts below the ground, which tell us more about the people who once lived there than we would ever have thought possible. I suspect that's why *Time Team*, the archaeology series I presented on Channel 4 for twenty years, was transmitted so early on Sunday evenings. It was a family programme, fun but serious minded, a bit of a lark and yet somehow dignified.

But things are seldom quite as they seem, and archaeology is no exception to this rule. Archaeological finds create a story, but that story can be flawed, or even downright wrong. Sites can be mis-recorded. Digs can be funded by people or institutions whose main interest is in perpetuating a particular point of view rather than empirically sifting through the evidence. Archaeological stories can be used to justify the possession of territory by people of a particular religion or ethnicity and the expulsion of other people who appear not to have lived in that territory for as long.

In other words archaeology can be highly political, and one of the reasons the discipline needs to be conducted with such rigour is that any mistakes or misrepresentations can become part of a narrative which is at best wrong and at worst malign.

The British Prime Minister David Cameron once made that mistake. He heard there was evidence of twenty Second World War RAF Spitfires being buried in a hole in the ground at Myanmar's main international airport, and as moves were afoot to accept that country into the international community after years of isolation, and as Cameron was about to visit Myanmar in what he hoped would be a diplomatic coup, an iconic dig fronted by British archaeologists seemed like a great idea. But, however seductive that notion might have seemed, it couldn't have been more wrong!

The Buried Spitfires of Burma is a cracking read told in a vigorous and amusing way. But it also uses the travesty of the Spitfire hunt to discuss the nature of archaeology, its social context, and the problems and challenges that surround any search to ascertain historical veracity. It's written with great flair, and buzzes with innovative storytelling ideas. But in these days of deliberate political misrepresentation, it's also a salutary reminder that whatever the temptations, we always have a duty to use our best endeavours to uncover the truth.

Sir Tony Robinson
January 2020

THE FACT

The shining yellow of the brand new JCB excavator matches the yellow glare of the late morning sun that presses down with an almost physical intensity on the parched plateau upon which stands Yangon International Airport.

As the steel-toothed bucket descends into the deepening trench, the archaeology team watches with a mixture of anticipation and excitement, while the cameras of Room 608 Productions wait to record the action, reaction, and even conflict of one of the most remarkable, and perhaps also the strangest, archaeological projects in years.

It is the team's third day on site, but after the walkovers, detailed geophysical surveys and the hand digging of some obvious surface features, this is the first opportunity for the team to undertake any serious digging. This is crucial because, as any archaeologist will tell you, the 'facts on the ground' serve to 'ground truth' any theory and their physical reality trumps any amount of desktop research, let alone speculation and wishful thinking.

The machine trench is now 30ft long; a livid red scar of soil and spoil on the scrubby expanse of tough green grass adjacent to the modern runway at Mingaladon.

The strength of the sun reminds everyone why only mad dogs and Englishmen would venture out at this time of day. But it is a tight timetable and the promise of solving the mystery that lies behind a 70-year-old legend which is driving the team on. The legend that describes what may lie buried beneath the red soil of Burma's only international airport.

Lincolnshire farmer and historic aircraft hunter David Cundall knows what lies there.

Earlier he reiterated to the team on camera that buried beneath this precise spot are at least six, and probably many more, Mark XIV Spitfire fighters that were buried here in their transport crates by American Seabees working on behalf of the Royal Air Force at the end of the Second World War.

Suddenly there is a crunching crackle as the teeth of the digger bucket bite into buried wood.

'Look at that fucker!' yells field archaeologist Martin Brown, swearing uncharacteristically in his excitement.

'Camera,' he calls to Adam Docker, the director of photography, whose state-of-the-art Red Epic high-definition camera has become the expedition's all-seeing eye.

Martin calls out to the rest of the team, 'Timbers, big fucking timbers!'

In the cabin of the excavator, Manny Machado manipulates the control levers with the finesse of a concert pianist, and the hydraulically driven muscles of the JCB hiss and strain in response.

'Everybody back, everybody back,' Martin warns, as the excavator's dipper arm clears the edge of the trench, balancing a hefty rough-hewn wooden beam precariously on the bucket like a 2 meter long toothpick.

'That's structural timber!' Martin shouts above the rumble of the JCB's engine. 'You don't have something that big for no reason. That's made to withstand a lot of weight and a lot of pressure.'

The archaeologists, STP workmen and TV crew alike lean in for a closer look, peering down into the excavation.

At the time nobody notices that, at what could be his moment of triumph and final vindication, David Cundall seems somehow to have moved away to another place.

PART ONE
THE LEGEND

Frederick the Great: Could you keep a secret?

Graf von Kalckstein: Naturally, Your Majesty.

Frederick the Great: Well I can too!

1

When the Second World War came to an end in August 1945 the legends began. One of the greatest of those legends, the subject of innumerable books, films, comics, and plastic models hanging from the bedroom ceilings of teenage boys, concerned the British Spitfire fighter.

In the legend the Spitfire was the aircraft with the film star looks, which won the Battle of Britain as the mount of popular heroes such as Douglas Bader and the Royal Air Force's highest-scoring ace Johnnie Johnson, and later of cinematic heroes played by David Niven, Kenneth Moore and Michael Caine.

Supermarine designer R.J. Mitchell's brainchild was even granted the honour of its own biopic, albeit somewhat romanticised, in the shape of Leslie Howards's 1942 film *First of the Few*. The film even premiered complete with its love theme to the Spitfire, Sir William Walton's soaring 'Spitfire Prelude', a work which remains a concert hall favourite to this day.

However, when the guns fell silent and the airmen went home the surviving Spitfires met the same fate as many veterans of war in that their peacetime masters did not know what to do with the thousands of aircraft now surplus to requirements, with the result that, on airfields in every theatre of war, from Scotland to Australia, aircraft that had cost tens of millions of pounds were lined up to be broken up and recycled.

But almost as soon as the cutting torches and wrecking bars had been put to work rumours began to circulate in the bars and NAAFI canteens of the Far East that some aircraft at least had escaped destruction and, like the legendary King Arthur, the Once and Future King, they were lying in secret underground vaults, ready to fly again in time of Britain's need.

By the 1970s, such rumours have become commonplace and are part of the currency of a new breed of aviation enthusiasts who have begun to track down and recover aircraft, particularly Spitfires which had gone missing for various reasons during the war. One of the most active and successful of these aviation wreck hunters is David Cundall's mentor, Jim Pearce. However, like many aspects of this story, there is another layer beneath the obvious and public. In fact, 'Jim' is a name Pearce has adopted. Documents in the UK's Companies House, which keeps the names of people who are directors of UK companies, records that his full name is Gordon Bramwell Edwin Pearce, who was born on Trafalgar Day, 21 October 1929.

Like many of the enthusiasts, Jim is too young to serve in the Second World War, but he does serve in the Royal Air Force in the troubled British enclave of Aden in the 1960s.

This is the time when Lt Colonel Colin 'Mad Mitch' Mitchell, of the Argyll and Sutherland Highlanders, is making his reputation in the British media as the swashbuckling leader of what is actually a grubby counter-insurgency campaign; a campaign that comes to be called 'the last stand of the British Empire'.

After retiring from the RAF Jim, it is claimed, undertakes certain unusual 'contract work' around the world for the British Government. He also takes advantage of the booming demand for agricultural spraying as the UK moves to large-scale industrial farming, based on the liberal use of agrochemicals, and he sets up a crop-dusting business based at the former wartime RAF Lympne, now renamed Ashford Airport, in Kent. Subsequently he moves to North Farm Airfield near the small village of Washington, which nestles on the edge of the rolling South Downs National Park in Sussex, north-west of Brighton.

Jim's new base even has its own grass airstrip, like those at local flying clubs across southern England where Fighter Command dispersed its Spitfire and Hurricane fighters during the height of the Battle of Britain in August and September 1940.

Looking towards the cropped grass of the runway it is easy to imagine the kind of scene fixed forever in monochrome by the photographers of *Picture Post*, with floppy fringed, pipe-smoking pilots lounging on the ground or sitting in deck chairs trying to relax, a black Labrador lying asleep at their feet. All the while waiting for the pulse quickening ring of the field telephone and the hellish clang of the scramble bell that will send them racing to their parked fighters.

If they are lucky they will live to fight and fly another day, and, as the sun sinks and the 'stand down' comes from 'Group', they will pile into the battered J type MG sports car that is parked behind the dispersal hut and, after a breakneck trip up the A23 to the fleshpots of Soho, they will drink cheap champagne at the Bag of Nails alongside other pilots out on the lash, including Richard Hillary of 603 City of Edinburgh Squadron, who will become the author of the classic Battle of Britain memoire *The Last Enemy*. Then they might move on to catch the risqué nude tableux at the Windmill Theatre; or, if they are very lucky, meet a date for a meal and a dance to the music of Ken 'Snakehips' Johnson and his West Indian Orchestra at the Café de Paris, on Coventry Street.

A quarter of a century later Jim's adventures in aviation take him much further afield than Soho. He also appears to have visited the United States regularly and to have operated in Yugoslavia, using contacts developed when purchasing crop-dusting aircraft for his business. The former Eastern bloc had developed an expertise in the design of such aircraft, perhaps because, Western intelligence agencies suggested, such technology could also be used to deliver chemical warfare agents on the battlefield.

By the late 1980s and early '90s, Jim's interest in aviation, and the contacts he has made on both sides of the Iron Curtain, leads to his becoming increasingly involved with the niche economy of the recovery and importation of Second World War aircraft from the former Soviet Union.

This is because, as so-called 'disaster capitalism' kicks in, everything is for sale from the state oil industry to lonely broken relics of the Great Patriotic War lying in the forests and marshes of western Russia. Thus, while his contemporaries on the aviation memorabilia scene remember him as a regular at the annual Shoreham airfield aero jumble, selling aviation relics at reasonable prices, Jim makes his real mark on the wider international historic warbird scene.

In February 1992 two Luftwaffe casualties of the Eastern Front, a Messerschmitt Bf 110 heavy fighter and an incredibly rare Focke-Wulf Fw 189 twin-engine reconnaissance aircraft recovered in 1990, arrive in the UK, and by the mid-1990s records from Companies House show that Jim Pearce appears to have been the director of two companies involved in Historic Aviation, FW189 Ltd, and Property and Aviation (UK) Ltd.

By 2012 Jim's reputation is well established, and while some have questioned the number of actual recoveries undertaken directly by Jim and his team in the field, the reputation is well-deserved.

Jim's operation is credited with importing several Focke-Wulf Fw 190 fighters, a sinister gull-winged Junkers Ju 87 Stuka dive bomber that spearheaded the Blitzkrieg in Poland and France, and its bigger brother from the Junkers stable, 'Germany's Mosquito', the highly versatile Junkers Ju 88 medium bomber.

Jim also imports from Russia a number of Messerschmitt Bf 109 fighters in addition to that first Messerschmitt Bf 110 heavy fighter and two US-built aircraft sent to the Soviet Union under Lend-Lease; a Curtiss P-40 Kittyhawk, which arrived in 1995, and a Bell P-39 Airacobra. This is an aircraft that Russian pilots appear to have appreciated more than their American counterparts, who were nervous of being the meat in the sandwich, sitting in a cockpit located between the engine and the propeller, with the propeller shaft between their legs and a notoriously difficult means of escape. That aircraft was brought to England in 2004.

Overall, as the website warbirdfinders.co.uk records, 'Renowned as one of the most experienced warbird recovery specialists in the world, Jim Pearce and his team have recovered over 50 of the most historic aircraft in museums and private collections throughout the world today.'

Jim's clients, who ultimately fund the recovery and importation efforts, include the helicopter and deer-farming millionaire Sir Tim Wallis's Alpine Fighter Collection based at Wanaka, New Zealand; the Brooklands Museum in Weybridge Surrey, which used £681,000 of public money from the National Heritage Memorial Fund to purchase Hurricane fighter Z2389 recovered from a swamp near Murmansk in north-west Russia;* and the Flying Heritage Collection (now renamed the Flying Heritage & Combat Armor Museum) belonging to the co-founder of Microsoft, the late Paul Allen.

As Jim's client list suggests, these highest of high-end designer objects, the ultimate in big boys toys, a historic warbird, demand both passion and deep pockets of any would-be owner. This is because, depending on its war record or lack of it, a Spitfire restored to flying condition might achieve a hammer price of at least $3 million, while its opponent, the still more rare Messerschmitt Bf 109, might fetch as much as $4.5 million. And that is before you factor in the running costs of getting these airborne thoroughbreds off the ground and back into their natural element, the sky.

It follows that while Second World War aircraft recovery and restoration can be a very lucrative business, with aircraft recovered and restored to order for well-resourced museums and well-to-do collectors, it is also risky.

---

*   www.brooklandsmuseum.com/explore/our-collection/aircraft/hawker-hurricane-mkiia.

Airframes are often passed from owner to owner as time takes its toll on enthusiasm and interest wanes or, most often, ambition exceeds available funding.

With this ongoing interest and an international following among owners, enthusiasts and historians, it is not surprising that the recovery and restoration of historic aircraft has also generated its own specialised media, both in magazines such the venerable *Aeroplane*, which traces its roots back to 1911, and the more recent *FlyPast*, and increasingly in websites and online forums such as that operated by Key Publishing, the owners of *FlyPast*.

One of the most active members on the historic aviation section of the Key Publications forum is Spitfire expert and author Peter Arnold.

Peter admits that he begins his career in historic aviation as a 'spotter' carrying a copy of the *Observer's Book of Aircraft*, subsequently upgrading his involvement to the real thing. However, his working life begins on the ground with the British sports car manufacturer Aston Martin, where he works as an engineer. It is while he is working for Aston Martin that his ongoing love of historic aviation leads him to rebuild his first airframe, a Vickers Supermarine Seafire (serial number LA564), in the 1970s.

This exploit leads to an appearance on the BBC's early evening magazine programme *Nationwide*, which can still be found on YouTube.

The pre-recorded package, which is fronted by one of the programme's lead presenters, Sue Lawley, seems to set out to portray Peter as an eccentric cross between Captain W.E. Johns' heroic RAF pilot Biggles and one of the louche characters played by the actor Leslie Phillips in British farces such as *Don't Just Lie There, Say Something!*. Like Phillips, Peter has for a long time sported an immaculately groomed moustache.

However, the TV producer's cheap shot serves to mask the fact that Peter has become a shrewd and effective operator who has seen an opportunity to indulge his own passion for the aircraft and at the same time supply an emerging commercial market, where a single propeller hub, essential to any Spitfire restoration, might be worth £60,000.

The result of this vision is that by the 1980s he begins to put together kits of Spitfire parts that can be sold on to the growing band of wealthy collectors such as Charles Church and later Steve Brooks. Men who share the same passion for Spitfires as Peter, but who can couple it with the cash to turn boxes of castings, pressings and manufacturer's plates into fully restored, airworthy aircraft.

As a mark of his success, at least four of the Spitfire 'projects' that pass through Peter's hands in the 1980s and '90s are flying again in the twenty-first century; Something of which he is understandably and justifiably proud.

He can be equally proud that along the way he amasses a body of knowledge and a sizeable collection of research notes and photographs, which ultimately lead to his co-authoring the standard two-volume work *Spitfire Survivors*, detailing the surviving examples of these iconic aircraft.

It is during this period that Spitfires also become currency on the international historic warbird circuit. In 1992 Peter is involved in the purchase and repatriation to Britain of a rare Handley Page Hampden bomber (P1344) shot down in northern Russia in September 1942. In return for the remains of the Hampden, the Royal Air Force Museum hands the importer, Jeet Mahal of Vancouver, British Columbia, Mark XVI Spitfire SL542 from its store.

The RAF Museum may have had the better of the deal, as in 2017 Peter will describe SL542 as a 'fairly mediocre low back'.

However, by 2002, while he remains active on the forums and retains his reputation within the sector as a researcher and consultant regarding all things Spitfire, Peter has sold on his last two active projects to new owners and is no longer a member of the elite Spitfire owners' club to which he has belonged for almost thirty years.

That he is able to re-join the club in May 2012 is thanks to the British Army's habit of dumping unwanted vehicles and aircraft on its training ranges, including those on Salisbury Plain.

In the mid 1960s a fellow collector obtains letters of permission to enter the range on the plain on days when there was no firing in order to remove anything of significant historical value from a griffon-engined Spitfire Mark XXII (PK519), built in 1945, which had been left on the range as a target.

Peter obtains the parts and is able to quote the permission to prove his legal ownership when he registers the aircraft with the UK Civil Aviation Authority with the result that, as David Cundall prepares to search for Spitfires at Mingaladon, the disarticulated parts on a wooden armature in Peter's garage now have an official civilian aircraft registration, G-SPXX.*

Peter Arnold and David Cundall appear to have begun to work together in the 1990s forging a partnership through their shared passion for Spitfires.

As David and Peter report it, one day in the mid-1990s, while the two men are talking about the possibility of fresh recoveries of historic aircraft with their colleague Jim Pearce, Jim tells them a story that began on RAF Mingaladon just outside Rangoon, the then capital of Burma, during the first days of peace in the autumn of 1945.

---

* G-SPXX (previously PK519) registered by Peter Arnold on 18 May 2012.

2

The Spitfires of Rangoon

A Novel of the Secret War in Burma

by Major William Wills DSO OBE

```
RAF Mingaladon Burma
1830 hours,
17 August 1945
```

As the setting sun exploded on the great golden stupa of the Shwedagon Pagoda, Squadron Leader Sylvester of 273 Squadron, Royal Air Force, reached into the breast pocket of his crumpled cotton drill tunic and withdrew a battered packet of cigarettes. This was a moment of peace and contemplation he allowed himself before sitting down once more to deal with the apparently endless paperwork of an operational RAF squadron at the sharp end of a supply chain of men and material stretching all the way back through the teeming docks of Bombay and Calcutta to the assembly lines of Castle Bromwich and Detroit.

Sylvester's lighter flared as he lit his cigarette, momentarily bleaching out the arc lights that he could see as he cast his eyes across the wide, flat range of RAF Mingaladon, towards the distant runway works by the Old Prome Road.

Sylvester inhaled, enjoying the moment, then blew the smoke out steadily so that it drifted away into the deep blue of the fast-falling evening.

Kipling had been right about the Burmese dawn coming up like thunder, but at dusk the daylight ran away like a waterfall over a cliff.

However, poetic thoughts aside, the officer's immediate concern was the planning for tomorrow's 'Nickel' drop, leafleting the Emperor's 'sons of heaven' in an attempt to persuade them that the game was well and truly up and the only sensible thing left to do was to emerge from the jungle with their hands up, white flags flying. Indeed, if the reports about the two special 'Atomic Bombs' that the Americans had just dropped, apparently destroying two whole cities, were even partially true, only a nation intent on committing collective national suicide would contemplate continuing hostilities.

As the last of the monsoon rain dripped from the heavy khaki canvas roof of the regulation British military tent that served as both Sylvester's office and home away from home, the moths gathered and danced in the sickly yellow light of a hanging paraffin lamp.

Sylvester's eye was caught by the light reflected in the pools of mud and water that booby-trapped 273's dispersal area.

He wondered if ACSEA and RAF HQ Rangoon would ever fulfil their promise to get his men out from under canvas and into properly built barracks to negate the worst effects of the monsoon. The rain and mud had been a spirit-sapping constant since the squadron had flown their already time-served Mark VIII Spitfires into Mingaladon from Ramree Island in the middle of May.

Even so, Sylvester was pleased with the way the squadron had acquitted itself under such difficult conditions. His men had responded to their situation with courage, professionalism and not a little ingenuity. The most recent example of this was the new method of dropping the Nickel leaflets by loading them into the flaps under the aircraft wings and then opening them over the drop zone. Even so, the latest instruction from those with scrambled egg on their hats was taxing and perplexing to even his experienced team.

He was lucky that George Shenton and Reg Ashmead had stepped so quickly and easily out of their regular duties and thrown themselves into the new task with such aplomb. Flight Sergeant Shenton in particular had proved himself to be not only a natural surveyor, he had a knack of getting on with the Yanks too and given the magnitude of the task they had been set that was of considerable importance.

Sylvester took a last drag on his cigarette then flicked it into the mud, where it fizzed for a moment before his boot drowned it with a deliberate twist of the toe. Then he turned back into his tent, sat down at his desk and began typing on his battered portable Remington typewriter.

273 Squadron
Flight Duty Rosta 17/8/45
Nickel Drops scheduled as follows

F/O Rivet	09.15–11.00
Flt Lt Shi Sho	'ditto'
Flt/Lt Colebrook	11.10–12.10
Flt/Lt Smith	'ditto'
Flt Sgt MacCarthy	11.45–13.00
W/O Lawler	'ditto'
Sgt Osborne	'ditto'
W/O Hughes	16.05–17.15
Flt Sgt Allen	'ditto'

G.B. Silvester Sqd Ldr

Sylvester added his florid signature, making the document part of the official historical record of the Royal Air Force.

Because it was so routine, he forced himself to read the list back to himself to make sure he had not made a mistake and he found himself smiling. They were all names who had been with the squadron long enough for faces to become attached to them. Even better, Sylvester knew that, unless someone was unlucky, flying into a Monsoon Thunderhead, or a flock of geese, or became careless and made one of those pilot errors that were so elementary it would be funny if it wasn't for the fact they got you killed, the whole squadron would be going home to England home and hearth.

They had survived.

He corrected himself. One of his pilots, Flight Lieutenant Shi Sho, was already home, although the young Karen had once told his commander that he would never really be home until his country was free. Sylvester thought there was something in the way he had said the words that made it clear he did not mean the Union of Burma.

Indeed, if you got them talking over a beer in the mess, the Lysander special duties boys running the jungle taxi service for Force 136 over on the remote north side of the airfield reckoned that, unless they squared their allies the Karen with, at the very least, real political autonomy, whoever ended up in charge of the Burma after the war – the Governor General on behalf of His Majesty, or General Aung San's Burmans from the revolutionary Free Burma Army with their Communist allies – they would be in for a whole heap of trouble.

No. 9 Operations Room: Rangoon Burma
1000 hours,
21 August 1945

'This really is most irregular sir,' said Flight Lieutenant Coton. 'I know you are our Allies and all that. But I can't authorise you to censor my official records. I mean, it's King's Regulations; I am responsible for their accuracy, if necessary all the way up to Air Chief Marshal Park himself. I would be court martialed if I was caught doing what you ask.' Coton tried to sound reasonable. 'Look, I will take this up with my superiors; perhaps if you came back tomorrow?'

'Flight lieutenant,' the American captain sucked on his cigar, 'let me make it easy for you.'

There was something in the tone that immediately made Coton realise he had made a mistake.

'Pass me your telephone.' It was an instruction rather than a polite request.

Coton lifted the heavy black Bakelite receiver and passed it to the American.

'Get me Government House.' There was a pause, during which Coton imagined the operator slotting in the jack plugs.

'Admiral Mountbatten please.' Coton sensed the click of the final jack plug slotting home to complete the circuit.

'Good afternoon, this is Captain Di Sandro, I am the S2 of the Construction Battalion up at Mingaladon. I need the Admiral to talk to,' he placed a hand over the mouthpiece, '... what was your name son?'

'Coton sir, Flight Lieutenant Max Coton.'

'That's right, Coton,' he returned to the call, 'I need the Lord Louis to talk to Flight Lieutenant Coton in No. 9 Operations Room.'

Coton had a moment to be irritated. Why did Americans insist on pronouncing his rank as 'lootenant'. But reality intruded again with a sickening jolt. This was really happening.

'Good afternoon Admiral, I am sorry to bother you,' said De Sandro with a tone that suggested familiarity with the person at the other end of the line. 'It's about the Special Operation at Mingaladon ... That's right sir, Merlin. I am with Flight Lieutenant Coton, he is the Commanding Officer at 9 Operations Room. He doesn't understand the need to amend his Operations Record Book ... That's right sir, thank you. I will put him on the line for you.'

He offered the receiver to Coton, who took it as carefully as if it were the best Waterford crystal from the officer's mess.

'Flight Lieutenant Coton, sir,' said the young officer diffidently. The rich voice on the other end of the line was far from diffident.

'Coton, unless you want to be the last man on the last boat out of Rangoon with the substantive rank of aircraftsman, I suggest you do exactly as the captain asks and then forget you ever met him. Do you understand?'

'Yes sir, of course, I am sorry sir.' The buzzing on the line told Coton that his first-ever conversation with the Supreme Allied Commander South East Asia, the King's cousin Admiral of the Fleet Lord Louis Mountbatten, was over.

'That's settled then.'

The American tore the most recent page from the Royal Air Force Form 540 Operations Record Book, lighting it with his cigar and dropping it into the ashtray on Coton's desk, where it burned and slowly disintegrated.

Coton watched the words disappear as they glowed orange, then charred grey, black and unintelligible. '16/8/45 Notice to airman ... US Construction Batt ... ived with hea ... equip ... Began burial ... Spitfires ... old runway Prome R ... Mingaladon ...'

The captain very deliberately stubbed his cigar out in the ashtray, reducing the burnt page to powdery grey fragments.

'So Flight Lieutenant Coton, Max, are you going to offer me one of your cups of tea?'

No. 9 Operations Room: Rangoon Burma
1200 hours,
21 August 1945

Flying Officer Wainwright resumed typing the entry on the Form 540, the Royal Air Force's standard Operations Record Book.

The entry read:

15/8/45 05.30 Japan packed up. Sunderland going out on armed recce must have heard news as he went out to sea to drop his bombs.

Official signal received stating offensive action against enemy Air, Land and Sea Forces to cease so far as it is consistent with the safety of our forces.

Wainwright paused to glance at the crib sheet, trying to ignore the fug from the American officer's cigar. Then he typed very deliberately:

16–20/8/45 Sorties still go on but there is nothing of interest to report.

'Thank you, son,' said Captain Di Sandro. 'You can fill in the rest. Good day to you.'

Di Sandro turned in the doorway.

'You've just written some history son. So you had better forget there ever was another version,' he said.

'Of course, sir,' said Wainwright.

Although on the evidence of what was going on at Mingaladon it would be difficult to forget that everyone at SEAC who had authorised this Op was clearly either drunk or a certifiable lunatic.

3

Nay Pyi Taw
Myanmar
14 April 2012

Political journalist Nicholas Watt of *The Guardian* newspaper is accompanying British Prime Minister David Cameron on his tour of the Far East, which includes a visit to the Union of Myanmar, where, just days ago, more or less democratic elections have seen former high-profile political prisoner and Nobel Peace Prize Laureate Daw Aung San Suu Kyi win a seat in parliament.

In the course of reporting the routine traffic of an official visit, including the private tour of the Yangon's greatest treasure, the magnificent golden Shwedagon Pagoda on Singuttara Hill, and discussing the pressing issues of the transition to democracy and the resulting lifting of sanctions by the European Union, Watt reports that President Thein Sein of Myanmar and Prime Minister Cameron also discuss another, more unusual, matter.

Watt tells his readers, 'David Cameron has reached an agreement with the Burmese authorities to dig up the remains of up to 20 RAF Spitfires that were buried in Burma two weeks before the atom bomb was dropped on Japan.'[*]

The Cabinet Offices refuse a Freedom of Information Act request for Cameron's briefing notes regarding the Spitfires on the grounds that their release could affect Britain's relations with another country, so it is not possible to say if the Prime Minister's office undertook any due diligence before publicising the story and giving the Prime Minister his media lines.

[*]   www.theguardian.com/world/2012/apr/14/david-cameron-spitfires-buried-burma

It is also fair to add that the visit to Yangon was a late addition to the Prime Minister's itinerary following the elections of March 2012 and the success of Aung San Suu Kyi's National League for Democracy, meaning there was limited time for the professional civil servants in the Cabinet Office or their Foreign Office counterparts to do any meaningful background research. However, it is reasonable to suggest that neither Cameron, in a previous career the Director of Corporate Affairs with media company Carlton Communications, nor the Prime Minister's media team, headed up by former Controller of English, BBC Global News Craig Oliver, are particularly concerned about the veracity of the story one way or the other. To them the buried Spitfires are a convenient 'good news' distraction for the press pack given their reporting of another, less patriotic, aviation story related to Cameron's visit to Myanmar.

Whereas Barack Obama had flown into Yangon Airport the previous November on board the most famous Boeing 747 Jumbo Jet in the world, Air Force One, with its state-of-the-art communications and luxury accommodation as befits the de facto Leader of the First World, for his trip Cameron's team cannot even borrow a suitable aircraft from the Royal Air Force, British Airways or even aviation enthusiast Richard Branson's Virgin Atlantic. Instead, No. 10 charters an aircraft which the press pack nickname imediately 'Camforce One'; an aging Jumbo Jet from an airline called SonAir, which no one seems to have heard of, even to take a cheap package holiday.

The hacks soon discover that Serviço Aéreo, S.A. aka SonAir, is owned by Sonangol, the Angolan state oil company, and more usually transports oil executives from Texas to Luanda, the capital of the oil-rich African republic. Research into SonAir's history soon reveals Prime Minister Cameron and his high-profile delegation of business leaders will be flying on an airline previously best known for being part of an investigation by the International Monetary Fund into the small matter of £20 billion of missing oil revenue.[*]

To be fair, the company was cleared by the investigation. However, the charity Human Rights Watch did not find the company's excuse of insufficient record keeping 'convincing'.

Nonetheless, making a brave PR fist of it, Mr Cameron tells the press pack that the reason behind the visit to the Far East is to 'get our exports up' and 'fly the flag for Britain'.

---

[*] Rowena Mason in *The Telegraph,* 11 April 2012, www.telegraph.co.uk/news/politics/9197170/David-Cameron-flies-the-flag…on-an-Angolan-plane.html

Which the Angolan aircraft does indeed do, at least from the flight deck window when leaving Heathrow.

Thus, as the Prime Minister's aircraft goes wheels up from Yangon, the media has been diverted by a photo opportunity with Aung San Suu Kyi, who at that point remains an international icon of political hope second only to Nelson Mandela, while flying top cover is the ghostly escort of a lost squadron (or two) of buried Spitfires.

Astonishingly, the Spitfires were not on Cameron's agenda as the result of months of diligent research by professional historians in the archives of the Royal Air Force, but are instead the patriotic project of a Lincolnshire farmer who dreams of watching the aircraft fly in squadron formation down the Mall.

```
Tracy Spaight
Westin St Francis Hotel, San Francisco
16 May 2012
1900 hours
```

A tall, robust fellow in his early sixties, wearing a blue blazer, khaki trousers and a white shirt, David Cundall descends the marble stairs and strides purposefully across the polished marble floor of the lobby of the Westin St Francis hotel. He has a weather-beaten face from years spent in the sun; his thinning blond hair is shot through with grey, but his intense blue eyes speak of youthful energy, while at 6ft 4in he towers over the businessmen and tourists milling about the lobby. His big frame and broad shoulders hint at Viking ancestry, which, I muse, is quite possible given his family origins in what had once been the Danelaw.

He walks towards the grand old Magneto clock in the lobby, our pre-arranged meeting place.

I'd chosen the St Francis because of David's interest in the Second World War. During the war, the hotel had been a marshalling point for thousands of American soldiers, including General Douglas MacArthur, before they shipped out to the Pacific Theatre and legendary confrontations with Imperial Japan at Midway, Guadalcanal and Iwo Jima.

'David?' I inquire as he approaches.

He smiles good-naturedly in greeting.

'Hello, Tracy! A pleasure to meet you.'

We shake hands.

David is a farmer by trade and heritage, growing potatoes and wheat on a 200-acre Lincolnshire farm, which the family has owned since the nineteenth century and which he inherited from his father.

Growing up in post-war Britain, as he tills the earth David looks to the sky, developing a lifelong fascination with Spitfires and the stories of the pilots who flew them in the Second World War.

Indeed, as David grows up in the 1950s many of those aviators he most admires, men such as Group Captain Douglas Bader, Squadron Leader Neville Duke and Wing Commander John 'Cat's Eyes' Cunningham, are still household names, their exploits portrayed in patriotic films or seen on newsreels displaying the latest British aircraft at the annual Farnborough Airshow. They are aircraft with such evocative names as Vampire, Meteor, Comet and, perhaps greatest of them all, the mighty, delta-winged, Vulcan nuclear bomber, which is soon placed on quick reaction alert at RAF bases in David's native Lincolnshire, the crews practising the scrambles, which, if performed for real would signal to local people that Armageddon would arrive in minutes.

However, much as he longs to, David cannot join their number; the needs of maintaining the family farm are such that he has to leave school at a young age.

But he never gives up on his dream of flying.

Unbeknownst to his mother, the young David flies whenever he gets the chance, earning his glider pilot's license at 16 and a powered flight licence at 17.

However, David's entrée to historic aviation comes about through an entirely serendipitous conversation when a friend tells him a story about a Spitfire that crashed on 3 April 1942 not far from his farm.

Intrigued, David tracks down the farmer who had seen it go down as a young lad while he and his mates were playing football. The farmer leads him to the spot and, as David tells it, his metal detector emits at once a high-pitched squeal indicating a strong metallic source.

This is the period, prior to the passing of the Protection of Military Remains Act in 1986, when aircraft wreck hunting in the UK is a free-for-all and, just a week later, with no licence or official permission required and certainly without any need to consult the government regulator English Heritage or any other archaeologists, David has a JCB excavator on site in response to this first excursion into the practical application of archaeological geophysics in the field. Not that he will see it like that.

Nonetheless, his research is rewarded when he finds the rudder 2ft below the surface and the engine block at 8ft. His witness and the metal detector are vindicated, and David is hooked.

The plane in question is Spitfire Mark Mk IIB P8438, of the famous 133 Eagle Squadron of the Royal Air Force. The squadron was made up of American volunteers who made the choice to pre-empt the decision of their own government and join the Royal Air Force Volunteer Reserve (RAFVR) in order to join the fight against fascism.

In the early months of 1942, 133 Squadron was operating out of RAF Kirton in Lindsey in Lincolnshire when, while on a training exercise, Pilot Officer Samuel Whedon flying Spitfire P8438 collided with the aircraft flown by his squadron mate, Pilot Officer William Arends. Both fighters crashed. Whedon managed to bail out, but, in one of those accidents that are somehow even more cruel when they occur in wartime, he was killed when his parachute failed to deploy properly.

California-born Arends was luckier. The canopy of his parachute bloomed in the spring sky and he made it safely to earth. However, his reprieve was short. William Arends died barely two months later on 20 June 1942, shot down in a dogfight over northern France by a 'Butcher Bird', the new Luftwaffe Focke-Wulf Fw 190 fighter, which at the time was cutting a bloody swathe through the RAF's now outclassed Mk V Spitfires. David also finds and recovers what is left of Pilot Officer Arends' aircraft a few miles away.

Both pilots are commemorated under the spreading wings of the Bald Eagle, which stands atop Dame Elizabeth Frinks' starkly simple twin obelisks of white Portland stone, which form the Eagle Squadron memorial outside the former US Embassy in Grosvenor Square, London.

Through the 1980s and 1990s David tracks down many more wrecks of Second World War aircraft, including another iconic type, a Lancaster bomber that crashed in Lincolnshire in 1944. The aircraft was returning from a raid over Germany, badly shot up and on fire, when the crew was forced to bail out before they could reach the airfield.

David and his friend, Dave Paltry (another Lincolnshire farmer), find the crash site at Owston Ferry.

According to witnesses, the plane plunged straight down, slamming into the ground at high speed. The fuselage disintegrated on impact into a mass of contorted aluminium confetti, while the four Merlin engines buried themselves 10ft into the earth. David manages to recover the engines and other parts.

Further digs will follow.

In 1990, he locates the crash site of a Hawker Hurricane fighter at Grinsby, in the Tetney Marsh. The pilot who flew the aircraft visits the dig and mentions that he'd left his wallet in the cockpit. Sure enough, David fishes out a muddy wallet from the cockpit and returns it to the owner!

Finally, in 1992, David finds another Spitfire, this time a Mark V, which crashed at Goole in Yorkshire. The crash was so violent that the plane buried itself 26ft down in the wet clay, tearing off the wings and rudder, and twisting the propeller blade into a corkscrew as it went, proving incidentally that the engine was still running at the point of impact.

However, as it turns out these early finds are simply the overture. David's latest find is the discovery of a lifetime, the all-singing, all-dancing Broadway finale to a career resurrecting aviation ghosts: he claims to have found twenty crated Spitfires, buried at RAF Mingaladon just outside Yangon at the end of the Second World War.

According to Adam Lusher's article in *The Telegraph*, it took David sixteen years to track down the planes, during which he suffered many setbacks, including failed surveys, running out of money, the arrest of the Burmese Prime Minister who backed him in the early 2000s, demands for large cash payments from his agents, and at one particularly low point in his quest having a gun pointed at his head.* David is now on the cusp of fulfilling his dream.

He is greatly assisted by the announcement, reported in the British papers, that British Prime Minister David Cameron has negotiated an agreement with Myanmar President Thein Sein for the recovery and repatriation of the planes. The news circles the globe and reaches my computer screen in my office in Emeryville, California.

I have a somewhat unusual job. I am a historian by training, but thanks to a lifelong interest in video games, I left the lecture hall for the video game industry and never looked back. In January 2012, I started working for Wargaming, a video game company that makes games about the vehicles of the Second World War. As the Director of Special Projects, my job is to come up with outside the box marketing ideas, including using interactive technology to 'bring history alive' at military history museums.

David's story fires my imagination. The Spitfire is, of course, just about the most iconic industrial object ever created. With the lines of a beautiful kinetic sculpture and the fighting power of a war machine; the distinctive roar of the Rolls-Royce Merlin engine that powered the aircraft through most of the Second World War is enough to make British people stop what they're doing and look to the sky, and, as those distinctive elliptical wings swoop into view, it seems most Britons cannot help but stand a little straighter, heart swelling with pride at Reginald Mitchell's fabulous creation. Perhaps some even dream of days

---

* www.telegraph.co.uk/news/worldnews/asia/burmamyanmar/9204921/British-farmers-quest-to-find-lost-Spitfires-in-Burma.html. David's story of being held at gunpoint is recounted in Lusher's later article: www.telegraph.co.uk/news/aviation/9806536/Burmas-buried-Spitfires-the-inside-story-of-one-mans-obsession.html

when the world seemed simpler, when what was right was right, and what was wrong was clear, when the Spitfire helped save the world from fascism.

If the planes are indeed there, then they are potentially worth millions on the collectors' market – and their heritage value to the British is incalculable. As Sebastian Cox, the Head of the Air Historical Branch at the Ministry of Defence, will later tell me, 'If these Spitfires are found, it will be the single biggest find of WW2 artefacts in our history.'

On current estimates just fifty-four of these iconic aircraft are maintained in flyable condition, most of them in the UK, and those that can still take to the skies are lovingly maintained and eagerly sought after by museums and collectors all over the world.

Intrigued, I track down David through a Google search and ring him up at his farm in Lincolnshire. It is 23 April 2012, St George's Day, England's National Day; a day for national symbols, red roses, Shakespeare's 'sceptred Isle' speech from Richard II and, since the summer of 1940, Spitfires.

Over the previous week David has been inundated with hundreds of calls from well-wishers, potential buyers, television reporters, rip-off artists and con men, and at least one clairvoyant (who claimed to know the location of additional planes), so it's rather surprising I get through to him at all. David assumes I am just another crazy caller (he's not a gamer, so has never heard of Wargaming. net), so we only speak for a few minutes before he rings off abruptly. Shortly afterwards I have to leave for the Smithsonian's somewhat awkwardly named Mutual Concerns Conference on 26 April (about historic aviation), and I will not be able to reach David again until two weeks later, on 8 May.

According to news reports, David has teamed up with a wealthy real estate developer and Spitfire enthusiast named Steve Boultbee Brooks, who owns the Boultbee Flight Academy (where one can learn to fly a MK IX Spitfire). Mr Brooks has immediately flown out to Burma to lobby the British Prime Minister David Cameron to support the project.

At the time, David Cameron (who also lives in Brooks's home county of Oxfordshire, north-west of London) is approaching the end of a trade mission to Asia on behalf of the European Union and his final destination is Burma.

For Cameron and the diplomats in the ornate offices of the British Foreign Office on Whitehall, a joint heritage project between the UK and Burma seems like just the sort of feel-good exercise in soft power that would help Cameron lift EU sanctions on Burma and generate some positive PR for his administration. He needs it. The trip to the Far East has attracted a lot of flak from the media.

And so, after hearing the story from Brooks, Cameron and his media team jump on board with the story, and in the course of his scheduled meetings, alongside trade and democratisation, he talks at length with President Thein Sein about the legendary Spitfires. The upshot of the talks is that the Prime Minister and the President reach an historic agreement to recover and repatriate the buried planes.

The agreement is announced on 14 April 2012 and makes headlines around the world. A spokeswoman for 10 Downing Street says, 'We hope that this will be an opportunity to work with the reforming Burmese government to uncover, restore and display these fighter planes and have them grace the skies of Britain once again.'*

However, what is not made clear at this time is that the person who accompanies the Prime Minister into the negotiations with President Thein Sein about the Spitfires is not David Cundall, but his new business partner, Steve Boultbee Brooks. On his return to England Brooks then appears representing the project on the BBC One early evening magazine programme, *The One Show*.**

In an appearance which was clearly inserted into the running order at short notice as a breaking story, the presenters appear poorly prepared and Mr Brooks also looks uncomfortable, possibly in part because he was repeating someone else's brief. He certainly seems confused about the depth and nature of the supposed geophysics targets and seems to quote David Cundall directly saying, 'We have seen the aircraft in the crates..,' when nobody, except David, was claiming this.

In Brook's defence, it is possible that he had not actually not actually seen the full geophysical data set. Geophysicist Dr Adam Booth recalls Brooks telephoning him for information at around this time, Adam believes possibly without David Cundall's knowledge.

This may be one of the reasons that the apparent bonhomie between the farmer and the property developer is short lived. David has a very public falling out with Brooks and – indirectly – with Prime Minister Cameron.

On 28 April 2012, the *Independent* newspaper in London runs a story with the headline 'Cameron's Claim on Spitfire trove ignites British Battle in Burma'. David alleges that Brooks is trying to seize control of the project, something Brooks denies.

In response, David tells the *Vancouver Sun*, rather undiplomatically and with characteristic bullishness, 'I can do it without Brooks, I can do it without anybody. I've been digging up aircraft for 35 years. I've pushed the boat out

---

* www.independent.co.uk/news/uk/politics/camerons-claim-on-spitfire-trove-ignites-a-british-battle-in-burma-7685290.html
** BBC One, *The One Show*, 16 April 2012.

financially. I've struggled like hell to keep it going. I've dug up Burma before, and I don't need them.'*

It is a mantra he will repeat in the future.

However, back in London in the late spring of 2012, 10 Downing Street is not pleased. Brooks makes it known he intends to launch his own recovery team without David – and get to Myanmar before the monsoon. This will be a David Cundall versus Goliath battle, particularly so because, with Brooks and his generously filled wallet out of the picture, David needs new financial backing urgently to have any chance of pursuing his dream. He is now much more receptive to my offer to fly him to San Francisco to discuss how we might assist with the recovery. We're interested in the project since our upcoming title, *World of Warplanes*, will feature the iconic aircraft. One week later David Cundall is standing in front of me in the old-world splendour of the Westin St Francis Hotel's lobby.

Over dinner at Santorini's Mediterranean Restaurant on O'Farrell Street, David tells me about his life. He is married with three children, who now have children of their own. From this perspective David is thinking about his legacy and turning to thoughts of fulfilling his childhood dreams, and his abiding dream and passion is the Spitfire.

His eyes shine as he talks about this iconic aircraft.

'The planes saved us in the Battle of Britain,' he says. 'Now it's time to return the favour and save them from rotting away in Burma.'

He tells me his dream is to restore enough of these planes to flying condition to create a squadron and have them fly at airshows around the UK. Of course, David plans to keep a few for himself, though he is quick to stress that for him the project is not about financial gain.

'I want to do something important in my life,' David tells me, looking me in the eye to emphasise the point.

I can understand him. David wants to make a contribution and to be remembered. Finding the Spitfires will lead to his coronation, even his canonisation, in the secular world of the historic aviation community, whose approval he seems to crave. Bringing the planes home might even garner him a knighthood. And incidentally, with airworthy Spitfires currently fetching around £2 million each, it would almost certainly make him a wealthy man, independently of the income from his farm.

Wargaming Office

---

* Quoted in Fox News www.foxnews.com/tech/dogfight-over-buried-wwii-spitfires-in-burma#ixzz2eZlLJq3Y

Emeryville
California
17-18 May

The next morning David and I take the train to East Bay to visit Wargaming's office on the top floor of a three-storey office building near the marina. I give him a quick tour of the building and introduce him to our senior staff. We all take our seats in the conference room. David takes out a thick sheaf of dog-eared and well-thumbed papers and begins to tell us his story:

> I first learned about the Burma Spitfires from my good friend Jim Pearce. Jim has recovered dozens of Second World War aircraft over the years, particularly in Eastern Europe, the Balkans, and Russia. He was busy in Russia in the 1990s and didn't have time to investigate the Burma Spitfires, so he passed the torch to me. Jim told me that he'd first heard the story from two retired American service personnel in the 1970s.
>
> They told Jim that they'd been in Burma in 1945 and had helped to bury a dozen crated Spitfires at Mingaladon airfield, just outside of Rangoon. This struck me as very unusual, but Jim had been right on many occasions, so I decided to pursue the story. I advertised in specialist magazines like *FlyPast* to track down others who had been stationed at Mingaladon airfield in 1945–46.
>
> I got a number of letters from retired RAF pilots and mechanics who attested that they had seen or heard about a burial at that time. I interviewed eight of these witnesses and they all pointed to the same spot on the map.

He takes out a map of Mingaladon airfield as it existed in 1945. We see a plan of three intersecting runways forming a large triangle, more or less in the shape of a giant letter 'A' scribed on a wide flat plateau, some 8 miles from central Yangon, then called Rangoon. 'Here, near the taxiway leading from the main runway to the maintenance hangars,' he says, pointing to the map. We all lean in to take a closer look.

'The news reports say that you have been searching for the planes for sixteen years – why did it take so long and how did you finally find them?' I ask. David collects his thoughts for a moment before replying:

> It took me two years to research the story and track down witnesses who remembered the burial. And you have to remember that Burma at that time was a closed country. It was very difficult to enter. I went to the Embassy many times to talk to the Ambassador. I finally got permission

in 1998, when I made my first trip. I returned in 2000 and 2004. All told I made about a dozen trips in those years. I spent about £130,000 of my own money on surveys and test digs. The government wanted more proof before they'd let me excavate, so I contacted Dr Roger Clark and Adam Booth (geophysicists) from Leeds University, whom I had worked with on previous projects. When I phoned him up, Adam thought I said Birmingham, not Burma, but he agreed to fly out to Mingaladon with me and survey the area with a magnetometer. And we found two large concentrations of metal right where the witness said the planes were buried.

David shows us the printout of a 100 x 180m scan of the burial site with a colour-coded scale showing electrical conductivity. He explains that red indicates concentrations of metal. Two large rectangular areas in solid red stand out clearly in the image against a sea of blue and light greens.

'We did this survey in the autumn of 2004.' David explains, 'I brought in an excavator to do a test dig. We'd dug down a couple of feet when suddenly the digger bucket crunched into wood. And before we could excavate further to find out what it was we were escorted off the site and not allowed to return.'

David adds, 'Soon after, the Prime Minister [General Khin Nyunt] was arrested on corruption charges.'*

In a moment the story has turned from being a fascinating and somewhat quixotic excavation looking for lost aircraft into a political thriller with overtones of Graham Greene.

David continues, 'My contract was cancelled, and they took my passport. I had to stay in the hotel for five weeks. I wasn't allowed to leave. Eventually they returned my passport and let me leave the country, but I wasn't able to come back until this year – in large part owing to the new sanctions imposed in 2007.** Now that sanctions have come off, and with the government's support, I can finally dig up the aeroplanes and repatriate them to the UK.'

'Why did the military bury the planes in the first place?' one of my colleagues asks, genuinely puzzled.

David replies confidently, laying out his stall:

There are two theories about that. The first is that it was simply to dispose of war material deemed surplus to requirements. At the end of the war, the navy was pushing planes off the decks of aircraft carriers into the sea because

---

*   At this time the State Peace and Development Council's chosen man is former Head of
      Intelligence Khin Nyunt.
**   This international isolation comes in the wake of the regime's violent suppression of the
      so-called Saffron Revolution.

they didn't need them anymore, and it was too expensive to ship them back to the UK. So they just dumped them. These Spitfires were part of the build-up for Operation Zipper, which was cancelled after the dropping of the atomic bombs made the invasion of the Malaya peninsula unnecessary. It's possible the planes were simply disposed of to make space on the airfield. But there's a second theory, which I'm inclined to believe …

His voice seems take on a subtle new tone, hinting that what he is about to tell us is privileged and maybe a little dangerous to somebody:

… and that's that the planes were buried for later retrieval by the Karen, who had supported the British in the war. The Karen peoples wanted independence and the planes would help them achieve it. But they were defeated in the 1948 uprising and the planes' location forgotten.

Our discussion continues for almost two hours, during which time David shows us stacks of documents, including a sheaf of letters from veterans who served at Mingaladon who all apparently remembered seeing or hearing about the burial, shipping manifests listing crated Spitfires brought to Calcutta in 1945, and the formal report on a further geophysical survey of the suspected burial site by a Yangon-based company called Suntec, which David had apparently commissioned to follow up the work of Adam Booth and Malcolm Weale.

He also shows us the Google maps satellite images of the modern airport, which we compare with the plan of the wartime airfield. It is a disorientating experience. Superficially the site is completely different. The wartime runways are gone, as are many of the surrounding structures, and the modern runway runs on a completely different axis. These changes make locating the burial site a challenge. David relates how a rival group (headed by former Israeli Intelligence operator Ziv Brosh) came in after David lost his contract and dug at the wrong end of the runway. They came up empty-handed.

After lunch, David is feeling a bit jet-lagged and decides to head back to the hotel.

I call him a taxi and our team reconvenes to discuss David's story. We recognise that the project risks are not inconsiderable.

Firstly, there is the possibility the story is a shaggy dog tale, and there are no planes buried at Mingaladon. But since the British Prime Minister has publicly backed the project, and even negotiated an agreement for the repatriation of the planes, we believe there must be reasonable grounds for taking the story at face value.

Surely 10 Downing Street's experts had vetted the story. Nevertheless, we discuss the question of what happens if we dig and there's nothing at the bottom of the hole. I make a joke about Al Capone's vault, which was opened on live television to reveal … nothing.*

Secondly, there is the possibility that the Spitfires are there but have disintegrated after being in the ground for seventy years. David tells us the crates had been tarred, the planes wrapped in greased paper, and the engines inhibited with oil – but even so tropical climates are not kind to wood or metal, particularly when it is buried in ground soaked by a monsoon every year.

And finally, the proposed excavation will take place in the former British colony of Burma, now the independent Union of Myanmar, a country that has been isolated for decades and which is only now emerging from years of military repression and sanctions. There are no guarantees that David and his Burmese business partners would be able to secure permission to dig next to an active runway at the country's only international airport.

In the end, we decide to move forward with the project. The initial funds required are small and we believe that it will make for a good story, whatever we find buried in Burma. We can take that view because we are not embarking on this project for financial gain. We don't need to; Wargaming does very well making video games. More to the point, we are not treasure hunters. Rather, we decide to sponsor the project because it fits well with our plans to reach aviation and military history enthusiasts, who share our passion for historic warbirds.

Jeremy Monroe (Wargaming's general manager) argues that the media rights are the most valuable part of the project, so we decide to ask for worldwide media rights to the story in exchange for financial support. We also ask for two aircraft (if any are recovered) in exchange for funding. Our thinking is that we will donate the planes to an historic aviation group, such as the Collins Foundation or the Commemorative Air Force, and thereby promote Wargaming at air shows around the country while ensuring the aircraft will be properly conserved, seen and enjoyed by the public.

The next morning, David agrees to our proposal and we sign a term sheet to back an expedition to Myanmar to excavate and repatriate the planes – pending permission from the Myanmar government.

It is agreed also that I will accompany David to Myanmar as Wargaming's representative.

---

*   *The Mystery of Al Capone's Vaults*, a two-hour television special hosted by Geraldo Rivera, was aired in 1986.

If David is right, and there really are crated Spitfires buried at Mingaladon, it will be a sensational discovery; nothing less than the aviation world's equivalent of Howard Carter's discovery of Tutankhamun's tomb in 1922. Indeed, David told me that he dreams to peer inside a buried crate and report that he sees 'wonderful things'. Only later do I realise that as the funder of this particular expedition I am in the position of Lord Carnarvon, who was, according to the tabloid legend at least, the first victim of the Curse of the Pharaoh!

On the last day of David's visit, to mark our newly established partnership, my colleagues and I, along with David, drive out to Moffett field in San Jose. We have arranged to fly around the bay in a vintage B-17 bomber operated by the Collins Foundation. After signing a rather scary liability waiver, we climb into the B-17, strap in and roar down the runway.

Soon we are flying over San Francisco Bay. It is exhilarating. Once airborne we are allowed to walk around the plane – taking care not to fall through the bomb bay doors. Moving to the glazed nose of the aircraft, I sit in the bombardier's chair and watch the hills of Palo Alto roll by through the targeting reticule. David poses for a photo with the 50 calibre machine guns. It is easy to imagine that we are flying over the wartime Ruhr valley, lead ship in a box formation of B-17s from Major General Ira Eaker's Eighth Air Force, keeping a sharp eye out for the swarms of marauding Focke-Wulf and Messerschmitt fighters and praying we don't get hit by the walls of German flak. David is beaming. This flight is a dream come true.

One week later, on Friday, 25 May, David receives an email from his Myanmar business partners urging us to come to Myanmar 'with all possible speed'. The 2012 monsoon season is about to begin. We have perhaps two or three more weeks of sunny weather before the rains will soak the ground, making it impossible to sink a borehole or conduct a test dig (as David had suggested) until at least the end of the year.

More alarming, the news that there may be an entire squadron of Spitfires buried at a former RAF airfield in Myanmar ignites a race to recover the planes, with competing teams putting in applications for digging permits. One of the groups is led by David's former partner and now arch rival, Steven Boultbee Brooks.

We book our flights and prepare to fly to Myanmar.

4

Andy Brockman
Shooters Hill
South-east London
Saturday, 14 April 2012

It is for people such as my colleague and friend Rod Scott that hands-free and speed dial was invented, and in the spring of 2012 he takes full advantage of these to fill the commute between his home near Oxford and his current posting in Bath. But today is Saturday. Thus it is more of a surprise when he calls in the late afternoon.

As a career soldier, a conversation with Rod normally starts with his requesting the latest situation report.

'What's new?' he asks.

It transpires that what is new for Rod is a post on a Facebook group to which we both belong, Modern Conflict Archaeology.

I tell him I have not looked at it today.

'Oh you'll love it,' he says and proceeds to tell me how the post describes the theory of a certain Lincolnshire Farmer called David Cundall.

I look it up.

'Hope for finding Burma Spitfires,' the article begins …

'British and Burmese authorities could work together to find 20 Spitfires buried in Burma at the end of the World War II, officials say.'

This report is apparently authoritative because the post is linked to another report on the BBC website.

I cannot help but get drawn into the whole story.

For me it has a delicious and irresistible mixture of mystery, politics and personalities, and above all it is about archaeology and Spitfires.

Archaeology is my job and the Spitfire has been a part of my life since I bought my first 1:72 scale Airfix kit of a Spitfire Mk V for 2s 9d in the model trains and kits department at the back of the ground floor of Barrett's of Canterbury, c.1967.

Just as the story is getting off the ground, however, it appears to stall and crash back to earth. *The Telegraph*, which clearly has the inside track on the story from Mr Cundall's point of view, reports a serious falling out between Mr Cundall and his business partner, Steve Brooks.

'It's Spitfires at dawn in Burma' claims the paper, adding, 'The hunt for valuable planes buried at the end of the Second World War is turning nasty.'*

While David Cameron's PR pitch to dig up Spitfires appears to have ground to an acrimonious halt, I decide to draw some lessons from the affair by writing an article about it.

The platform will be Markus Milligan's new online venture into archaeology news *Heritage Daily*, for which I have recently begun to write.

On 12 May 2012 the article is ready and is published under a title paying tribute to the *Commando* comic books I had read, shared and swapped with my school friends in the early 1970s. I title the piece 'Achtung! Spitfires!'

Less graphic novels in the modern sense than comic strip yarns, *Commando* comic books were founded on gung-ho adventures where square-jawed British servicemen fought against the odds to defeat various gratuitously offensive national stereotypes.

The artists of the *Commando* stories would regularly take you inside the cockpit of a German bomber as the gunners called out the warning, 'Achtung! Spitfires!' before having their day spoiled by a hail of .303 rounds loosed off by a laconic member of the Few.

The article was really intended as an exploration of the issues the Burma Spitfires story and its treatment by the media raise for those of us who work in the archaeology of conflict. It certainly is not intended as a job application. However, as it transpires, not only is the article prescient, on 7 September 2012 it will provide me with a career-changing reminder of the power of the internet to create new links and networks.

---

*   www.telegraph.co.uk/history/world-war-two/9228910/Its-Spitfires-at-dawn-in-Burma.html

5

It is a guilty secret buried in the history of modern scientific archaeology that, particularly in its early days, archaeology and treasure hunting were almost indistinguishable.

Consequently, the galleries and store rooms of many of the great museums of the European Enlightenment from St Petersburg and Berlin to London and Paris are full of artefacts excavated and exported from their home soil by pioneer archaeologists like Sir Austin Henry Layard, who exported the reliefs from the Assyrian palaces of Nineveh to London; Heinrich Schliemann, who took what he thought to be the jewels of Queen Helen from Troy to Berlin; and Thomas Bruce, 7th Earl of Elgin, who claimed to have reached a deal with the Sublime Porte of the Ottoman Empire to remove half of the sculptural freezes from the ruined Parthenon in Athens.

In those pioneering decades of the nineteenth century, with the newly unified Greek and Italian governments clamping down on the export of classical antiquities, the most lucrative treasures for anyone hoping to obtain personal and corporate sponsorship for an archaeological expedition were those that could be connected with the Bible.

Treasures such as the greatest lost treasure of all, the lost Ark of the Covenant last seen in the Kodesh Hakodashim (Holy of Holies) in the Temple of Solomon in Jerusalem, in 587 BC.

The Port of Jaffa
Ottoman Province of Palestine
August 1909

As he strides down the gang plank of Mr Clarence Wilson's superbly appointed steam yacht, the *Water Lily*, Captain the Honourable Montagu Brownlow

Parker is just about as textbook a representative of the British Empire as you could ask for.

In August 1909 he is 31 years old. A war hero in the South African War fighting the Boers, he has retired from the British Army with the rank of captain having served with the elite Grenadier Guards; a commission befitting the son of the 4th Earl of Morley, a title to which he will succeed in 1951.

Of course, a retired soldier who is still young and vigorous needs something to do with the rest of his life and Captain Parker has decided that something is archaeology. His chosen location is the Holy Land of Palestine, where an ambitious archaeologist can both make a name for himself and fill a museum.

Captain Parker has chosen archaeology in the Holy Land not because he is a religious zealot like his fellow soldier and religious warrior hero, Colonel Charles George 'Chinese' Gordon of the Royal Engineers, who in 1883 identified the site of the crucifixion, at least to his own satisfaction, as the Hill of the Skull, which can be found today in Jerusalem just off the Nablus Road, overlooking a bus station. It was a discovery that came just two years before he found his own martyrdom at the hands of the Mahdi's Ansars in Khartoum.

Neither is Captain Parker inspired by this new academic subject of archaeology and excited by a role as a clandestine intelligence operator like the young Welsh-born, Oxford-educated archaeologist Thomas Edward Lawrence, who is currently finishing his BA thesis with an 1,100-mile walking tour of the Biblical Lands. In December 1913, Lawrence will be sent to northern Sinai and the southern Negev desert by the Palestine Exploration Fund, ostensibly to research archaeological sites but actually to spy on the Ottoman Turkish defences of Southern Palestine. It is experience he will put to good use a few years later in his wartime guise of Lawrence of Arabia.

Captain Parker is in Palestine as an independent expedition leader because last year, in London, he met Dr Walter Henrik Juvelius.

Finnish-born scholar Dr Juvelius is a trained surveyor and a poet with two published collections of poems to his name. Now, aged 44, he earns his living as the director of the workers' education centre in Viipuri (Vyborg), but his hobby, about which he is passionate, is researching Biblical texts and Jewish chronology and he has an intriguing proposition. In a secret manuscript copy of the book of Ezekiel, which he has found hidden in a library in Constantinople – he cannot say exactly where for fear others may find it – he has discovered a coded account that gives the location of a fabulous treasure buried close to Temple Mount in Jerusalem.

Buried by the priests of the great Temple of Jerusalem to keep it from the conquering army of Babylonian King Nebuchadnezzar in 587 BC, this unparalleled material and spiritual treasure may even contain the single most important object borne out of the desert by the Children of Israel, the Ark of the Covenant, which is said to contain the words of God himself, given to Moses on Mount Sinai.

Dr Juvelius estimates the value of the treasure to be as much as $200 million, but he has not got the means, style, connections or language to convince the people with the kind of money he needs to invest in a project to go in search of the Temple treasure. A young and energetic English aristocrat of proven courage and ability is somehow a more credible salesman than a Finnish academic tinged with mysticism.

By the start of the summer Captain Parker has raised $125,000 from investors who allegedly include the Duchess of Marlborough and, in a sign of the international appeal of Biblical studies, the Armour family of Chicago meat packers.

For that reason Captain Parker does not care that, according to Dr Juvelius, there is a curse six and sixty-fold upon any person who dares reveal the location of the sacred treasure.

Instead, he is convinced the partners in the JMPVF Syndicate, Dr Juvelius, the Swedish tunnelling engineer Mister Millin, Captain Parker himself, Mr Vaughn and Mr Fort, will soon be both rich and famous.

One of the reasons he is so confident is that a large portion of the money and the promise of 50 per cent of the find is about to be invested in the Ottoman officials whose permission is needed to undertake the excavation, including the governor of Jerusalem, Azmey Bey Pasha.

Captain Parker knows precisely how to do business in the Ottoman Empire.

He is also aware that if he makes a mistake in Jerusalem he can mortally offend the followers of the three great religions of the Book all at the same time.

6

From before a time no one could remember, the skies of Burma had belonged to creatures born with wings, and particularly the legendary golden Hintha bird who represents the ultimate liberation from the cycle of life and death.

However, in contrast to the thousands of years of legend and religious philosophy that gave life to the Hintha, it took just eight years for the new science of aviation to travel from Kittyhawk, where Wilbur and Orville Wright took their first flight, to a plateau above Rangoon.

The edition of *Flight* magazine published on 22 June 1912 records that the first powered flight in Burma took place in the Mingaladon township, where Rangoon's international airport and principal RAF base would grow up twenty years later.

It is a Sunday morning on the course of the Rangoon Golf Club.

Mr W.C. England blinks and squints as something on the edge of his vision flashes in the early morning sun. He straightens and wipes his face with the oily rag he has just used to mop the leaky seal on the 40hp ENV aero engine that he has been tuning. His once white overalls are oily and red with the dust of Rangoon in the dry season.

Mr England is the manager of the Burma Motor and Engineering Company. In autumn last year, 1911, he took leave to visit England and seized the opportunity to qualify for his pilot's ticket with the Claude Grahame-White Flying School at the London Aerodrome in Hendon, north London. On his return to Burma he had been accompanied by his brand new Howard Wright biplane, reduced to its component parts and safely crated up for the long sea journey.

Arriving safely at Rangoon docks, it has taken Mr England six months' work to get his precious aircraft ready for flight. He has stripped and replaced all the canvas covering, and he has even ordered a new carburettor from England because the original could not provide enough power to get the aircraft airborne in the still, hot and dry air of Mingaladon. But now he is satisfied with his work. He is convinced that the aircraft is better than before, more stable and more responsive in the handling. He even finds it does not attract the ants and termites that the naysayers told him would reduce the airframe to sawdust before he could even get her into the air.

He clambers aboard and fastens the leather safety belt around his waist.

Mr England opens the throttle and the Howard Wright gathers speed, the double wheels of the landing gear bouncing hard across the ruts formed from the sun-fired hoofprints of grazing cattle. But the discomfort is soon over and Mr England smiles at the thrill of flight as the aircraft lifts off into the high blue without him even having to apply any elevator.

Climbing easily to 150ft, he turns the aircraft back and forward across the golf course to give the golf club members and friends a good view. If any of them volunteer the desire to fly he will order a new and more powerful aircraft so that he can offer demonstration and cross-country flights carrying a passenger, perhaps even making a circuit of the Shwedagon Pagoda itself, which he can see golden in the distance across the Insein Lake.

Throttling back, Mr England settles the Howard Wright back onto the ground and begins to taxi the aircraft back to its shed, while in the still air high above the Mingaladon Golf Course, far higher than Mr England can even dream of reaching, and on the edge of human perception, the great Hintha bird of Burmese legend turns easy circles. Her golden feathers splinter the sunlight like the diamond on the top of the Shwedegon Pagoda that she too can see shining like a setting sun over the Burmese capital of Rangoon away to the south-west. Then she swoops across the golf course more clearly to see the interloper into what has been her space.

The flash of the Hintha bird's feathers catches Mr England's eye once again and his body tenses instinctively so that his feet kick against the rudder bar, flicking the aircraft around. In a moment he is aware of the ping of a broken wire and a splintering crunch as the aircraft tilts alarmingly to the right.

Swearing, Mr England cuts the engine and jumps down to inspect the damage. He kicks at the hard-baked clay of the anthill which he has struck, pulling out the right-hand landing carriage assembly by its roots.

It can be repaired.

Next year, Mr England promises himself, it will be better. At the end of the monsoon season he will arrange for a runway to be rolled at Mingaladon so that it dries hard and flat. That will make taking off and landing less like driving over badly laid bricks with the added obstacle of anthills.

He must do this because it is progress, it is the future, it is evolution. Such are the gifts that the British can give to the peoples of the Empire. Aviation has come to Mingaladon and one day, Mr England is convinced, you will be able to fly from Rangoon to London in the way that today is only possible for the migrating birds.

And high above, the Hintha bird banks, looks down, wonders and laughs at this clumsy attempt to conquer her realm with wood and canvas, driven only by a tiny stuttering device of hot metal and the dream of flight.

Tracy Spaight
En route to Myanmar
30–31 May 2012

One hundred years on from Mr England's first flight in Rangoon, David and I are flying in a modern long-range Airbus. The journey bears little resemblance to the glamour and luxury of the first generation of long-range jet airliners flown by British Overseas Airways Corporation to link a shrinking British Empire and Commonwealth in the 1950s, let alone to the sedate flying boats of Imperial Airways that pioneered air travel to Rangoon in the 1930s.

Today there are none of the smiling supermodels working incognito as stewardesses shown in the early airline posters, no grilled filet mignon au beurre served on bone china, and no jet-setting movie stars like Richard Burton and Elizabeth Taylor, whiling away the miles at 30,000ft with relays of vodka Martinis and whisky sours. But whatever the discomforts of modern air travel, they pale in comparison to what travellers endured in centuries past.

In the sixteenth century, Ferdinand Magellan's scurvy-ridden crew take eight months to reach the fabled Spice Islands of Southeast Asia and after a circumnavigation taking three years only one ship out of a squadron of five, the *Nao Victoria*, and just eighteen of the original 270 members of the expedition, complete the voyage to return to Sanlúcar de Barrameda in Andalusia, the same port from which they had set off. The rest died of starvation, of tropical diseases, or like their commander, under the war clubs and bamboo spears wielded by Chief Lapu Lapu's war band in the Philippines.

However, the bravery of these pioneering travellers pays off, and by the mid-nineteenth century South East Asia is much closer in time to London and New York, so that Jules Verne's Phileas Fogg can take every state-of-the-art mode of transport, and an elephant, to travel 'around the world in 80 days'. In a truly modern touch, Mr Fogg's greatest danger is of missing a connection.

That said, while the danger of drowning, or of being murdered en route, had reduced substantially by 1912, when Mr England travelled back to Burma with his aircraft, an unaccompanied white male of means travelling out on one of the Peninsular and Oriental Steamship Company's crack steamers, faced new risks.

One was finding oneself bored rigid for nights on end by the traveller's tales of a would-be rubber planter hoping to make his fortune up country in Burma, while another, potentially more permanent, risk was being netted over a game of whist by a member of the 'fishing fleet'. This was the annual migration of English Home Counties boarding school 'gels', taking the passage to Bombay and through its gateway to the world of the British Raj in the hope of snaring an eligible husband in the Indian Army or Colonial Service.

Of course, whether packing a steamer trunk with the recommended items from the Army and Navy Store in Victoria in 1912, or hold baggage in a Samsonite case in 2012, it is important to add those hard to obtain extras that are essential to the success of the trip. When we land in Kuala Lumpur, stiff and tired, on the morning of 31 May we suddenly realise that neither of us have brought gifts to present to the Myanmar minister we are meeting! Some things do not change as swiftly as the technology of travel and the etiquette of business is one of them.

In fact, gift giving is an essential and delicate matter in building a business relationship in Asia. The gift has to be appropriate and thoughtful, but crucially not so expensive that it might be construed as a bribe. That would be insulting as well as illegal. Ideally, it should be something from one's home country, which might have been a problem in Kuala Lumpur. Fortunately, some home products are now global in reach and the airport duty free shop has bottles of 40-year-old Scottish Royal Salute whisky, which David tells me the minister enjoys. I buy a bottle and we board our flight to Yangon.

In 2012 Yangon from the air looks very different from Bangkok, Hong Kong, Kuala Lumpur, Singapore or other metropolises in Asia. The city boasts a population of nearly 4 million people, yet there are no gleaming glass and steel skyscrapers, nor soaring suspension bridges across the Yangon or Bago rivers, like the Nanpu Bridge in Shanghai. Aside from a few mid-rise buildings and hotels constructed in the 1990s, Yangon still retains much of its colonial-era charm, with hundreds of decaying, but still beautiful, Victorian and Edwardian buildings lining the Strand and the many crowded thoroughfares.

In the late nineteenth century, Yangon – then called Rangoon – was known as the Garden City of the East. The British occupied the city in the wake of the Second Burmese War in 1852, after which it became the capital of British Burma in 1886.

Under British administration, the city was transformed from a sleepy port town where the Pazundaung Creek and the Yangon river came together into a major commercial and political hub, with broad tree-lined streets and spacious gardens, such as the Cantonment Gardens. The General Hospital, the Secretariat Building, the Strand Hotel, Yangon University, the post office, and telegraph exchanges, Yangon's central train station and the magnificent Trinity Anglican Church all date from this era. With the opening of the Suez Canal, demand for Burmese rice, rubber, teak and other exports soared – enriching many British firms, who monopolised the trade and in the process fuelled Burmese resentment and nationalism.

The influx of workers and entrepreneurs from India, many of them Muslim, was also a source of current and future tensions lasting into the twenty-first century, culminating in August 2017 with the ethnic cleansing of an estimated half a million (c.50 per cent) of the Burmese Muslim population of Rakhine Province by the Burmese military, with, at best, the public aquiescence of the now State Councillor (de facto Prime Minister) Aung San Suu Kyi.*

Nonetheless, these are halcyon days for the British Empire, and its poet of imperialism, Rudyard Kipling, put its 'civilising' ethos into verse. But whatever the benefits of Pax Britannica, British high-handedness, discrimination and disrespect for local customs (one complaint was that the British refused to remove their shoes when visiting Buddhist temples!) angered the Burmese, who increasingly pushed for self-rule.

This darker side of colonial rule was captured in George Orwell's *Burmese Days* (my inflight reading), whose main character, John Flory, defines colonialism as 'the lie that we're here to uplift our poor black brothers rather than to rob them'.

When the Japanese promised to drive out the colonial powers and create a 'Greater-Asian Co-prosperity Sphere', many Burmese were thus inclined to listen. However, after the invasion in 1942, it quickly became apparent that the

---

*   UN Human Rights Commission Report www.ohchr.org/Documents/Countries/
     MM/CXBMissionSummaryFindingsOctober2017.pdf

Japanese had no intention of granting Burma its independence – so under a charismatic young officer called Aung San, the nationalists switched sides, forming a coalition with the British to help drive them out. Yangon was heavily damaged in the fighting.

Today the surviving colonial era buildings are in varying states of decay, with the cumulative effects of monsoon rains, sweltering heat and tropical creeper vines crumbling the masonry and eroding the once proud facades. Most streets are unlit at night. Pavements – as I will soon discover – are uneven and perilous, especially after dark. If you're not careful, you can easily bump into or trip over the bamboo scaffolding that adorns many buildings, or worse, fall into a 3ft-deep hole filled with raw sewage.

Decades of neglect and lack of investment have turned the city into the Havana of Asia, with old cars and overcrowded buses lumbering up the streets, crumbling infrastructure and intermittent power outages, exacerbated by the aerial spaghetti of do-it-yourself electrical cabling that span the back-streets. To its credit, the new government is taking steps to preserve and repurpose older buildings, rather than simply bulldozing them and building high-rises and shopping malls – as many other countries in the region have done. Yangon may yet bloom again.

We finally arrive on the afternoon of 31 May. Daw Tin Ma Latt and U Soe Thein meet us just outside customs. Tin Ma Latt (we call her Auntie Latt) is a vivacious 67-year-old Burmese woman brimming with youthful energy. She has long black hair and favours red longyi and blouses, with a pin depicting her departed reverend monk.

As a young woman, she was a classmate of Aung San Suu Kyi, Nobel peace prize winner and daughter of the country's assassinated independence hero General Aung San. Tin Ma Latt herself was born into a prosperous family, claiming descent through her maternal grandmother's side to King Mindon and the Shan Princess.

Her companion, U Soe Thein, is a retired professor of geology with a slightly not-of-this-world air and wispy grey beard, so that he comes across as the epitome of the absent-minded professor. Both work with Shwe Taung Por (STP), a company founded by David's Burmese business partner, Htoo Htoo Zaw. We pile into STP's van and drive to the Chatrium Hotel, where – after an early dinner – I promptly fall asleep.

The next morning, Tin Ma Latt, Prof. Soe Thein and Htoo Htoo Zaw arrive at the hotel to discuss the project. Htoo Htoo Zaw is a businessman with good government connections. He is in his mid-thirties, a successful entrepreneur with several businesses, and a penchant for western business casual – particularly polos and designer sunglasses. He carries two cell phones with him at all times. I arrange for a meeting room so we can talk in private.

Accompanying them is a wizened Burmese monk named Poe Poe, clad in a saffron robe. Without a word he takes a seat at the end of the table, sitting cross-legged and barefoot, staring off into space during the meeting. He appears to be on another plane of existence entirely.

Htoo Htoo speaks to us (and Auntie Latt translates) about his plan to secure the contract and ensure it does not go to a rival group. He promises to drive to Nay Pyi Taw (the new capital) in the morning to meet with the ministers. Htoo Htoo says that he wants to do the project for the honour of his country, to show that the Burmese are capable of managing a high-profile heritage project. He jabs his finger in the air for emphasis. We ask some questions about the agreement and discuss next steps. The Shwe Taung Por group departs around 1600, with their monk in tow.

With a few hours till sunset, I decide to take a cab to Singaturra Hill, upon which stands the majestic and awe-inspiring Shwedagon Pagoda, an enormous 2,600-year-old Buddhist stupa. It is the spiritual centre of the city and the heart of the nation. The Burmese are overwhelmingly Buddhist but also follow astrological beliefs that originated in Hindu Brahmanism. My Burmese guide that day – a charming old woman in a red longyi – asks me my birthday. She consults her book and announces that I was born on a Tuesday. She leads me to the Tuesday 'planetary station', where I discover that my guardian spirit is a lion.

As instructed, I dip a silver cup in the marble basin and pour water (five times) on the Buddha's head to cool him off.

I silently ask him to smile upon our venture.

The hilltop marble courtyard is surrounded by many brightly decorated stupas, but the central stupa – rising to 326ft – is the main attraction. Inside the stupa are relics of the Buddha, including eight strands of his hair. The entire massive structure is covered with more than 50 tons of gold. Topping the stupa is the *hti* or umbrella, which is covered in gold and studded with diamonds. On the very top of the spire is a single 76-carat diamond. Shwedagon is simply breathtaking.

Yangon too is beautiful, from the piety of the monks in their maroon robes to the riot of colour in the Theingyi markets. In the coming days I will spend many mornings strolling through the market while waiting for word on meetings with the various ministries. Here the market girls with their brightly coloured skirts sit in front of woven baskets and mats piled high with strong-smelling durians, sweet and juicy jackfruit, papayas, bananas, mangos, and the exotic and alien-looking red spikey mamon japones, with their white flesh.

Further down the street, fishmongers set out trays of shrimp, squid, rohu, tilapia, and more exotic species I couldn't begin to identify.

Other streets are filled with stalls laden with Asian eggplants, chillis, beans, bamboo shoots, gourds and jengkol. The morning air here is redolent with the sweet smell of overripe fruit, turmeric and cooking oil from pavement stalls. Women carry baskets on their heads, men peddle bicycles loaded with sacks and monks walk serenely through the crowds, carrying their rice bowls for alms.

Nearby, across the Strand road, dozens of brightly painted boats, like Italian gondolas but with sputtering diesel engines, ferry passengers across the Yangon River.

While walking along the Strand, I meet a young boy who looks to be about 8 years old. He is selling postcards with images of Shwedagon on the pavement outside the Zawgyi Café on Bogyoke Aung San Road, near the Scott Market. 'Where you from,' he asks me in a bright and cheery voice. He has two sunny yellow circles painted on his cheeks – the thanaka cosmetic women and children wear to protect themselves from the sun.

'I'm from the United States,' I tell him.

'What's your name?' I ask.

'Niko.'

'It's nice to meet you Niko.'

'How's business?' I ask him, gesturing to the postcards.

'So so,' he replies in surprisingly good English. 'Not so many tourists today.'

'Do you want to buy some postcards,' he asks, looking hopeful.

I buy five postcards and give him a couple of bills.

'Thanks!' he says.

'See you around Niko!'

He gets on his bike, which he later told me proudly that he bought with his own money. Niko is an impressive kid: confident, open and entrepreneurial. If all goes well he represents the future of Myanmar. As I head back to the hotel, I wonder if he's in school. Education at the state-run schools is compulsory (for five years), but the high fees make it difficult for many families to afford. Many drop out. Only a meagre part of the government budget is spent on education, perhaps because students are often in the vanguard of democratic movements, and an education is dangerous to the military government's maintenance of power and control.

The Road to Nay Pyi Taw
2-8 June 2012

Htoo Htoo returns the next day from Nay Pyi Taw and informs us that the ministers are confused about the British government's relationship to the Spitfire project. The confusion arose from Prime Minister David Cameron's visit to Myanmar in April, when he met with President Thein Sein. In the meeting, the Prime Minister had spoken at length about working together with the Burmese to recover the Spitfires and repatriate them to Great Britain as a way to bring the two countries together.

The Burmese now ask whether this would be a government-led initiative or one organised by private parties – and if the latter, then which group? For our contract to move forward, the Myanmar government requests that we secure a letter from the British Embassy endorsing David's application to excavate the Spitfires.

This could be somewhat problematic as David has very publicly told the Prime Minister he does not want or need his assistance and No. 10 could be forgiven for washing its hands of the whole affair. However, David has told me in San Francisco that all this is sorted, and we have merely to go to Myanmar to execute a contract that has been negotiated months before by STP. I'm annoyed at David once I discover the true state of affairs, but I resolve to focus on the task at hand and help secure the contract. First, I help draft a letter to President Thein Sein's office in which we summarise David's long quest to find the Spitfires. We print, translate, and notarise the letter, and send it out on Monday (4 June) by courier.

Next, we telephone Second Secretary Fergus Eckersley at the UK Embassy in Myanmar. We explain that we are in Yangon and need a letter from the British government endorsing the project. Eckersley says that the British Ambassador (Andrew Heyn) is very busy. Furthermore, none of the other applicants (there are two other British applicants) have requested such a letter, so he would have to discuss it with the ambassador. This does not look promising. That evening, we call David's contact, Isabel Hunt, in the UK, who prior to taking on her role as communications director at Leeds University was a director in the strategy team at the British Home Office.

She promises to exploit her extensive contacts in the Whitehall civil service machine by making some discreet phone calls on our behalf to gather intelligence about our rivals and to convince 10 Downing Street to authorise the UK Embassy in Yangon to write us a letter of support.

Time is running short, the monsoon rains are coming and our competitors are gaining – we have heard a rumour that agents of David's rivals are already in Yangon. As a result, we decide to camp out on the doorstep of the imposing stone edifice of the British Embassy in Yangon on 5 June.

Unfortunately, Fergus and the ambassador are not in the embassy when we call, but the guard (it appears that the embassy guards are all ex-Gurkha soldiers) helpfully informs us that they might be at the Strand Hotel or the British Club.

We check the Strand first. It is a delightful colonial-era building with white walls trimmed with teak and polished marble floors, islands of wicker furniture and wooden ceiling fans spinning lazily overhead. There's also a whimsical lost and found with a dusty pocket watch and a lady's fan that clearly date back to the colonial era. However, back in the twenty-first century the ambassador and Fergus were not to be found here either.

In the afternoon, we phone up Fergus again, explain our predicament and ask if we could get together to meet. Fergus agrees and graciously invites us to the Queen's Diamond Jubilee celebration, which will be held that evening at the British Club. We make plans to attend.

The British Club is a members only club frequented by diplomats and expat Brits. It is surrounded by a wall of white masonry and has a stout wooden gate with a guard house. A Union Flag with an image of the Queen, encircled by the words 'To Commemorate the Queen's Diamond Jubilee', announces that we are in the right place.

We find Fergus and the ambassador on the back lawn, talking with guests. They welcome us and we chat about the project over glasses of beer. Fergus proves to be an extremely charming fellow. He is fresh out of Oxford. This is his first posting in the Foreign Service. We have clearly put him in a difficult position as he is under injunction to treat all parties equally, despite David's claim to precedence and the fact that Mr Brooks had neither been to Burma prior to his visit in April, nor done any of the research required to locate the planes. I refrain from pointing out that the embassy had previously shown favour to Mr Brooks by facilitating his meeting with the Prime Minister, who subsequently allowed him to fly back to London aboard his plane it is alleged.[*] Although, in fairness, they did not know about David's involvement with Brooks at that time.

Fergus reiterates that the embassy cannot endorse any particular party nor involve itself in commercial projects. I consider this and then ask if the embassy would be willing to endorse the *idea* of recovering and repatriating the Spitfires, without specifically endorsing David's application over the others. He replies that this would be acceptable, provided we agreed to allow the embassy to offer such a letter to each of the other applicants. We accept this proposal, and on Thursday morning, 7 June, we pick up a large Manila

[*] Newspapers reported that Brooks returned on the Prime Minister's plane.

envelope stamped 'On Her Majesty's Service' at the embassy. Carrying the letter down the embassy steps I feel like James Bond.

We open the envelope and read the letter in the lobby of the Strand Hotel next door. The letter reads in part 'the Embassy would be extremely keen to see cooperation between the UK and Myanmar on such a joint heritage project' but 'the decision on how to proceed is entirely for the Myanmar government'. It is not the strongest letter of support, but at least we got one. We hope it will be enough.

We leave the Strand and drive directly to Nay Pyi Taw, which lies about 220 miles north of Yangon, at the end of a stretch of highway that the *Asia Sentinel* dubbed the Highway of Death on account of the number of fatal crashes that have occurred upon it since its opening in 2009. It is advisable not to go faster than 60mph, not so much because it is illegal but because one's vehicle might flip over on the uneven surface and poorly banked turns. The road is made of concrete slabs rather than asphalt, which makes for a bone-jarring ride and a lot of wear on the tyres.

Motorists are well-advised also to keep their car in good repair, as there is nothing between Yangon and Nay Pyi Taw except for rice paddies and the occasional small village of thatched huts. There's really only one place to stop: The Mile 115 café (which serves up some excellent Burmese cuisine!). We would make four round trips on this road over the next five weeks, for a total of 1,700 miles of bone-jarring driving.

We check in to the Junction Hotel (we are the only guests), dress for dinner, and await the Minister of the President's Office and former General, Soe Maung at the Café Flight, which seems an appropriate venue given the nature of our request. The restaurant has an aeroplane parked out front.

This particular gate guardian is Fokker F-28 Fellowship XY-ADW (formerly owned by Myanmar Airways) and it had an embarrassing end to its long airline career. In 2009, the aircraft skidded off the runway at Sittwe, damaging the wing and landing gear. As an insurance write-off, the aged aircraft was subsequently acquired by the café owner.* He removed the airline seats and put in couches and tables. It is now a dining room – but too small sadly for our group.

Instead, we sit in the main building and wait. Soe Maung and his wife, Nang Phyu Phyu Aye, finally arrive around 7 p.m. in a black Audi with tinted windows. They are accompanied by a security detail. Soe Maung is dressed in a traditional Burmese collarless dress shirt of dazzling white and

---

*   All Burma IT Student Union (ABITSU) website, Myanmar to Launch café flight service
     using destroyed aircraft, 2 June 2010.

a *longyi*, the ankle length kilt worn by most men in Myanmar. David, Moe Moe, Htoo Htoo, myself, and Tin Ma Latt greet him in a receiving line, and then troop in behind him for dinner. David makes a presentation and Tin Ma Latt translates for him, while passing maps and images for the minister's review. U Soe Maung asks questions about the recovery plan and how the planes will be restored. He promises to help us, because he believes in the project. Before he departs, we take a group photo, with David and the minister in the middle shaking hands. We drive back to Yangon in good spirits.

We spend the weekend trying to find a suit for David, who rather daftly didn't think to bring one for his government meetings. Our first stop is Junction Mall, a multi-level shopping centre with a few dozen shops, mostly stocked with Chinese brands. I am dubious that anything will fit him here, since he wears a size 46 long jacket and a size 13 shoe. He is like Gulliver among the Lilliputians. After a fruitless search we finally give up and head back to the hotel. There I ask the concierge to help find a tailor who could make a bespoke suit – quickly. We finally find one, Golden Star, that said they could do it in two days: David is delighted – as a farmer spending most of his life on the land, in all weathers, he doesn't have the opportunity to wear a suit very often, so he enjoys having one made. Next, we go shopping for dress shoes – and hit a complete dead end. After our seventh or eighth shop we give up and agree it is like trying to find shoes for a yeti. We finally settle on a pair of leather dress sandals, which though too small at least stay on his feet.

There's not much else I can do until we have news from Nay Pyi Taw, so the next morning I set out south along Alan Pya Phaya Road, which runs down to the Strand. I cross the bridge over the railroad tracks and pause to give a thousand Khat note to a one-legged man sitting on the curb. I see him every day and give him a 1,000-khat note every time I cross, perhaps to assuage my conscience about spending money on presents when people are going hungry and children are sleeping on the overpass. There is a lot of poverty here – a testament to the former military government's decades of mismanagement. The man smiles his thanks.

I turn right on Bogyoke Aung San Road and enter the Bogyoke Market, a huge colonial-era bazaar filled with antiques, jewellery, bolts of cloth, jade carvings, and Burmese handicrafts of every description. I wander through the shops for hours admiring jade and wood carvings and browsing antiques from the colonial era. I buy some small presents for friends and (for myself) a carved jade lion, my guardian animal, after haggling (as is the custom) with the shop owner. He will join my desktop crew of a Thai elephant, a sitting Buddha and a terracotta warrior, which I acquired on past travels. I sit for a while and watch a procession of young monks asking the shopkeepers for donations, vendors hawking their wares and money changers pursuing tourists.

Money is emblematic of the contradictions of modern Myanmar. The country has been isolated from the world community for decades, and since 2007, it has lived under economic sanctions imposed by the UK, US and EU in response to the former military government's crackdown on pro-democracy demonstrators. One of the effects of this political isolation (which is just now lifting, along with the sanctions), is that the banking system is not integrated with the rest of the world. The most obvious manifestation of this is the absence of cash machines. Neither does anyone take credit cards or travellers cheques. You have to carry around bricks of cash to pay for everything, including your hotel.

In the US, a $1 bill is worth one dollar, whatever its condition – provided it is not torn in half, and even then – with some judicious application of tape – the bill is still legal tender for all debts, both public and private. However, in Myanmar, the value of foreign currency depends on its condition and the amount of money you wish to exchange. Generally, the larger the denomination of the bill, and the better its condition, the better the rate offered. To get the official 850 kyats to the dollar exchange rate, you need to exchange at least one or more $100 bills, in mint condition. No creases. No blemishes. No fold marks. No dog-eared corners. No ink stains. Newly minted, crisp, perfect bills fresh off the printing press.

The highest exchange rate I was able to get outside the airport was 830 Kyat to the dollar.

Basing the value of money on its physical condition is reminiscent of how money changers operated in the European Middle Ages. To increase the amount of currency in circulation, medieval monarchs often decreased the amount of precious metal in their coins, while continuing to circulate them at face value. Additionally, 'coin clippers' would shave off bits of metal from the edges of coins – pocketing the precious metal they accumulated – and then dump the now smaller coins back into circulation, again at full face value. Not surprisingly, medieval money changers learned to ignore the face value of a coin and instead weigh it, study its edges and then exchange it into local currency.

Myanmar has come full circle. At Bogyoke market, I meet an old Burmese man with a long scraggly white beard, who is carrying a bulging wallet. He offers me 830 kyat to the dollar, if I exchange $100. I agree. In return for the near perfect $100 bill I gave him, he counts out a stack of ragged 1,000-kyat notes so crumpled and worn that they feel like soft-ply Kleenex. I complain in mock-seriousness that the Myanmar bills are in poor condition; therefore, I should get a higher exchange rate. He gets the joke and laughs good-naturedly, 'Myanmar money no problem!'

7

The Spitfires of Rangoon

A Novel of the Secret War in Burma
by Major William Wills DSO OBE

```
Biology Laboratory
Pasteur Institute
Rangoon University
13 May 1945
```

'What the hell are you doing here? This is a restricted area,' said the British major angrily as he entered the room, Webley service pistol in hand, the monsoon rain still dripping from the peak of his service dress cap.

The room was a laboratory on the lower left front of the Pasteur Institute of Rangoon University on the corner of Pyay Road and University Avenue Road in Kamayut Township, immediately north of Yangon.

Founded in 1904 as an outpost of the famous Pasteur Institute in Paris, with the aim of trying to control outbreaks of rabies, the site was one of the best-equipped laboratories in Burma, or at least it had been when the Japanese occupied the city in 1942. It had clearly suffered along with the rest of Rangoon, although whether as the Japanese pulled out or after the Allies arrived was impossible to say.

The American captain coolly indicated a large refrigerator.

'I'm probably checking out the same rumours you are.' He saluted and held out a hand,

'Leonard Short, Captain US Army Medical Corps,' the captain added by way of explanation, 'I've just flown in. I am a US Military Observer attached to Lord Louis' intelligence staff.'

'Your identification please Captain.' The major replied coldly. Short pulled an identity card and set of orders from his tunic. The major scanned the contents and handed the papers back to their owner.

'Pleased to meet you,' he said, holstering his pistol and shaking hands. 'Bill Baron. Let's just say we are in the same business.'

Baron offered the American his own identity card saying, 'I'm sorry. SEAC didn't see fit to tell me you chaps were working this far south.'

'I wasn't told you British had anyone looking at this matter either.'

Baron laughed. 'I understand from your compatriots in Kandy that the official US Army term for this is a SNAFU?' '

'Correct Major,' said Short, reflecting, 'Which means I guess it is up to us to come up with a modus operandi as there's no point in us duplicating work. What have you found out so far?'

'Look around,' the Englishman invited, 'What can you see?'

'OK,' says the captain, 'It's a University biology laboratory, pretty smashed up; papers, test tubes, Petri dishes the usual, not huge quantities though …'

'Ah now that's interesting.'

'Pray tell,' Baron said cryptically.

'I noticed when I came in. There is no obvious sign of any additional security. There's clear glass in the windows for a start. They weren't too concerned if anyone walking past looked in.'

'That was my conclusion too.'

'Can I take a look in the fridge?' asked Short.

'Be my guest. No nice cold beers I am afraid.'

Short pulled open the heavy refrigerator door. Inside were rows of 16oz bottles, some intact and full of liquid, some broken as if someone had taken a rifle butt or army boot to the glassware.

'Oh, now that is also interesting.'

'Very,' Baron responded, 'and whoever smashed this place up is bloody lucky that stuff isn't the active agent.'

'Yeah,' said Short, 'otherwise we'd be dealing with a full on cholera epidemic instead of just the monsoon mud.'

'We have one of the locals who worked here in custody, chap called Dr Samyal. Apparently, the headman was a chap called Dr Kamico. Heard of him?' Baron asked.

Short shook his head.

'Samyal says that the Japs were only at it for about four months before we arrived, which makes sense given how little they actually left behind,' Baron said. 'For want of any other evidence we've classified this as a defensive effort by an outpost of the Army's Epidemic Prevention and Water Purification Department, rather than anything more sinister.'

'So, contrary to the rumours, there is no Bacteriological warfare laboratory in Rangoon,' said Short, summing up.

The Englishman shook his head, 'It's pathetic really. I think this rumour gets filed in the same place as the intelligence the Air Force picked up that the Japs had built huge underground hangars up at Mingaladon.'

'They didn't?' says Short.

'No, just dispersals, trenches and bunkers. The Sons of Heaven are very good at bunkers. Some of their deep shelters are remarkably strong and it is all done with local materials, good red earth and teak beams.'

8

Buried in Burma

Tracy Spaight
Yangon
Myanmar
15 June 2012

When Rudyard Kipling penned 'The Ballad of East and West', with its oft-quoted line 'never the twain shall meet', he was describing the gulf of understanding between the British and the independence-minded tribes living on the North West Frontier of the British Raj. In the case of Myanmar, the divide is not so wide as Kipling's somewhat jaundiced quip might suggest, but we impatient Westerners, eager to fast-track things and sign contracts, soon discover the Burmese have their own ways of thinking and doing things.

Business in Myanmar requires a Zen Buddhist approach. On 14 June, after another week of anxious waiting, Htoo Htoo Zaw meets with us at our hotel. He tells us (through Tin Ma Latt) that the case has been transferred to a committee composed of seven different ministers. Now we have to convince the Minister of Industry, the Minister of Planning, the Minister of Transportation (which encompasses Civil Aviation), the Minister of Foreign Affairs, the Ministry of Environmental Conservation and Forestry (there are trees near the dig site!), the Military, of course, and other government departments that they should award us the contract. If they do, then it must then be reviewed by the attorney general and finally approved by the president's office. Clearly, we're going to be here a while.

In addition to the bureaucratic hurdles, rival groups are petitioning the government for permission to dig. These include Steven Boultbee Brooks, the wealthy Spitfire collector with whom David had fallen out back in April. The other we believe to be Keith Win, who worked with David back in 1998–2000. One of David's acquaintances, who works at the UK Embassy, confirms that she has seen these two applications. In addition, we learn from Htoo Htoo that an Israeli team, a Japanese group and a Singapore-based consortium have all approached the Myanmar government about excavating. We need to enlist allies if we're going to secure the contract.[*]

Therefore, it is to bolster David's application that we secure a letter of support from the geophysics department at Leeds University, since Dr Roger Clark and his then graduate student Dr Adam Booth had both worked with David in the past – and Adam Booth had accompanied David to Myanmar in 2004.

We also secure letters from *The Sunday Telegraph* and the British Spitfire Association. As a precaution, David also engages the London-based law firm Simmons and Simmons to establish his precedence and fend off rivals.

And finally, we use the good offices of Isabel Hunt to again appeal to 10 Downing Street.

With a view to taking the story public and protecting Leeds, and therefore David's, interest in the project, Isabel also reaches out to Adam Lusher of *The Telegraph*, offering a feature article with the Leeds academics, adding in conclusion:

At this stage, it feels as if No 10 must be encouraged into doing the right thing, else money and contacts may prevail. I understand that the excavation proposals are being submitted to the Burmese tomorrow (Monday). If there was a chance of *The Telegraph* picking up the story at this stage, David may have a better chance. I know *The Telegraph* has been involved for some time, and David mentioned your editor's letter of support.[**]

We wait for the anticipated meeting in Nay Pyi Taw. However, days pass without any word from the ministers.

Time starts to drag. Every morning begins incongruously with the maudlin sounds of Lara's Theme from the movie *Doctor Zhivago* playing in the hotel

---

[*]   Journal of Tracy Spaight, entry for 15 June 2012. 'Htoo Htoo Zaw asks if Wargaming will
        match Mr Brook's offer, which included a large deposit. I tell him no.'
[**]   Email from Isabel Hunt to Adam Lusher copied to Tracy Spaight, 3 June 2012.

restaurant. Omar Sharif and omelettes. The music repeats every hour and makes me yearn for the wintry landscapes of the film. I fill my mornings walking around the city and in the afternoons (when it gets too hot) writing blog entries.

I have dinner with David most evenings. He's an engaging storyteller with a well-honed sense of the dramatic. In most of David's stories he is the underdog farmer, trying to make his way in a world full of officious Department for Agriculture bureaucrats; obnoxious and litigious neighbours and business associates or, in one particularly amusing story, someone trying to pull the Nigerian Prince/General internet scam whom he claims to have toyed with for months.

Finally, on 17 June, the promised meeting is set and we pile into a minivan with Tin Ma Lott, Htoo Htoo and Moe Moe for a second trip to Nay Pyi Taw.

We arrive around 4 p.m. and while Htoo Htoo heads off to a private meeting with Soe Maung to discuss our case, the rest of us go out to dinner at the Junction Centre Shopping mall.

The mall is another of the capital's Potemkin developments whose shelves are loaded with goods, but whose stores are largely empty of customers.

Htoo Htoo joins us just as we are finishing our meal and tells us (through Auntie Latt) that we will meet the Deputy Minister of Planning the next day.

Early the next morning, we send up another letter to the Office of the President requesting a meeting. We press our suits and wait. And we wait some more.

The phone does not ring.

Two days later, on 19 June, we drive over to the Ministry of Planning's complex, not for the anticipated meeting but to deliver a formal letter with a *request* for a meeting.

We are allowed to enter the compound, with its high chain link fences topped by razor wire and guarded by armed security. Htoo Htoo delivers the letter while we wait outside the minister's office. In the afternoon it begins to rain. Not a spring shower, delicately pattering on the roof and window panes, but a full-force torrential downpour which continues for hours. The 2012 monsoon has finally arrived.

As we drive back to Yangon, our spirits dampened by the latest setback, I tie myself into knots trying to decide whether or not to fly in the New York-based documentary film crew (Room 608), whom I have retained for the project. If we're going to make a documentary then we need to capture the challenges of navigating the government bureaucracy and the uncertainty about whether we will beat out David's rivals to secure the contract. If we don't film this now, as it happens, then we won't have the beginning of the story. But if we do start filming, and we fail to secure the contract, then the film won't have an ending – and Wargaming will be out a fair bit of money for flying over the crew! I decide to reach out to my colleagues in our Emeryville, California, office to discuss the situation. We decide it's a gamble whatever we do – so we may as well bring the crew over to Myanmar and hope for the best. I call Room 608 and tell them it's on. We make flight arrangements.

The next day I get another surprise. We must leave the country, since we've been here for so long that David's visa has run out – and mine will expire in another week. Normally extending a UK visa isn't a problem, but because a Korean man killed his wife at the Trader Hotel last night – brutally stabbing the poor woman – the government has frozen all extensions. So now we must fly to Bangkok and apply for a new visa at the Myanmar Embassy (it's the closest one). We thus get new passport photos and buy plane tickets to Thailand, and I arrange to have the film crew meet us in Bangkok, since they would be flying in to Suvarnabhumi airport en route to Yangon in any case.

So, on 24 June, Moe Moe picks us up at the Inya Lake Hotel (our latest residence, a Soviet-era hotel that would not have looked out of place in East Berlin in the 1970s) at 7.30 a.m. and we drive to Mingaladon airport. We arrive in Bangkok around noon, where we meet Mark Mannucci and Anna Bowers from Room 608 as we exit baggage claim.

Mark is an urbane New Yorker who looks much younger than his 57 years. He is excited to start the project. Anna is in her mid-twenties, but she is already an accomplished filmmaker. Soon we are joined by the rest of their team.

Good-natured cameraman Ethan has a full shaggy mop of Muppet hair and short beard of a Grunge band drummer coupled with an attention to detail and fierce dedication to his craft. Canadian Ian is cut in the same mould as the creative geeky set from Silicon Valley, while sound recordist Brian is someone who listens rather than talks, which is perhaps fitting given his role. It is a good team.

David and the film crew pile into the van so Mark can shoot a short interview on the way to the hotel. He wants to capture David in a relaxed setting, so he will be more conversational and less practised in his responses.

'Tell me how your quest began,' Mark says.

'The story started for me in 1996 with a friend of mine who told me about it,' David begins.

9

The Spitfires of Rangoon

A Novel of the Secret War in Burma

by Major William Wills DSO OBE

```
The Prime Minister's Bathroom,
Potsdam Conference, Berlin
20 July 1945
```

'Admiral of the Fleet Mountbatten, Supreme Allied Commander South East Asia, etc, etc ...'

Patrick Kinna, the Prime Minister's stenographer, tapped away at the portable typewriter perched on his knees.

The famous nineteenth-century literary critic William Hazlitt had once written that watching the great actor Edmund Kean play Richard III was like '... reading Shakespeare by flashes of Lightning'. To hear British Prime Minister Winston Churchill declaiming dictation was to hear the rhythms and cadences of one of his great set-piece speeches in the House of Commons, and having worked with Churchill since the darkest days of 1940, Kinna was used to the Premier's verbal and personal idiosyncrasies. Churchill had notoriously once received the late President Roosevelt in his guest bedroom at the White House stark naked, saying, 'You see Mr President, I have nothing to conceal from you.'

Tonight the Prime Minister reclined luxuriously in his bath and, raising the golden tumbler of whisky and soda to his lips, he took a deeply satisfied swallow.

'Following our conversation of this instant regarding potential developments in the Far East War during the August of 1945, it is necessary to make certain arrangements for the period after hostilities have ended.

'In Burma, our brave Karen allies are holding themselves firmly aloof from the other parties and are apprehensive of the future lest self-Government in Burma should place them at the mercy of the Burmese majority.'

Churchill mused aloud, 'They are a courageous people the Karen, our Special Operations Executive could not operate in Burma without their assistance. Hmmm ...

'Continuation ... However, there should ... there should be no illusion that His Majesty's Government is not committed to complete self-Government for Burma, within the British Commonwealth, as soon as circumstances permit.

'The agreed transitional period will follow military rule when the Supreme Allied Commander is satisfied that internal order and transportation links have been established in a functional manner and external enemies have been defeated. Thereupon, the Government will establish direct rule under the pro- visions of the Government Burma Act of 1935, with the Governor of Burma in Rangoon, acting under the authority of the Secretary of State for Burma. His Majesty's Government is of the opinion that we need look no further ahead than December 1948 to achieve Burmese independence. It is also the intention of His Majesties Government that the Karen people will enjoy the constitutional status of an autonomous state within the future independent Burma.

'Therefore, in order that the Karen autonomous state has the capability to defend itself in the face of either a Communist insurgency, or oppressive actions by a future independent majority Burmese Government, you are authorised to strike off charge thirty-six Spitfire aircraft which are surplus to the requirement of Air Command South East Asia and hand them over to the Karen National Organisation.

'Note – Rather than deplete operational squadrons you have the authority to intercept aircraft in the Royal Air Force supply chain and divert them to this purpose.

'The aircraft concerned should be concealed on Burmese territory in such a manner as to be quickly available to the Karen if and when they are needed. The precise manner of this concealment is to be decided by SEAC, according to SEAC's operational capabilities at the time.'

The practical details laid down, Churchill adopted the tone of the most severe grade of Prime Ministerial gravitas, as though to imbue Kinna's typing with all the power of his office.

'The Prime Minister stresses that this operation is one of the utmost secrecy, because any hint that His Majesty's Government was taking steps to arm one piece of the Burmese jigsaw with modern weapons over and above any other party, especially that of General Aung San, would be interpreted as an act of gross duplicity, with the consequent risks to the British Government's ability to achieve a peaceful transition to Burmese majority rule.

'Sign it, "Churchill" and add "Action This Day".'

'There ...' The Prime Minister strikes a match, sucking the pungent cigar back into life.

'Mr Kinna, please ensure that cable is marked for immediate onward transmission to Mountbatten's Headquarters for his and Park's eyes only. It is imperative you do not make any copies and you must ensure that this copy is destroyed as soon as it has been transmitted. Mmm ...' Churchill muses.

'Now, what else is there?'

Kinna consulted his notebook.

'President Truman wishes to discuss the framework for the final application of the Tube Alloys project Prime Minister; and Marshal Stalin is still most concerned about the attitude of the Poles towards their western border.'

'Yes, well the Polish are rightly suspicious of the Marshall, especially after he divided their country with Herr Ribbentrop and murdered thousands of their intellectuals. Those concerns will be on the agenda for tomorrow at the Cecilienhof.'

Churchill's eyes seemed to mist like the glass on the bathroom mirror.

'Kinna, when I was a little boy, I would line up my toy armies, on the carpet at Blenheim Palace, and I would win deathless glory on the battlefield day after day, face to face with my enemy; and I did face my enemy in real life when I took part in the last cavalry charge by the British Army at Omdurman in the Sudan and when I escaped from the Boers in South Africa. It saddens me that the little boys who are born in the wake of this terrible war will only be able win such glory vicariously, through imitating the deeds of others in their games, or by touching the relics of weapons and aircraft that can no longer be used.

War by press button from 25,000ft, or at great geographical distance, is somehow not the act of a civilisation in touch with its humanity.'

Headquarters South East Asia Command
Kandy, Ceylon
14 August 1945

The two senior officers, one wearing the immaculate dress whites of an Admiral of the Fleet and the second in the Khaki drill of the Royal Air Force, strolled in the evening twilight in the tropical gardens of the King's Pavilion.

'I thought Boy Browning looked at death's door when you met my plane.'

'Yes sir,' said Air Chief Marshal Sir Keith Park. 'Well he had got up off of his sick bed. We all wanted to assure you that everything is in hand for the capitulation.'

Park's companion paused in his walk as if taking in fully the scented silence of the garden.

'Would you have done it?' asked Admiral of the Fleet Lord Louis Mountbatten, cousin of King George VI and Supreme Commander, South East Asia Command.

'Done what sir?' Park replied.

'Given the order for two of your crews to each destroy a city, and Lord knows how many tens of thousands of people, in a millisecond?'

'Without hesitation,' said Park.

'Oh I know the arguments,' Mountbatten continued. 'It will end the war, save lives and more to the point it will demonstrate to Uncle Joe Stalin that he hasn't got free rein in Europe or the Far East.'

'Well it is bloody cynical to come in and make a strategic land grab just as the Empire of the Sons of Heaven is falling apart,' says Park alluding to the intelligence reports that no fewer than three Red Army fronts, under the command of Marshal of the Soviet Union Aleksandr Vasilevsky, were currently scything through General Otozō Yamada's Imperial Japanese Kwantung Army, in a classic pincer attack across an area of Manchuria and Mongolia the size of Europe.

'Don't worry Keith, I am not getting sentimental,' Mountbatten said reassuringly. 'Don't forget it was my family the Bolsheviks murdered.' There was a moment of pregnant silence, then Mountbatten mused, 'My cousin Maria was such a beautiful creature you know, I was crackers for her. Still think of her every day.'

It was 1913, Europe's last golden summer of peace before the conflagration of the First World War, when the young Prince Louis of Battenberg, as he was then, holidayed with his Romanov cousins at the Battenberg family palace of Heiligenberg in the Rhineland of southern Germany close to Lake Constance and the Swiss border. In the process, among the terraces, paths and gardens of the 'Holy Mountain' he developed a teenage crush on the Tsar's third daughter, the then 14-year-old Maria Nikolaevna. He would keep a photograph of her in his bedroom for the rest of his life.

But in Ceylon on 14 August 1945, Mountbatten broke from his reverie.

'Keith, I need to discuss Winston's plan to arm the Karen National Organisation. Now he has inherited the scheme, with the new Government in place I have to reassure Atlee and Bevin that you can actually do it?'

Park grinned, 'Look, I defended London with 11 Group when I wasn't just fighting the Luftwaffe but Bader, Leigh-Mallory and their bloody Big Wing theory as well, and we didn't do so badly on Malta when the press said the Royal Air Force was down to three Gladiators and sheer bloody-mindedness. We might have to improvise, beg steal and borrow, but the Royal Air Force can do it. I just wonder if anyone in Whitehall has actually thought this thing through.'

Park paused, then, almost pleading, said, 'For God's sake Dickie, forget the politics of it. You know as well as I do what kept the whole SEAC caravan on the road was airborne logistics.

'It was my Dakotas that kept Bill Slim's troops moving and supplied with everything from ammunition and tea to the Mules to carry it. We've been fighting a new kind of war here and you know who the biggest enemy was?'

'The terrain and the weather?' ventured Mountbatten.

'Precisely. Has Winston any idea what he is asking us to do?' Park asked with plaintive frustration.

'Sourcing the aircraft, that's not the problem,' he said. 'I am standing down the single-engined fighter squadrons first anyway. We don't need them anymore and anything we have on Lend-Lease will become too expensive to maintain once the Yanks start charging full commercial prices again.

'Besides, the maintenance units have already broken up over 400 strike-offs with the effect that half the housewives in downtown Rangoon are cooking supper in woks made from my surplus aircraft. What I don't have are any airfield engineers.'

Park lit a cigarette.

'Dickie, you know as well as I do with limited space on the sealift from India and the logistics train set up for Operation Zipper, all we have in theatre in Rangoon are the repair and salvage units and the Royal Engineers who were already there, and they have their work cut out just trying to fix everything from the airfield to the docks to the railways, simply to get the wretched country running again.

'And that is before we start trying to sort out secure billets for the troops to keep them dry and stop them raising hell because we haven't got the transports to get them home fast enough when they are supposed to be demobbed.'

'And we still have several months left of the monsoon,' Mountbatten said.

'Exactly, you saw what Mingaladon is like when you landed there in June. It's a soaking wet bomb site.

'Our tactical air campaign did far too good a job. Half the taxiways are so wrecked they are downright dangerous and my pilots have to wade through mud up to their ankles just to get to their aircraft.

'You know there is a dog-leg on the taxiway out of one of the engineering dispersals where if you get the angle only slightly wrong, or your brakes lock up and the wheels slip, next you know you are 30ft down at the bottom of a *chaung* with the snakes and spiders for company, and a lot of embarrassing paperwork.'

Mountbatten placed a friendly hand on Park's arm.

'Keith, we both know this is political. Get your senior engineering officer and the Commandant of the Royal Engineers to put together a plan. I don't care how far-fetched it is, just give me something that shows our political masters we are taking it seriously and that we could do it. But hurry. As Winston said, it is "action this day"'.

'When isn't it,' Park laughed.

'And it's Top Secret,' Mountbatten added gravely. 'I have a chap in Burma who, shall we say, runs errands for me. I will loan him to you to handle security. If we can find him and bring him back from up country that is.'

Mountbatten paused for a moment, then turned to face his Air Force commander.

'You know Keith, the war fighting is almost over and what we are undertaking now is peace building; hopefully making a better job of it than last time.' Mountbatten paused again, clearly ambivalent about the way to phrase his next thought, then said. 'With President Truman's new atomic gadget I suspect that if we get this wrong, and our successors have to do all this again in twenty-five, or fifty, or a hundred years' time, there will not be many of us left to write the memoirs afterwards.'

10

Tracy Spaight
Bangkok and Yangon
25 June 2012

'He said that the planes were buried at the end of the runway [at Mingaladon] in crates,' David explains. 'So I did some research. I went to the public records office in London (Kew) and found out that at least twelve Mark XIV Spitfires arrived in Rangoon and were more or less immediately struck off charge, which is remarkable.'

'What does struck off charge mean?' Mark interjects.

David replies:

It basically means they didn't want them. They disposed of them. Scrap. Further investigations – I advertised in magazines – and I got eyewitnesses coming forward to say that they saw these aircraft buried on 17 August 1945 at this location. So I then applied for a visa and permission to survey. I tried at the Myanmar Embassy in London. And unfortunately I got refused. And it took me a year to get permission to survey.

'What happened then?' Mark asks:

Well, I made a mistake. I didn't do my research properly. These aircraft were buried near the end of the runway, as Jim said. But I went to the end of the runway to look for them and they weren't there! I went to the other end of the runway and they weren't there. And at Mingaladon [in 1945] there were three runways. So I checked each end of each runway and I found nothing. So I did more research and I found out there was a runway extension of 600m. I calculated where the old runway finished. So I then worked out how to survey that area. And eyewitnesses told me they were buried something like 4–5ft deep in boxes. So I took a machine out that went down 20ft and I found nothing. I was getting rather disappointed and wanting to give up. And then I found out more information.

At the actual end of the runway there was a deep river bed, at least 36ft deep. And to enable this runway to be extended, they had to build up this level to the same level as the old runway. That made the boxes 25–26ft deep. So I went back with Leeds University – this was in 2004 – and we took equipment that could scan deeper and we located them!

'So you're convinced the planes are there – can you tell me that,' Mark says, trying to get a quotable line for the film.

'I'm totally convinced they're there,' David says with conviction. 'I've got British, American and Burmese eyewitnesses. They're all saying the same spot. The reason for the delay is the planes are much deeper than originally thought. I took out the wrong piece of equipment. But now we know the depth. We know where they are.'

'Why weren't you able to recover the planes in 2004?' Mark asks.

Well I turned up and we started digging. And we were told that we had permission. After an hour or so this jeep came up with this man. He asked, 'What the hell are you doing?' And I said I'm digging up the planes. And he said he hadn't been paid. He wanted $50,000. I said I didn't have it. And then someone else came and he wanted $50,000. And I said I don't have that sort of money. And I was told to go back to the hotel. I spent five weeks in the hotel, technically under house arrest. They had my passport so I couldn't go anywhere. I was promised meetings but nothing really happened.

And then all of a sudden when they decided to release me, I was escorted out of the hotel and into a car, and I was taken to a location where this man came. The interpreter told me it was General Tan Shwe! The general was angry with me because he did not know anything about the agreement or the contract. And the translator came and told me the general was threatening to execute me. Which alarmed me a little bit [he laughs]. But I talked him out of it. I told him, 'If you let me go I'll go back to Singapore. I'll raise more money and we'll do a deal together.' And he fell for it. I was on the plane back to Singapore within a few hours.

'Set the stakes for me. These planes are worth how much?' Mark asks.

'If we find all the aeroplanes, we're probably looking at $120 million, maybe as high as $200 million. These Spitfires are unique. They are brand new. They've only flown once. They've been packed in crates. They're greased. All the joints are tarred to keep the water out. We think there are thirty-six at Mingaladon.'

'Why do you think they'll fetch $120 million?' Mark asks.

'Well, the last Spitfire was sold in the United States for $5 million. It had a history. Battle of Britain history. These don't have a fighting history. But they are 100 per cent original. They've been buried for sixty-seven years. So essentially we're getting a brand new aeroplane, sixty-seven years old.'

'It's literally buried treasure, is what you're saying,' Mark summarises.

'It is buried treasure,' David agrees.

'Why didn't you return to dig them up before now?' Mark asks.

'Burma was ruled by a military government for over fifty years,' David explains. 'Britain did not get on too well with them.

'After the 2007 uprising we imposed sanctions and they didn't like that. The sanctions prevented me from digging up and exporting the planes. Now that sanctions have come off, we finally have a chance to recover these aircraft.'

While David is excitedly telling his story on camera, I'm lying on the rear seat of the van trying to keep quiet and stay out of the shot. I'm listening to David and thinking about the military government's heavy-handed suppression of the 2007 protests. The videos I'd seen on YouTube of baton-wielding military police beating protesters are deeply disturbing. While there have been many reforms since 2010, and the country recently held its first democratic election in decades, the military still has considerable sway over the civilian government. I wonder about the ethics of working with them.

The van comes to a quick stop, nearly depositing me on the floor and jolting me back to the present. We have arrived at our hotel. David and I still need to renew our visas, so we take a taxi to the Myanmar Embassy.

Meanwhile, the film crew checks their equipment and prepares for our morning flight to Yangon. While transferring video footage from the day's shoot to the back-up drives, Ethan discovers a problem with one of the Red Epic HD cameras.

It's bad luck. Mark recommends we replace the camera before going into Myanmar, since if the second one goes down we won't be able to shoot. Anna tries but can't locate a replacement in Hong Kong or Singapore, so the Los Angeles-based film house they work with agrees to fly in a new camera from California, along with a courier to transport it – a young woman named

Oksana. We do some sightseeing in Bangkok while awaiting Oksana's arrival (a day later). Early on the morning of 28 June we head back to Myanmar.

```
Nay Pyi Taw, Myanmar
29 June 2012
1600 hours
```

As I lie on my bed at the Junction Hotel, staring listlessly at the old-style ceiling fan spinning lazily overhead, I wonder whether we'll ever get this project off the ground. After our arrival in Yangon yesterday, we drove straight from the airport to Nay Pyi Taw in anticipation of a meeting with the Minister of Planning today – only to learn that the meeting has been cancelled yet again. Like a character in Rod Sterling's 1950s television programme, the more I see of Myanmar's capital city the more I have the inescapable, but disorienting, feeling that I have stumbled into the Twilight Zone.

Nay Pyi Taw is truly a surreal place. The name means 'Abode of Kings', and the location was reportedly chosen by Than Shwe, the former head of the military junta ruling Burma from 1962, on the advice of his astrologer. Like Burma's warrior kings of the past, Than Shwe decided to build an expansive new capital, and to locate it some 200 miles north of the old capital of Yangon, or Rangoon. The new capital would be beyond the reach of foreign invaders (a perpetual worry for the regime) and, perhaps more importantly, it would be far from the masses of poor Burmese, university students and Buddhist Monks who might rise up against the leadership. On 8 August 1988 the so called 8888 Uprising brought an estimated 1 million Burmese into the streets of Rangoon in protest against the corruption and incompetence of the military government. The result was a bloody military coup by what became the State Law and Order Restoration Council (SLORC) and the rise of a charismatic democratic politician, Aung San Suu Kyi.

At 6.37 a.m. on 6 November 2005, when the stars were in the most auspicious alignment, and Aung San Suu Kyi was still under house arrest, construction of Nay Pyi Taw began in total secrecy.

It is still under way.

Seven years on, the capital boasts brand new government buildings, including the impressive Pyidaungsu Hluttaw complex, several museums and gardens, a water park and an immaculate eighteen-hole golf course for the regime's aging generals. The city is divided into several zones, including a hotel zone (for foreign visitors), a military zone (closed to the public and consequently the subject of whispered rumours about networks of buried bunkers, tunnels and roads that double as runways), and residential zones, where the four-storey apartment roofs are colour-coded according to in which ministry the occupants work. It is a very orderly and regimented place, with broad streets and sweeping vistas that make social disorder – much less barricades – impossible. Georges-Eugène Haussmann would be proud. Indian journalist and academic Siddharth Varadarajan described the city as 'the ultimate insurance against regime change, a masterpiece of urban planning designed to defeat any putative "colour revolution" – not by tanks and water cannons, but by geometry and cartography.'*

According to Wikipedia, the city has a population of more than a million and is one of the fastest-growing cities in Asia. But driving around the twelve-lane motorway that rings the city, it's hard to see where all these supposed inhabitants live. The place looks deserted, aside from the sweepers and gardeners who sweep the streets and prune the bushes. There is no traffic aside from the occasional lorry or bicyclist in a bamboo hat. The government set aside space for foreign embassies, but thus far only one country has moved its embassy from Yangon. The rest have refused to move.

Towering above the surrounding trees and grasslands that comprise most of the space inside the city's beltway, the Uppatasanti Pagoda is a replica of the enormous gold-covered Shwedagon Pagoda in Yangon, spiritual centre of Burma and pilgrimage site for millions of Buddhists for almost 2,600 years. The five-year-old Uppatasanti Pagoda, in contrast, is the former military government's attempt to legitimise their rule and connect the new capital with the country's Buddhist faith and royal history. The pagoda looks impressive from a distance but up close the hurried construction is apparent. It too is a simulacrum, like the miniature Eiffel Tower at Walt Disney's Epcot Centre.

And unlike the original architectural and cultural marvel in Yangon, the general's clone pagoda has few visitors.

Most ironically to a Westerner, and most symbolic of the cultural schism I am now trying to bestride, a pair of white elephants are stabled near the pagoda.

In Burmese belief, they are auspicious, but in the west, a white elephant means something that is useless and expensive to maintain. This was probably not the meaning the government meant to convey, but it is a fitting symbol for the regime's foray into urban planning. Nay Pyi Taw reportedly cost more than $30 billion to build. This is a colossal expense for one of the poorest countries in Asia, where millions live without electricity, running water or basic health care.

*   svaradarajan.blogspot.com/2007/02/dictatorship-by-cartography-geometry.html

While Nay Pyi Taw is usually anglicised to 'Abode of Kings', the literal word by word translation from Burmese means something closer to 'Royal City of the Sun'. My mind wanders back to an undergraduate course on the classical river valley civilisations, where I learned about another absolute ruler who sought to redefine reality for his people by redefining their physical and cultural landscape. Pharaoh Amenhotep IV wanted to found a new religion focused on worship of the sun god Aten and to do that he needed to cut himself free of the power base of the Egyptian priestly caste in the millennium-old capital of Thebes. He thus rebranded himself as Akhenaten and abandoned Thebes for el-Amarna on the east bank of the Nile. Many dreams do not survive the death of their dreamer and so it was with el-Amarna. With Akhenaten's death, the city was abandoned and soon buried beneath the desert sands. Whether Nay Pyi Taw will be swallowed up by the jungle or emerge as a thriving metropolis only time shall tell.

While our meeting with the Minister of Planning has been cancelled, the enterprising Htoo Htoo has managed to secure a second meeting with General Soe Maung. Htoo Htoo reserves a large private room for the group at the Café Flight. The staff cover the table with a gold cloth. Soe Maung and his wife arrive at 7.30, again chauffeured in a late model black Audi. He graciously allows us to film the dinner meeting.

We exchange pleasantries over dinner, with Tin Ma Latt translating. Once the dishes are cleared, Professor Soe Thein gives the general a copy of our presentation, which he leafs through. David begins his pitch.

Addressing the general, and pointing to Adam Booth's survey from 2004, David says, 'This is electromagnetics and it's taken at 25ft below ground level. The red areas indicate metal.'

David then holds up another colour image. 'And this is a ground radar image of all the boxes. These are boxes,' he says, pointing to green lines on the image, 'and you can see, on this one here, this red mark here, this indicates the engine. The top of the engine cowling, the pilot seat, and you see it's coming to a point, and Spitfires come to a point at the tail end.'

Soe Maung studies a photograph of a restored Spitfire, which is on the cover of David's presentation. 'Will they look like this picture?' he asks.

'Oh yes,' David says.

I'm conscious of the fact that the planes – if they are there at all – will likely be in poor condition after spending more than half a century underground. They certainly won't look like the immaculately restored Spitfire in the photograph. But this is not the time to gainsay David. The government is keen on the project in no small measure because of the potential commercial returns.

According to the proposed contract, they will receive 50 per cent of the proceeds from the sale of any recovered aircraft.

David addresses the general again. 'Sir, we've carried out all the surveys. The monsoons are coming, which will make digging much harder, but if we could have an agreement in writing as soon as possible it would be wonderful.'

Soe Maung nods and then turns to Tin Ma Latt, who translates for us: 'The president appointed extremely busy ministers to the committee. They're overextended. So it's going to take time. I feel bad they [our group] have been waiting so long. In Burmese, I'd say I feel *anarde*.'

Tin Ma Latt says to Soe Maung, in Burmese, '*Anarde* doesn't exist. There's a word in Japanese, but how would I translate that into English?'

She thinks for a moment and then says to us. 'Abba is feeling bad that you have to wait so long.'

Soe Maung, perhaps sensing that she has not captured his meaning fully, says, 'Please tell them I'm doing my best to make it happen.'

The meeting is over. We look at each other across the table. There's nothing for it but to wait while the gears of government grind slowly ahead.

Holy Trinity Church
Yangon
3 July 2012

The reminders of the Second World War can be found all around Yangon, if you know where to look. Perhaps the most prominent are contained within the graceful pile of the Anglican Holy Trinity Cathedral. With its soaring white bell tower and spire, the cathedral stands on the Bogyoke Aung San Road, just past the Scott Market. Designed by architect Robert Chisholm, the cathedral was begun in 1886 and the white stone and red brick structure was largely completed in 1894. The bell tower was finished later in 1913. The interior of church is an architectural gem, with white marble floors, soaring columns separating the nave from the arcades, rows of polished wooden pews lining the centre aisle, side chapels in both transepts, and a beautiful rose-stained glass window above the west entrance. Thankfully the church survived the bombing of Yangon by both the Japanese and the Allies during the Second World War, even surviving the indignity of being transformed into a sake brewery by the Japanese during the occupation.

After the Second World War, the church was restored and a chapel created in the north transept, dedicated to the Anglo-Indian 14th and 12th armies that had fought in the Burma Campaign. The chapel walls are covered with the regimental plaques, which represent a roll call of the British and Indian regiments that fought against the Japanese. Among them are the Royal Lincolnshire Regiment (David Cundall's home county), the Lancashire Fusiliers, King George's Own 19th Lancers, 4th Prince of Wales Own Gurkha Rifles, The Royal Scots Fusiliers, The Punjab Regiment, The Madras Regiment, and the Somerset Light Infantry. Among the dozens of others is a memorial to 273 Squadron of the Royal Air Force, one of the units that flew Spitfires out of Mingaladon in the summer and autumn of 1945.

We visit the cathedral on 3 July, as we are keen to film in the chapel. The vicar, the very Reverend Reginald Bennett, is extremely gracious. He welcomes us into his church and gives us permission to film after morning service.

On top of the lectern adjacent to the chapel altar, preserved under glass with loving respect, is a large leather-bound book whose pages record in beautiful calligraphy the names of thousands of British, Australian, and other Commonwealth troops who fought and died in the Burmese Campaign in 1942–45. Most were in their late teens or early twenties. There are dozens of names on every page, and there are hundreds of pages. Nothing brings home the reality of the war more forcefully than those endless rows of names.

According to historian Louis Allen, himself a veteran of the Burma campaign and author of *Burma: The Longest War*, there were more than 70,000 Allied casualties in the victorious Burma campaign, while more than 200,000 Japanese soldiers were killed or wounded. The civilian death toll across the Union of Burma was even higher. The vicar explains to us that every year, on the Sunday closest to 11 November – Remembrance Day – he says a mass for the fallen and holds a moment of silence to remember their sacrifice. We film the plaques and shoot close-ups of the book. When we have finished shooting, we meet the vicar again and present him with a donation to further his ministry and preserve this beautiful building. He says a prayer for us and wishes us success in our quest.

Nay Pyi Taw
5–6 July 2012

Two days later, on 5 July 2012, Moe Moe (Htoo Htoo's sister) calls us to say that Htoo Htoo has news for us from the government. We agree to meet that afternoon in the lobby bar of the Park Royal Hotel. David and I take seats in a corner alcove and the film crew sets up lights and a camera to capture the meeting on film. Htoo Htoo, Moe Moe, and Tin Ma Latt arrive and take their seats. Moe Moe relates the news.

'Htoo Htoo has heard from Abba [Soe Maung] that the president reviewed our proposal,' she says, looking pleased.

'He wrote "get it done quickly" in the margin. It is now back with the Minister of Planning,' she says, unaware that the President has echoed Churchill's famous exortation, 'Action this day!'

David breaks out in a huge smile and hugs Moe Moe, who tries to duck the big man's embrace. 'Thank you very much,' he says. He shakes my hand vigorously. 'This has been quite an adventure,' I tell him. 'An adventure I'll never forget,' David says, beaming with happiness. We order drinks to celebrate.

The following morning at 4 a.m. we head to Nay Pyi Taw one more time, for a promised meeting with the Minister of Planning. We arrive at 9.30 a.m. and have breakfast with Htoo Htoo. We change into our suits and drive over to the ministry compound. We wait in the nicely appointed and mercifully air-conditioned waiting room where we … wait. We wait for hours until finally an assistant enters and tells us that the minister regrets that he is too busy to meet with us today, and would we please come back next week. We're disappointed but try to be gracious about it. We've been here thirty-seven days. I tell David that I can't stay here any longer. I have to get back to the office and my family. It's time to go home.

As I am stepping out of the taxi at Yangon airport, I get a phone call from Tin Ma Latt asking if we can meet with the Minister of Planning on Monday! 'On Monday?' I ask, taken aback. She must have forgotten we're leaving today.

'I'm afraid that's not possible,' I tell her.

'David left this morning for the UK, the film crew flew back to New York, and I'm about to board my plane. We're going to have to reschedule for a later date.'

I suggest that we get a meeting on the minister's calendar in early August and David can return to meet with him. I thank Tin Ma Latt for her efforts and drag my suitcase to the ticket counter. I hand the ticket agent my passport and itinerary. She searches for a long time, but is unable to find me in the system. She finally suggests that I go back to the hotel and we can try again tomorrow. I'm frustrated but keep my composure, since it's not her fault. I use my last $300 to buy a new ticket to Singapore. I have to pay cash because they can't process credit cards. I race to the gate and barely make the flight.

As the plane roars down the runway, I catch a glimpse of the old taxiway and the area David had circled on his maps. I wonder if we'll ever have a chance to find out what – if anything – lies beneath.

Rangoon
Thursday, 2/Friday, 3 May 1945

With its cell blocks radiating out from a central point like spokes from a wheel, Rangoon prison is a stark expression of the European idea of Enlightenment law and order transplanted to the Far East, and it holds some dark memories.

During disturbances that began on 24 May 1930 the predominantly Indian prison staff shot dead thirty-four prisoners, most of them ethnic Burmans from the majority population, wounding around sixty others.

In a direct reversal of fortune, under the Japanese occupation the jail houses hundreds of Allied servicemen, most of them British, but with contingents of Australian and Dutch personnel and lately American aircrew, shot down during operations in the Rangoon area.

However, grim as the jail is, the sight that greets the Mosquito crew as it circles the cell blocks is as comically absurd as it is full of promise and hope.

The lone figure standing on the roof of the prison is back in the front line of the war for the first time since his capture in the spring of 1942. However, this time Lt John Wilde's chosen weapons are not grenades and a service pistol but a bucket of whitewash and a brush.

Daubed across the roof, and soon to be the subject of a famous photograph, are four simple words that act both as a situation report and a plea not to be bombed.

'Japs gone, British here.'

The risk of bombing is a real one. In January 1943 the jail is hit during a bombing raid on targets in Rangoon and some forty prisoners are killed. Mostly the unlucky victims are Dutch, but the casualty list also includes some British and American personnel.

The risk of friendly fire also remains tragically real for the 450 prisoners of war who are evacuated from the jail and marched up country by their guards a few days before 14th Army arrive. Their comrades left in Rangoon do not yet know, but when they are finally released in a village near Pegu on 29 April, the senior officer, Brigadier Clive Hobson, is killed when a flight of Indian Air force Hurricane fighter-bombers mistake the released prisoners for Japanese soldiers and make three passes, beating up the column with their cannon.

While the first rooftop daubing is entirely practical, on the roof of another cell block is another altogether more cryptic, phrase, 'Extract digit.'

In fact, this wording is designed to show that the sign is not a Japanese trick. The phrase is RAF slang instructing the reader to 'pull your finger out', that is to 'get a move on', with the liberation.

At the same time as the Mosquito crew are noting the writing on the roof of Rangoon jail, Wing Commander A.E. Saunders OBE, the commanding officer of the Mosquito fighter-bombers of 110 (Hyderabad) Squadron, is a few miles away circling the former RAF Mingaladon. The only sign of movement Saunders and his navigator can see on the pockmarked and shattered airfield is the fluttering of a white flag.

Saunders brings his aircraft into land.

In moments the sortie to Rangoon has become a one-way trip because the tailwheel of the Mosquito fails to extend and the tail of the aircraft is damaged in the landing, preventing Saunders from taking off.

Undaunted, Saunders heads into town and reaches the jail, where he meets the PoWs' senior remaining officer, the generously bearded Wing Commander L.V 'Bill' Hudson RAAF, former commanding officer of 82 Squadron, captured when his Mosquito was shot down the previous December.

Hudson shows Saunders a note written in English, left by the retreating Japanese, that reads:

Rangoon, 29 April.

To the whole captured persons of Rangoon Jail.

According to the Nippon military order we hereby give you liberty and admit to leave this place at your own will.

Regarding food and other materials kept in this compound, we give you permission to consume them as far as your necessity is concerned.

In a flicker of defiance and the Samurai spirit, the note concludes:

We hope that we shall have an opportunity to meet you again at battlefield of somewhere. We shall continue our war effort eternally in order to get the emancipation of all Asiatic races.

With this first-hand knowledge of the situation the resourceful Saunders makes his way to the docks and succeeds in commandeering a sampan, in which he makes his way out to meet the invasion fleet with the welcome news that Operation Dracula, the assault on Rangoon, will be more of an exercise with live ammunition than a potentially bloody contested landing.

Meanwhile, in a dripping cavern deep below the runways and dispersals of Mingaladon, the multi-headed nāga snake, magical guardian of the western direction, is enjoying the sensation of stillness, the receptors on his skin free from the months of torment brought on by shockwaves of exploding 500lb high-explosive and delayed action bombs as SEAC's tactical bombing campaign lays waste to the runways and Japanese installations on the surface.

Helping to sooth him are five British servicemen, F/O Bellinger, F/Lt Emeny, Sgt Davis, 2/Lt Moore and P/O Osboldstone. The five liberated prisoners from Rangoon jail have volunteered to stay behind and help prepare RAF Mingaladon for the waves of transport aircraft that will soon fly in the vast array of supplies the invading force needs and fly out the freed prisoners.

Sgt Norman Davis's offer to stay is particularly selfless as the RAF flight engineer has had a particularly hard time since he was captured after bailing out of a stricken Liberator over Rangoon in early 1944. Not only was he defined as a 'criminal prisoner', as were all aircrew, and thus subjected to additional torments such as being forbidden to wash and shave; being both short and distinctively red-haired, the Japanese guards also fixed on him as a focus for their bullying, subjecting him to more than one mock execution.

By the evening of 3 May 1945, Mountbatten's Operation Dracula can be judged a roaring success and 26th Indian Division has fanned out across Rangoon to take full control of the city. Its advance units are heading north to link up with the rest of Bill Slim's 14th Army.

Sadly, one of the few RAF casualties of the fall of Rangoon is Wing Commander J.B. Nicholson VC, Fighter Command's only Second World War Victoria Cross recipient, who is killed along with all but two of the crew when the 355 Squadron Liberator bomber in which he is flying as an observer is forced to ditch at sea following an engine fire.

Within three months, Wing Commander Saunders and his navigator, Flt Lt James Stephen, will also have, in the words of Pilot Officer John Gillespie Magee Jr's famous sonnet 'High Flight', 'slipped the surly bonds of earth'. On 11 July 1945 the Burma Communications Squadron Expediter Mk I in which they are flying as passengers disappears without trace over the Bay of Bengal.

11

The Spitfires of Rangoon

A Novel of the Secret War in Burma

by Major William Wills DSO OBE

RAF Mingaladon
17 August 1945

As the shafts of sunlight broke through the dark monsoon clouds, the black-painted Special Duties (SD) Lysander turned slowly, seeming to hang in the air on its high-mounted wings like a listless mechanical vulture.

'Hello Tower. Hello Tower. This is Victor 57, Victor 57, turning on finals requesting permission to land? Over.'

The laconic voice of the controller at Mingaladon crackled in the earphones of the Lysander's pilot, Flight Sergeant Castledine of C Flight, 357 Squadron, Royal Air Force.

'Hello Victor 57, Hello Victor 57. You may land long on runway 06, wind nominal. Caution there are runway works at the north-west end of the runway. Repeat caution there are runway works at the north-west end of the runway. Over.'

'Roger Tower, acknowledged. Victor 57 landing long on runway 06. Listening Out.'

It was all so matter of fact.

Glancing behind to the two passengers in the rear of the Lysander's glass house cockpit, Castledine said cheerily, 'At least the rain's stopped so I can see where we're going ... Make sure your straps are buckled up tightly please gentlemen.'

As the Lysander began its final descent onto the runway, the passengers could see that the side of the hill was teeming with people and machinery, giving the slope below the runway threshold the appearance of an ant nest that has just been given a good kicking, the piles of crates being the precious pupae about to be carried away to safety by the scurrying workers.

'What are they doing down there?' asked the major with the rough beard and earthy smell of an officer who has been too many weeks up country in the jungle.

'Can't say, sir,' shouted Castledine above the noise of the Lysander's Bristol Mercury radial. 'It's all very hush hush. Apparently, they are Yanks doing some sort of special job for our Lords and Masters at SEAC.'

'There are some of your chaps down there too Colonel,' Castledine added as he juggled the stick pedals and trim wheel to slow down the brilliantly versatile, but famously tricky, aircraft for landing.

Colonel Kusahara Mitsuo grinned.

'I am very pleased,' he said, using the excellent English that he learned before the war studying engineering at Harvard and which was the reason he was chosen for his liaison role with the British, 'that the Geneva Convention prevents you employing officers like me for hard labour.'

Kusahara and the major from Force 136, who Castledine knew only as Bill, laughed, which Castledine thought was a bit rich given the way the Japanese had treated British officers who were prisoners of war.

The carter glanced up as the shadow of the Lysander passed across the Prome No. 1 road. His teenage son jumped on top of the cargo of dark teak beams, which were still slick with the monsoon rain.

'Hello pilot! Hello pilot!' he waived and shouted.

'Oi you, get a move on!' shouted the corporal in the sweat-stained jungle greens. 'You know you're not supposed to be hanging around here.'

The carter fumbled in the waistband of his longyi and, bowing his head, handed over the papers.

'Oh right.' The corporal turned to the other soldier manning the barrier. 'Let him through Taff, it's another delivery for the Yanks.'

Their souls stuck in the animal realm on the bhavacakra, the Buddhist wheel of life, the long-suffering oxen plodded off up the track through the cloying monsoon mud; past the remains of the silted up slit trenches left over from the futile attempts to defend the airfield in 1942, and past the incongruous sight of the naval lieutenant sitting on a crate, a watercolour pad on his knee; heading towards the D3 bulldozers belching fumes and the massive earthworks that scarred the side of the Mingaladon plateau.

12

Funded personally by Kaiser Wilhelm II of Germany and his wife, the Empress Auguste Victoria, after their visit to Palestine in October 1898, the Empress Augusta Victoria endowment on the Mount of Olives is one of Jerusalem's most modern buildings, offering the European pilgrim, tourist, or visiting archaeologist all of the latest comforts, including electric light courtesy of its own diesel generator.

According to the Baedeker guide to Palestine and Syria, the site also offers panoramic views of the Old City of Jerusalem.

Especially imposing is the view of the Haram al-Sharif, upon which stands the Dome of the Rock and the al-Aqsa Mosque.

Experienced Jerusalem hands also know that the view is at its most spectacular in the early morning sun and that spring is the best time to visit the city because the vegetation is still green and fresh.

However, this does not matter to Captain Montagu Parker, who has moved into the brand new complex, which is still under construction, because it offers him a secure base appropriate to his social station for 12 francs per day without wine.

From here he can hire his expeditionary force of workmen, cooks, bodyguards and maids and, clad in the formal suit that the Baedeker also advises for such meetings, he can also set out to meet the governor of the city, Azmey Bey Pasha, and the local dignitaries whom the governor will introduce.

All hope to bask in the reflected glory of the captain's success in finding the fabled treasure.

Two commissioners from Constantinople have also arrived in Jerusalem. The Ottoman Government is continuing to take a close interest in Captain Parker's expedition and if he is successful it intends to hold him to the terms of his licence.

However, other parties who are not part of the government are also taking a close interest in Captain Parker's preparations.

Jerusalem is a giant rumour mill and the community of archaeologists and Biblical researchers who are based in the city are becoming alarmed by Parker's activities.

The most serious question under discussion in the libraries and coffee shops of the city is just what damage could this unknown Briton, who seems to be more a treasure hunter than an archaeologist, and who seems to take his guidance not from scholars but from telepaths and a clairvoyant, inflict upon one of the world's most sensitive archaeological sites?

Soon the telegraph to Constantinople is humming with requests that the government intervene, if necessary over the head of the governor.

Tracy Spaight
New York
August 2012

After returning from Myanmar in July, Mark and Anna of Room 608 start logging and reviewing the footage they shot with David.

In one of the interviews, David claims that the burials were undertaken by members of the United States Navy Construction Battalions (the Seabees), although he may have confused them with the similarly named, though organisationally different, United States Army Engineers Construction Battalions (CBs).

We decide to follow up on this lead.

As part of routine fact-checking, Anna contacts the United States Naval Archives to inquire about what documents they hold regarding the Seabees activities in Burma, only to be told that the Seabees were never in Burma.

The US Army Construction Battalions, on the other hand, did operate in Burma – but only in the far north of the country, where they built the Ledo Road to bring supplies to Chiang Kai-Shek's forces. Inquiries to the University of Santa Barbara, which holds a collection of photographic records from US CBs, also draw a blank, meaning that, based on documentary records, these units were nowhere near Mingaladon in 1945–46.

If this is indeed the case, it blows a rather large hole in David's story.

Mark, Anna and I discuss the situation and decide that we need to engage an expert to help us navigate the complexities of British and US military archives to either validate or refute David's claims. This decision ultimately leads us to Andy Brockman, who specialises in an academic field none of us even knew existed: Second World War conflict archaeology.

```
Andy Brockman
Shooters Hill,
London
17 August 2012
```

In the course of the article in *Heritage Daily*, I suggest that, whatever we believe about the likelihood of Spitfires being buried in Burma, the story and its investigation should be taken seriously, which is why I place this statement on the record:

> Strange and rare objects <u>are</u> found dumped or still in situ; the parts of the Livens Large Gallery Flame Projector excavated at Mametz on the Somme by Dr Tony Pollard and the Glasgow University Centre for Battlefield Archaeology and the subject of a *Time Team* documentary is a case in point [*The Somme's Secret Weapon*, Channel 4, 14 April 2011]. However, such cases are <u>archaeology</u>, not material for recovery for the sake of recovery.

I add:

> If the Burmese site was to prove to be genuine, and a prudent archaeologist never says never, it would be archaeology of major importance; both in terms of the material culture of war in late World War Two and in demonstrating that those urban myths might contain a kernel of truth.

I conclude by arguing this search should not be yet another subject of private excavation ripping aircraft or aircraft parts out of the ground with JCB Limited's 'big yellow trowel', with no archaeological recording or publication, except perhaps a documentary on the History Channel.

In particular, the likely disposal of finds to the private market, potentially for a large profit, is counter to ethics and best practice in heritage conservation and archaeology, as well as the spirit and possibly the letter of various aspects of UK legislation and International conventions on the recovery and export of government property and culturally important heritage items.

That alone suggests that were the story to prove to be even partially accurate, any expedition should be taken seriously by the mainstream conflict archaeology community, which should engage with the project and assist in ensuring the work is undertaken ethically, properly recorded, and fully reported and published.

I add a second line of argument, which places the expedition in the wider context of UK archaeological practice. I suggest that over the past forty years mainstream archaeology has not taken the desire of people in the wider world to value and excavation sites related to wartime aviation seriously and that we are now playing catch up over such issues.

The problem is highlighted by the fact that, for example, there are now probably no Mark I or II Battle of Britain-period Spitfires left in the UK mainland archaeological record. This is because the available crash sites have all been 'excavated' without records being kept, and items from digs claiming to be before the 1986 Protection of Military Remains Act, which imposed a licensing system for military aircraft excavations, are often available on eBay.

In essence; as currently configured, if Mr Brooks and Mr Cundall do not find anything under their Burmese airfield except scrap and monsoon mud, they might regard their project as a failure, the money wasted. However, looked at archaeologically, properly researched, recorded and published, the unlikely duo will have undertaken an archaeological research project that retains value, albeit by proving a negative.

It is that discussion that seems to prompt the email that appears in my inbox from Anna Bowers of the New York-based Room 608 Productions.

Anna explains she came across my article while researching a documentary about David Cundall's claims and asks if she can book a call to discuss my perspective on the story.

We agree to talk.

13

Captain Montagu Brownlow Parker has a public relations problem.

There are long-established archaeological entities in Jerusalem represent-ing the great and the good of Biblical archaeology in Europe and the United States, and they are deeply suspicious of the motives and technical ability of the young Englishman.

Dammit all, they say, a member of his team is one Major Foley who is famous less for his archaeological prowess than for being a member of the infamous Jameson Raid into the Transvaal of South Africa, which was a key factor in the outbreak of the Boer War.

The Jewish population of Jerusalem is also less than pleased with the rumours Captain Parker is looking for no less than the Temple of Solomon and the Ark of the Covenant itself.

After all, Baron Edmund de Rothschild, of the French half of the famous banking family, is financing his own search for precisely that fabled object. He too has the ear of the authorities in Constantinople and he can make trouble.

There are also accusations that Captain Parker is committing sacrilege on other sacred Jewish sites.

In an attempt to head off this pincer movement of criticism, which could derail his entire project, Captain Parker hires his own archaeologist and, not lacking in ambition, he hires the best.

Captain Parker's academic cover is the moustachioed 37-year-old Frenchman and Dominican monk, Père Louis-Hugues Vincent of the pres-tigious l'École Biblique et Archéologique Française de Jérusalem.

Père Vincent will record and report on the archaeology uncovered by the expedition.

Captain Parker does not think it is necessary to brief the priest/archaeologist on the other less orthodox aspects of the project, while Père Vincent makes the calculation that the risks of being associated with such a strange endeavour are outweighed by the opportunities to undertake archaeology in locations in Jerusalem that were previously unavailable.

A photograph of the pair taken in 1911, in what is now known as the Warren Shaft, shows the bearded Parker, wearing knee-length riding boots and a dark jacket, while Vincent sports a dapper pale suit and carries a cane. They sit apart, with Parker gazing at the ground as if not wanting to be challenged by face-to-face contact with a potentially critical audience, while the priest fixes the glass eye of the camera with direct confidence.

Unfortunately, the winter rains come early to Jerusalem in 1909 and the autumn dust is transformed into sheets of cloying mud. In November Captain Parker calls off work for that season and returns to London.

Next year, he will ally faith in Dr Juvelius and the Irish clairvoyant Mr Lee, with a more muscular approach to the excavation under the direction of Père Vincent. With that in mind, Parker sets about hiring tunnelling engineers who have been helping most recently to extend the London underground.

14

Andy Brockman
London and New York via Skype
11 September 2012

It is a common trope in dystopian fiction that documents disappear into a bureaucratic black hole never to be seen again, unless it is to be weeded and shredded to avoid future political embarrassment, rewritten as propaganda by faceless drones such as George Orwell's Winston Smith, or culled to save storage space.

In 2018 the British Home Office provided a real world case study proving the fiction when it was revealed that thousands of landing cards of legal immigrants arriving from the Caribbean, last seen in an office block in Croydon, had been destroyed. The resulting Windrush Scandal saw at least eighty-three UK citizens wrongly deported and hundreds of others subjected to months of stress and even the denial of medical treatment. Which returns us to the dystopia we began with.[*]

It follows that every researcher who visits the National Archives at Kew (the UK's repository of Government papers) and from the visit produces a citation, essay, book, or broadcast, engages in an activity that might be by turn an act of resurrection, subversion, or defiance in the name of history and maybe some combination of all three.

It is also the case that, thanks to the amount of material dating from the Second World War that has been declassified, including files that were

---

[*] The entire sorry episode is described in the book *The Windrush Betrayal* (2019) by award winning journalist Amelia Gentlemen.

once given the highest security classification such as those relating to the code-breaking work at Bletchley Park and its use politically and in the field, our understanding of events from Dunkirk and the Battle of Britain to the Dambusters raid and the responses to the German V weapons programmes have been transformed.

However, perhaps because most archaeologists are trained to handle objects, not historical documents, and also because the history of archaeology is littered with unfortunate examples of archaeologists driven to find 'evidence' that proves the 'truth' of famous documents from the Bible to Plato's Atlantis and Hitler's Aryan race, the relationship between archaeologists and historical records is complex and sometimes ambiguous.

For a start, it is a core tenet of modern scientific archaeology that 'facts in the ground' trump everything. For example, when in 2006, Martin Brown, who would later become Field Director on the Burma Project, excavated the Shornecliffe Redoubt in Kent for Channel 4's *Time Team*, the work was guided by several beautifully drawn plans produced by Colonel William Twiss of the Royal Engineers in 1794 when the redoubt was built.

Unfortunately for the visual impact of the programme, but in a perfect example of why it is necessary ultimately for archaeologists to dig to test a hypothesis, it transpired that some of the most significant features in the drawings made by Colonel Twiss, such as underground ammunition magazines and associated defensive gun emplacements, had never actually been built. This was probably because changes in military tactics during the French Revolutionary War, or the Army's budget, necessitated a redesign, the records of which, if they existed at all, had not reached the archives.

However, the simple fact remains that no archaeologist can knowingly ignore information from historical archives where that information is available.

When it comes to the archaeology of the Second World War, that archive material can extend to tens of thousands of pages, any one of which might contain a line, plan, or photograph that could illuminate the purpose of abandoned concrete or, like the phantom magazines of Shornecliffe, be contradicted by the truth in the ground.

So it is that a week after that initial electronic handshake across the Atlantic, and following a subsequent conversation on Skype, I email Mark and Anna in New York with an initial assessment of how David's story sits within the documented history of the immediate post-war period in Burma.

I have already discussed the paper trail that we will need to examine for the project with Wargaming/Room 608's UK-based researcher Meghan Horvath, who has been working in the archives of the Royal Air Force

Museum at Hendon in North London. We have agreed that, in addition to the aircraft record cards she has already been checking and copying, we will need to trace the records of the units that served at Mingaladon as well as political and military intelligence files held at the National Archives at Kew and perhaps elsewhere.

Now I tell Mark and Anna that I have also checked the background material on RAF Mingaladon (and Burmese airfields in general) and, based on what I have found, I want to raise various issues that might help them contextualise their approach to the site and to filming conflict archaeology in general.

First, I note Mingaladon has a complex history, down to the airfield's present use as a dual military and civilian airport. Thus, it is going to be virtually impossible to extract material from a relatively narrow window of time in late 1945–46 without a detailed desktop study of all the available information, documents, air photographs, properly located geophysics, satellite imagery (if available) and a forensic assessment of David's witness statements.

However, based on the information I have seen so far, the basic research questions, Who? What? When? Where? And Why? do not seem to have been asked of David Cundall's evidence.

Regarding the geophysics from David's two contractors, Suntac and Malcolm Weale, I explain that archaeological geophysics on its own (even coupled with alleged 'witness statements') is not enough evidence upon which to base an expensive project because it is very difficult to differentiate between objects and periods except in the most general terms. Indeed, geophysics plots can be subject to multiple interpretations and many archaeologists, though not it must be said most geophysicists, regard their interpretation as something of a dark art.

'In other words,' I write in summary, 'any geophysics the project has or will undertake is as likely to pick up geology, a Japanese air raid shelter, dispersal pen or barracks as a feature from the period when the RAF was in control.'

It follows that the team need to be sure they have the right advice available on site to interpret what the geophysics actually shows, not what they want the geophysics to show.

I illustrate the point with the story of the excavations at Stalag Luft III when a TV production company placed an expensive shaft in the wrong place to intercept one of the famous tunnels dug for the so called 'Great Escape', because they did not wait for the lead archaeologist to arrive on site and thus spent what should have been the big reveal explaining to the audience why they had not found the tunnel.

I also remind them that safety is critical on any archaeological site and because Mingaladon was a front-line airfield throughout the Burma Campaign, and continues in military use down today, the threat from contamination and unexploded ordnance (UXO) is higher than for many other locations and I would not recommend digging at Mingaladon without properly qualified explosive ordnance disposal (EOD) cover.

Contrary to the impression given in some television history programmes, this is not a job for amateur researchers who say they understand the subject just because they have been in the armed forces, read the manuals, or buy militaria on eBay.

To demonstrate the importance of taking these risks seriously, I cite the cases of amateur collectors and battlefield diggers in France, Belgium and Eastern Europe who have been killed by their finds, and of Sam White of Richmond, Virginia, who died in 2008 when the black powder in the shell he was trying to defuse at his home exploded, making Mr White probably the last fatal casualty of the American Civil War.

In the end, while I realise the audience hook and narrative thrust of this project is about a historical mystery (albeit one I feel is almost certainly based on an urban myth), I suggest that the best chance of getting usable material out of the project is to have the means of recognising and interpreting the material that will be found and that will allow the production team to move seamlessly from a known (documents, photographs and actual archaeology) to the unknown (the Spitfires legend), while making sense of both for the audience.

I believe such an approach would also provide a more certain and useful return for the programme funder, Wargaming.

Instinct tells me also that this fascinating project is not going to end up in the place everyone expects at the moment, so to provide the opportunity for a soft landing I also contribute a final idea about framing the project suggesting, 'I would pitch the "quest" within the story as, "Is the Legend of the Burmese Spitfires True?" rather than, "Let's find the lost Burma Spitfires."'

I wonder if I have just talked myself out of a job.

But I need not have worried.

Further conversations via Skype lead to further research, including reading the wartime Cabinet minutes published online by the National Archives at Kew, and soon I am able to send Mark and Anna the detailed assessment of the situation they have requested.

I suggest visiting the National Archives in order to access the intelligence briefings and bomb damage assessments of Myitkyina and, particularly

Mingaladon, as well as reading the operations record books of the various maintenance units and repair and salvage units that were stationed at Mingaladon.

Most important of all, I want to look at documents that are not referred to anywhere by David Cundall and supporters of the burial story, the records of South East Asia Command itself, including those of its RAF Commander, Sir Keith Park.

Mark Mannucci discusses the situation with Tracy Spaight at Wargaming and the result is an email asking me to undertake a formal desktop assessment.

Mark adds that another researcher who has worked with David, Andrew Pentland, claims to have pinpointed sixty aircraft destined for ACSEA that may include the aircraft that are alleged to have been buried.

Reflecting on this dialogue it seems that, despite my scepticism about David's story, Mark and Anna seem still to want to have me involved.

This is encouraging because they (along with Wargaming) are clearly taking the research element seriously and are not just running with David Cundall's version of the history, as accepted, apparently without question, by Prime Minister David Cameron and the bulk of the British and international media.

15

Andy Brockman
South Kensington
London
28 September 2012

By mid-September, it is clear that the Myanmar government will award the contract to David Cundall, so Tracy Spaight gives the green light to Room 608 to record more interviews in the UK and we agree to meet.

The crew arrive from New York on 27 September, and I travel across London to meet them at their hotel in South Kensington, a stone's throw from the three great Victorian foundations, the Science, Natural History and Victoria and Albert museums, and geophysicist Adam Booth's employer, Imperial College.

We introduce ourselves and talk generally for a while. I also restate my general take on the various research issues, but we don't speak for long.

Mark, Anna and the team are tired after the flight and they want to have some food and then get to bed. However, I feel the meeting has gone well. I am invited to join them for a meal, but I decline. I do not want to appear too eager. Besides, we have agreed to meet again over breakfast in the morning.

While I am on the tube heading home, with a non-disclosure agreement signed as the price of seeing David Cundall's research, Anna emails the crucial document to me, adding in a cover note that it seems an imperfect piece of research but it is also the origin of the buried Spitfires story and thus must be considered.

I soon realise that what we come to call the 'Cundall Dossier' is like no research report I have read before.

With its apparently disconnected witness statements, uncontextualised quotations from documents, and apparently random collection of plans and sketch maps of RAF Mingaladon, David's document reminds me of nothing so much as my favourite method statement in any historical account, that which is often attributed to the ninth-century AD Welsh monk Nennius.

In the preface to his *Historia Brittonum*, Nennius, or more likely that famous literary editor 'anonymous', wrote, of the organisation of the sources set out in the book, '*Ego autem coacervavi omne*', which translates loosely as, 'I have made a heap of everything I found'.

However, by the Middle Ages, this 'heap' of sources describing the attempts of the Britons to hold back the tide of the invading Germanic tribes during what archaeologists and historians then called the Dark Ages, had become a foundation text of the Matter of Britain, the great national myth of King Arthur, set out first in Geoffrey of Monmouth in his *History of the Kings of Britain*, and latterly in Thomas Mallory's great work *L'Morte d'Arthur* (*The Death of Arthur*).

In the account set out in the *Historia Brittonum*, Arthur is the victor of twelve battles the length and breadth of Britian, which turn the tide of the invasion. However, critically wounded in his last fight at Camlann, the warrior hero is taken aboard a magical boat and vanishes into the mists of the Island of Avalon, while his great sword Excalibur is flung into the dark waters, only to be snatched up by the Lady of the Lake.

The tragedy of Arthur's death is leavened by the hope, or the promise, that he is not really dead and that one day, if Britain should ever be in mortal peril, the Once and Future King will return to save the nation.

It is a myth played for all it is worth by the Welsh-born Henry Tudor in his campaign to overthrow the Plantagenet Richard III, to the extent that he fights at Bosworth in 1485 under the Red Dragon of Wales, which also appears in the account of Nennius. Victorious, the new King Henry VII names his eldest son Arthur.

Reading the dossier, it is impossible not to draw parallels between how a people trying to define and defend their culture in the changing world of the Middle Ages created and then clung on to the myth of Arthur and his magical sword, and with what David claims is the mysterious disappearance of a modern Excalibur; the Spitfire fighter, wielded by the knights of the Royal Air Force during a later Battle of Britain in 1940, where a modern Germanic enemy fought not with the spear and scramseax of the sixth century AD, but with the output of the factories of Messerschmitt, Junkers, Dornier and Heinkel.

Andy Brockman
Lepain Quotidien
South Kensington
London
29 September 2012

We, the Room 608 team plus Tracy Spaight from Wargaming (who arrived late last night), reassemble over breakfast in Lepain Quotidien in Exhibition Road. With its bare brick and wooden floor, this is one of the many designer cafés that serve the local business community and tourists in South Kensington and one of the most popular.

It is a fine early autumn morning and judging by the buzz in the big open plan dining room the mood, and business, is good.

I eat scrambled eggs on toast, drink coffee and try to get the measure of my new colleagues. Tracy Spaight, in particular, is not what I expect in an executive in a rapidly growing international software company. A smartly turned out, youthful looking 43, Tracy is, I discover, a historian by training and was a teacher before he entered the gaming industry in the mid-2000s. He also comes across as something of an anglophile, having spent a year as a visiting scholar at Cambridge in the late 1990s. I will discover later that beneath the calm and, for me, reassuring determination to do right by the history as Head of Special Projects at Wargaming, there is also a creative spirit steeped in California's technology counterculture. Tracy is co-founder of Cyberia, one of the larger theme camps at the annual Burning Man festival.

Today we discuss the research and in the light of my concerns about the nature of the evidence I have just read in the 'Cundall Dossier', I offer some suggestions about how to approach the upcoming interviews with the alleged eyewitnesses that lie at the centre of the claims David has made.

For example, I recommend including questions such as details about military careers, locations and operations, which can be checked against primary sources such as war diaries and RAF operations record books.

I do this because, as I read the contents of the dossier I detect none of the scepticism or need to provide corroboration from unconnected sources that I would expect to find in a standard research report. Indeed, as far as I can tell, thus far, no one has applied any checks and balances.

A witness states they are a veteran of the Burma campaign and that they saw Spitfires buried at Mingaladon in 1945, and they are believed automatically. While the absence of any verifiable evidence for the burial has become, at least in David's mind, evidence of a conspiracy at the highest levels of the British Government and military to cover up the burial.

Then, as we talk, Mark Mannucci asks me matter of factly if I would be prepared to go to Myanmar when David Cundall returns there, almost certainly early in the New Year of 2013, during the dry season.

I say 'yes', hoping that it does not show that the prospect makes me more than a little nervous. It is not just that the prospect of becoming a member of the team investigating one of the most high-profile historical mysteries to emerge in the twenty-first century is somewhat daunting.

Neither am I concerned now about engaging with a country and a government that until a few months ago was under severe sanctions which would have made our expedition both unethical and illegal. At this time both the UK government and, crucially, Aung San Suu Kyi's National League for Democracy (NLD), are encouraging such engagement.

The thing is, I have managed to reach the age of 51 and attained a level of knowledge about aircraft and the archaeology of aviation without ever having left the ground in anything other than the London Eye.

Tracy Spaight
Leeds University
30 September 2012

Mark and Anna and I, along with Adam Docker (our Director of Photography) and our London-based researcher Meghan, meet at 9.30 a.m. at King's Cross station to catch the 10.08 a.m. train to Leeds.

We're heading to the University of Leeds to interview Dr Roger Clark and Dr Adam Booth, both of whom have worked with David Cundall on various aviation recovery projects over the years.

We find them at the Mathematics/Environmental Sciences building, one of the drab post-war concrete and steel modernist structures that present such a startling contrast with the nineteenth-century Gothic architecture favoured by the university's founders.

We exchange greetings while the film crew sets up their equipment. Dr Clark is the older of the two. He was Dr Booth's thesis advisor in 2004. Adam Docker indicates that he's ready to shoot, so we start the interview.

'What's your relationship to these buried Spitfires?' Mark asks Roger:

Well, I guess it goes back to rather than longer ago than the Spitfire project, in that David Cundall cold-called us, it must be twenty years ago now, wanting to borrow some geophysical equipment for a site survey, which is not an unusual call. We get them occasionally. When I asked him what it was for, he said that he's a kind of amateur aviation archaeologist, likes looking for crash sites to see if he can get some bits of old planes back, which resonated with my own interest. I grew up next to an RAF airfield, so I said, sure.

And I guess about fifteen years ago, he mentioned he had yet another project under way, but this time in Burma. It was a slightly delicate matter. It wasn't a very popular country then, but when he offered us the opportunity to be involved in it, once we saw the way he was doing it, you know, from the ground up with the locals and through the embassy and all the rest of it, we figured we would help.

'How did he present the project to you?' Mark asks:

Pretty much the same as every other project he's done, whether it's a crash site or a dump site at an airfield in Southeast England, he'd done the desk study, looked at the RAF records, identified somewhere where there may be something worth digging up, and would we advise, help, lend the equipment, come and do the geophysical survey to support the desk study that he's done and the eyewitnesses that he'd interviewed and so on and so forth, see if there's actually anything unusual under the ground.

'Well, what did he say?' Mark asks, eager for Roger to continue:

He's always been a Spitfire fan, and he, I mean, I can't remember the exact words but I mean, he just said, 'You know, the next project on the line is that I think when the RAF left Burma, they buried some unused Spitfires still in their packing crates, and there's a chance they might be there. And I want to go for it, if there's a need for geophysics, are you interested in helping and so on?' And that's a great heritage story, as I said, it resonates with my own interest in aviation.

'Why is it a great heritage story?' Mark asks.

'Because Spitfires are one of the iconic British aircraft of World War II,' Roger replies. 'The design is elegant, as well as the function it served very successfully, and to have a few more in museum condition or even flying condition around the world would be wonderful. It would be great to get them back above ground, where they belong.'

'When he told you these planes might be buried underground, did it sound crazy to you? Did it sound plausible?' Mark asks.

'It's one of the more exotic suggestions that David has come up with,' Roger says drily. 'We've done some very unglamorous sites as well, wet fields in Yorkshire that turned out to have a crashed Spitfire under it and stuff like that, but this would be quite a big one, I have to say.'

Adam jumps in, 'I can't say I've got anything to really base the idea on, it was just, there's David with this idea, geophysics can help him out, verifying or refuting the hypothesis and why not? Let's go for it.'

Adam explains he became involved off the back of one of Roger's projects with David at an RAF base near Bristol. David needed some geophysical work done to try and find some engine components, and, as Adam was between projects, he undertook some electromagnetic work trying to find the targets David was seeking.

Sometime later Adam received a phone call from David asking if he would be willing to fly out to Burma. The suggestion was so left field that Adam misheard and for a moment thought David was talking about England's second city, Birmingham.

The misunderstanding resolved, Adam joined David's hunt at Mingaladon.

'What did he explain to you that he had been told by the eyewitnesses about the way these planes were buried?' Mark asks.

'I don't know all that much detail except that they had been shipped out to the Far East, ready for, for proper combat use, but by the time they got there, the, the kind of strategic situation was such that Spitfires weren't much use. The battle front had moved a long way away, they were never assembled,' Roger says, repeating David's claim that the aircraft were in packing crates, sealed in canvas, and with their engines inhibited so they wouldn't rust.

Mark turns back to Adam. 'How did you examine the site?' he asks.

Adam explains that, to a geophysicist, a Spitfire is essentially a lot of metallic components, so searching for a buried Spitfire becomes a problem of identifying what physical properties you're going to look for and choosing the right equipment to identify and record those properties.

The essential point is that while metals are electrically conductive, the soils they are usually found in are electrically resistive. The task then becomes one of testing the electrical conductivity around the target so that if the equipment reveals an area of high conductivity in the right place it is possible that a conductive object, like an aircraft, is buried at that location.

'Locate us in time. When did you go?' Mark asks.

'You went in summer 2004,' Roger says as Adam tries to recall the specific date.

Adam explains that he was at Mingaladon for twelve days, divided into a few days becoming used to the lay of the land, followed by a week of surveying. Wanting to tie up the loose ends, Adam also prepared a preliminary report.

'What did you think at that point,' Mark asks.

With no reason to doubt the evidence David has shared with the two academics, Adam says his conclusion was that there was a large electrical anomaly suggestive of metal in the ground. Coupled with David's documents and eyewitness reports, that anomaly could be David's buried Spitfires.

'You've found them,' Mark concludes, prompting the sound bite he needs for the film. However, the academic in Adam cautions, 'No, we've, well found a geophysical anomaly that's consistent with, but not exclusively indicative of, there being Spitfires ... they could dig a trench and find some other metal objects down there.'

Adam explains that while state of the art, the equipment deployed in Yangon is not a Spitfire detector. The anomaly could equally be coils of barbed wire.

He concludes that the contribution he and Roger have made to David's research is simply one more risk reduction factor to add to David's accumulation of facts that seem consistent with his story.

'There is something unusually electrically conductive down there.' Roger Clark says. 'It's not natural. I mean, when you see the actual geometry of the anomalies, it's not a geological formation. There's something down there.'

Roger finishes the thought. 'If in late 2004, David said to us, should I go and do a lot more geophysics, or given I've got a chance to, to auger a borehole or something like that, well, you might as well just dig a hole.'

'You are not saying that the eyewitness and anomaly reports are sufficient alone. They really have to be tied together,' Mark says, again looking for the telling soundbite.

'The observations say there is likely to be metal buried in the ground. Now what that metal is is anyone's guess, but with the eyewitness reports as well, then the two stories start to become consistent,' Roger says.

We relocate to Roger's office and set up the camera to show the maps of the electrical conductivity at the site that Adam surveyed at Mingaladon in 2004.

Adam explains for the camera:

What we're seeing here are two maps of electrical conductivity responses, and you can see it's multi-coloured, and the, the blue colours, they are areas that have a low conductivity, uh, you move through green, which is intermediate conductivity all the way up to red, which is very high electrical conductivity. And we have an area of 100m by 180m, and what we can see is that the area is largely green coloured, so there's a background of intermediate electrical conductivity, but in both of these maps, you can see that there are discrete regions of red colours, so that's where we're interpreting the, the high electrical conductivity responses, potentially diagnostic of metal in the ground, to be.

'So those red areas might suggest …' Mark says, his voice trailing off.

'The red areas, because they're such high conductivity, they might suggest that there is metal in the ground at those locations.' Adam says.

Roger comments, 'What is particularly striking is that certainly this one here, this T-shaped one, and to some extent the other [L-shaped section], are not natural shapes. You certainly don't find anything as, as orthogonal and, and, and square as this one in nature. It's clearly a man–made feature of some sort.'

Next, Adam relates his survey grid to an air photograph of the modern Yangon International Airport, explaining that the area is in the order of a 180m long and 100m wide.

'Why did you pick that spot?' Mark asks.

Adam is clear that the decision to survey that area came from David and that in turn he had based his decision on the reports he had gathered over the years from his witnesses.

Adam states that David placed most faith in the response of an eyewitness he had flown in to visit the site and who took David to that location, saying, 'This is where they'll be buried.'

Remarkably, events at the end of the expedition provided evidence that David might just be right.

'I was asked to recommend a position for a trial excavation,' Adam says, which he was able to do based on the anomalies in the electrical conductivity data.

'So a guy came in with an excavator,' he continues. 'He dug down for a while, and you know, stood on the edge of this trench going oh, come on, you know, and suddenly, instead of the grind of the bucket of the excavator against the soil, there's a crunch as it hits wood!

'And blimey, you know, there really is something down there,' Adam says, seeming to relive the moment. 'You don't normally find wood inside the ground.'

But at that point, to Adam's obvious frustration, the excavation was closed pending further negotiations with Burmese officials.

'You are sure it was wood? You were there?' Mark asks with emphasis. Adam is sure.

'I was there. I heard the crunch of, of a metal bucket going through wood, saw a few jagged edges of wood sticking up out of the ground, very, very encouraging,' he says.

'That was your eureka moment. What did you think?' Mark prompts:

I thought, I hope that there's Spitfires within that crate and it's not a whole
load of buried Jeeps and buried wreckage or whatever. But yet, you know,
to have directed the excavations to these anomalies to then find it's not just
a heap of earth in the ground, there is something buried in there, there's got
to be something beneath that wood, there's got to be something under there,
yeah, that's, it's a really great moment. And then suddenly, I don't understand
why, but the digging doesn't go any further, the hole is backfilled and we're
all, you know, we're escorted off the site.

   There's no real hostility there, but you know, it's quite clear that the survey is
over, and there was something else going on that I was never really told about.

We conclude the interview by discussing the likely state of the planes, after
having been in the ground for almost seventy years.

   Adam speculates that if the soil actually seals the crates preventing water
from getting in, and if the supporting teak beams have not collapsed under
the weight of soil, then the potential for preservation is actually pretty good.

   'Let's equally moderate this a little,' Roger interjects, 'even if there's been a
lot of damage, the heritage value of what you bring out is enormous.'

   He reinforces the comment by pointing out that there are many successful
restoration projects that have recovered aircraft from such unforgiving locations as the bottom of Norwegian fjords and the steppes of Russia. Some of
those projects, like the P-38 Lightning fighter now called *Glacier Girl*, which
was recovered from under the Greenland ice cap, are flying again.

   'I'm as into this as David is,' Adam says. 'I have to say, I want there to be
some Spitfires buried there.'

   While remaining grounded in his science, Roger too is caught up in the
thrill of the chase, saying, 'It's been a delight to support David in this one, and
we'd like to be there for the conclusion. Whether it's professional satisfaction,
that it's a bunch of metal objects that happen to be old trucks or whether it's
actually the fantastic heritage story of some old Spitfires, it's inspired a lot of
people around the UK.'

   'I really do just want to see what lies beneath. There's got to be something
there, and I want to know what it is. Hopefully it's a Spitfire!' Adam adds.

   After the interview, Mark and Anna, along with the film crew, head back to
London. They want to get an early start to interview Second World War aviation wreck hunter Jim Pearce, who first set David on the Burma Spitfire trail
in the 1990s. Meghan and I stay overnight in Leeds, so we can visit David's
farm near Scunthorpe in the morning.

16

Tracy Spaight
David Cundall's Farm
Lincolnshire
1 October 2012

The Cundalls live in a charming two-storey brick farmhouse with a brown door and brown-trimmed windows. The house is surrounded by a thick green hedge and mature trees, with farm buildings off the lane. The fields opposite the house stretch as far as the eye can see, to a distant line of trees marking the edge of the property.

David welcomes us and ushers us into the kitchen, where his wife offers us cups of tea. We chat for a bit about our visit to the University of Leeds. Then we ask to see David's research, which he obligingly brings out in a large shopping bag and empties it all over the kitchen table.

Meghan and I exchange surprised glances. His research is a big, disorganised heap of letters, photocopies, maps, photographs, and notes scribbled on notepad paper all jumbled together. We spend the morning sorting it into piles and David helps us understand what we are looking at. I take photos on my iPhone of each piece of paper. We plan to organise it all into a timeline on my laptop later.

After lunch in the local pub, David mentions that his neighbour, Dave Paltry, accompanied him on some of his early UK-based excavations of crashed Second World War planes – and that he might have an old VHS tape showing the dig. The tape would, of course, be hugely useful for the documentary, so we ask if David can arrange for us to drop by for a visit. This he arranges with a call and drives us over.

Dave takes us out to his barn to show us a Spitfire gear they had recovered on one of the digs.

Next he digs up the VHS tape, which we watch in his living room. It is 1990. The grainy tape shows a more youthful David at the bottom of a hole he's just excavated with a digger. He has a big grin on his face. David has just found the propeller and they are about to lift it from the earth.

Dave agrees to let us borrow the tape, so we can make a copy for the film.

London
1 October 2012

Meghan and I catch a train back to London that evening and have a late dinner with Mark and Anna in South Kensington.

Everyone is tired, but we're also excited about our progress. Meghan and I describe what we found in David's astonishingly disorganised 'bag of research'. I take out my phone and read some of the letters, while we await our entrées.

One is an undated typed letter from a Mr Kim Wylie to a Mr Norman Couling, who was apparently stationed at Mingaladon right after the war. Mr Wylie and his partner, Mr Daniels, explain that they were preparing an article about the RAF in Burma when they came across a story about twenty-five Spitfires, still in their transport crates, being buried at the end of the war at RAF Mingaladon.

'According to the story,' Wylie writes, 'a large trench was dug with earth moving equipment and all twenty-five crates were placed in the trench and covered over. Is it possible that you saw or heard anything about this?'

It appears the letter (and research material from David Daniels) was sent to David in 2007, by one E.V.G. Albrecht, Esq., along with his write-up on Mingaladon in 1947.

I read another letter, this time from a Mr Nick Bushnell to David Cundall, in which Mr Bushnell confirms an earlier conversation that he had had (six years before) with a volunteer at the Spitfire Museum in Manston, Kent.

'He informed me he had witnessed the burying in a hollow of numerous crated Spitfires at the end of the runway at Mingaladon.' He adds that, 'The information was given to me prior to your advertisement in Spitfire magazine.'[*]

And finally, I show the group a photo of Stanley Coombe's original letter to David, in response to David's advertisement in FlyPast magazine.

---

[*]   Letter from Nick Bushnell to David Cundall, 16 July 2007.

'I remember the Spitfires being buried at Mingaladon,' Stanley writes. 'There were at least six, still in their crates, never unpacked. They were used to fill in at the east end of the runway when it was extended. The ground had to be built up about 25ft and the road diverted.'

Whether the Spitfire burial is a shaggy dog story or a genuine recollection of an event that actually happened, it seems clear from the letters that veterans who were stationed at Mingaladon in 1945–46 had heard rumours, or seen things, which they interpreted as Spitfires being dumped or buried. And it's also clear that modern researchers have been chasing the same stories as David Cundall since at least the 1990s.

Mark and Anna have also been busy. They spent the morning interviewing David's friend and fellow Second World War aircraft recovery enthusiast Jim Peace at his home in Sussex. However, they are disappointed in the interview, as they explain that Jim turned out to be rather cagey and ill-humoured on camera.

Mark brightens, however, when he reveals that they have located a second witness to the burials!

The archivist at Hendon, after learning of our interest in post-war RAF Mingaladon, contacted them to say that shortly after Meghan's recent visit, an elderly gentleman named Maurice Short had stopped by to enquire about donating his papers about his service at Mingaladon in the Second World War.

Talk about serendipity!

Mark and Anna spoke with him on the phone this afternoon and arranged to record an interview at his home on Thursday.

Andy Brockman
Shooter's Hill, London
2 October 2012

This morning our turn-of-the-century terrace house, which survived a Luftwaffe bomb four doors down the road, is a film location and I am walking Mark and Anna through the evidence I have gathered searching out the online sources and from visits to the National Archive at Kew.

After recording some establishing shots of me 'working' at my desk, we discuss the space required to bury a crated Second World War fighter (the ballpark figure is around 2,000 cu ft per aircraft, or 24,000 cu ft for David's squadron of twelve Spitfires), and I suggest that David and other supporters of the burial theory have never explained how long it would take to bury the aircraft and quite how much effort would be involved.

Even a crude calculation demonstrates burying a crated Spitfire is not a simple job and you can see why dropping a concrete block on the aircraft, or setting to with a bulldozer, was more popular with the RAF ground staff and probably a lot more fun!

I also point out both the US and British forces in Burma carried out an extensive programme of disposal of surplus material.

US material from Burma was largely withdrawn to bases in north-east India and either disposed of on the civilian market or sold to the Government of India (who according to a contemporary press story took 600,000 tons of equipment in one deal alone). It was a process that was overseen by the Foreign Liquidation Commission (FLC).

Massive quantities of surplus ammunition were dumped in the Bay of Bengal, while anything assessed as too dangerous to move was disposed of on site, which in some cases will have meant it was buried.

It is noted in contemporary reports that the extreme conditions in Southeast Asia caused additional problems and dangers for the armourers and ammunition technicians. For example, white phosphorus used in incendiary and smoke grenades and air-dropped munitions was prone to function spontaneously because of the high ambient temperatures.

Placing this activity in context, the records suggest the Allied powers perceived a need to demilitarise a potentially unsettled Burma, as Major General Thomas A. Terry, US Army, the Commander of US Forces in the China/Burma/India [CBI] Theatre, wrote in late 1945:

> In Burma, for example, the unsettled condition of the country makes the sale of our goods extremely difficult. Therefore, I reluctantly gave orders to bring some 20,000 tons of valuable surplus out of Burma. This means additional work for all of us, but I could not allow these supplies to be abandoned. Such an action simply could not be justified to the American people.

In addition, I explain, far from being a casual process, FLC operated a clear hierarchy of potential end users for unwanted war surplus from bases such as Myitkyina.

US Government agencies had first call, followed by non-profit charitable, educational and religious institutions, such as the Red Cross and missionaries; then American manufacturers or distributors whose firms bore the trademark on an item; then foreign governments for rehabilitation, relief and reconstruction; and bringing up the rear, private foreign interests.

By contrast, as the then colonial power, Britain needed to maintain a military presence in the Burma Theatre, and at the same time preparing to hand over to a post-war, civilian-led government.

Therefore the British were under less pressure to remove war surplus material from the Burma Theatre in a hurry and instead wanted to try to create a stable political environment. No easy task in the fractious ethnic and political melting pot of Burma.

However, when it comes to aircraft, the bulk of Spitfires in Burma can be shown either to have been transferred with their units back to India when service in Burma ended, or transferred to other units or locations.

As an example I quote the operations record book, photographs and newsreels, which all show that on 19 August 1945, 607 County of Durham Squadron disbanded at RAF Mingaladon and their Mark VIII Spitfires were transferred directly to 8 Squadron of the Indian Air Force. At the close of hostilities in Burma, 8 Squadron and its aircraft flew back to India.

I add that on 11 September 1945, another Spitfire squadron quoted as being directly involved in the burial by David, 273 Squadron, also flew out of Mingaladon with all their aircraft.

This time they flew east, their destination Saigon, where they were tasked to offer a show of force in support of French forces attempting to reassert their authority in French Indochina.

The key point I try to put across on camera is that the burial of crated aircraft, intact, does not accord with any known practice in Burma or elsewhere, as it is wasteful in terms of time, material and effort. This is particularly so as any crated aircraft that did turn up would be packed and ready to go straight back on the ship on which it had arrived.

We also discuss the fact the British Cabinet papers for 1945–46 do not contain any mentions of the need to keep military equipment out of the hands of particular groups such as the Burmans or to transfer equipment to other ethnic people such as the Karen. In other words, the suggestion at the heart of David's 'burial on the orders of Mountbatten' theory finds no corroborating evidence in the records of the tier of government that gave Mountbatten his instructions.

Instead, the documented concerns were first the necessity to disarm the large Japanese forces that were still in theatre at the time of the surrender in August 1945 and then to keep Burma united and stable under a renewed British administration until the Burmese could undertake self-rule.

Finally, we discuss the issue of the geophysics upon which David places such importance. While not questioning Adam Booth's work in 2004, I set out what I see as two important caveats. First that the sample grid is relatively small and was predicated on finding metal objects at the depth at which David claimed they were present, and we do not know how representative the sample is of the wider area of the former RAF airfield.

More significantly, I also point out that RAF Mingaladon was a combat zone for three years and the area that David thinks is the Spitfire burial site was a primary target for the RAF and USAAF bombers dropping 500 and 1,000lb bombs capable of spreading a lot of metal when they explode and of penetrating 30ft deep and as much again laterally if they do not.

It follows that just because the geophysics picked up metal at depth it does not mean that metal is a Spitfire. Indeed, the odds are it is not.

As we talk there are moments of intellectual jousting when Mark asks me to paraphrase a carefully constructed argument, or equivocation, into the soundbite he wants. To which I reply I can't say that, but what I can say is … and produce a more concise version of what I have just said. I also observe again the truism that a prudent archaeologist never says never.

Frustrated with my reliance on the contemporary documents and keen to find a hole through which a squadron of buried Spitfires can sideslip to keep the legend airborne, Mark puts it to me, 'It's not a digital world, OK, the records got lost?'

'What if I tell you,' I say, 'that some of the things mentioned in the operations record book of one of the squadrons that witnesses for this story are drawn from, 273 Squadron, are a couple of parties: one for VJ Day and one for some Australians and some Canadians who are being repatriated through Rangoon harbour. That's the level of reporting that's in that operations record book, and I think that if they are talking about the parties that they are having, if something as remarkable as burying thirty-odd crated Spitfires happened it would be there.'

'Yeah, maybe,' Mark says in a semi-exasperated throwaway.

There is a pause as the remark registers, then Mark, Anna and I burst out laughing.

17

Tracy Spaight
Duxford Airfield
Cambridgeshire
3 October 2012

'I can think of nothing more useless to the Karen in 1945–46 than a crated Spitfire. The best thing the Karen could have done with a crated Spitfire was to take the Spitfire out of the crate and turn the crate into a hut to live in.'

Historian at the Royal Air Force Air Historical Branch, Sebastian Cox, suppresses a smile as he seemingly undercuts the political and military rationale of David Cundall's entire theory.

We are filming in Hangar Two at RAF Duxford in Cambridgeshire, the home of Douglas Bader's famous, and controversial, Duxford Wing during the Battle of Britain. Duxford is now home to a branch of the Imperial War Museum and is Britain's largest aerospace museum.

A short distance away, Hangar 4 houses the museum's excellent Battle of Britain exhibition, which includes sandbagged emplacements, recovered German aircraft shot down over the UK, and my favourite, a sign that exhorted Brits to donate their aluminium cooking pots with the message 'out of the frying pan, into the (Spit)fire!'

The grade II listed building survived the second World War unscathed but was damaged by the special effects crew in Guy Hamilton's classic 1969 film *Battle of Britain*. In one of the most memorable scenes, Reichsmarschall Hermann Göring asks one of his Luftwaffe officers what he needs to defeat the RAF in preparation for Operation Sea Lion, the invasion of Britain.

The officer, who is based on real-life cigar-chewing ace General der Jagdflieger Adolf Galland, replies brazenly, 'Give me a squadron of Spitfires!'

This infuriates Göring, who turns on his heel and stalks away without saying a word.

Apocryphal or not – General Galland himself said that the comment was actually an expression of his exasperation at Göring's failure to listen to his fighter commanders and that for operational flying he actually preferred the Bf 109 – the scene captures the grudging admiration many German pilots had for R.J. Mitchell's elegantly deadly fighter.

Squadrons of Spitfires (and the unsung Hurricane) would shoot down hundreds of Luftwaffe bombers and fighters in autumn 1940, playing a lead role in thwarting the planned invasion and giving the British time to rearm after the disaster at Dunkirk.

As Churchill so memorably put it on the floor of the House of Commons on 20 August 1940, as the Battle of Britain still raged in the skies of southern England, 'Never in the field of human conflict was so much owed by so many to so few.'

With that mythic pedigree it is no wonder the plane has an almost iconic status for the British so that even today, more than seventy years later, the Spitfire is spoken of with awe and respect. They are preserved with the skill and reverence reserved for the most sacred of historical relics as part of the foundation myth of modern Britain.

At the former RAF Bentley Priory at Stanmore in north-west London there is even a stained-glass window commemorating the Spitfire's role in winning the Battle of Britain in almost religious terms.

More prosaically, Kent brewer Shepherd Neame manufactures Spitfire beer that, as its famous, and deliberately bad taste, advertising campaign claimed, is, 'downed all over Kent, just like the Luftwaffe'.

The British love the Spitfire.

However, the importance of Duxford is that it does not just show the claws of the RAF in action; it also shows the brains which directed them.

Behind Hangar Two in an inconspicuous low building is the 1940s operation room with a giant tabletop map of South-east Britain, around which sat the enlisted women of the Women's Auxiliary Air Force, who plotted the positions of British and Enemy fighters with croupiers' rakes, overseen by a minstrels' gallery of officers.

Overlooking and controlling all is the iconic sector clock, colour coded in fifteen-minute segments so that the controllers could tell at a glance how old the plot was by the colour of its identifier.

Here museum visitors can close their eyes and listen to the recreation of a bombing raid on the airfield, complete with radio chatter, anti-aircraft fire and earth-rattling explosions.

Back in Hangar Two, Sebastian is sitting calmly in a director's chair in front of a beautifully restored Spitfire Mark Vb.

The middle-aged scholar is smartly dressed in a navy suit and sky blue striped tie.

'When did you first hear the story of the Spitfires?' Mark asks.

'I first heard about it in the late 1990s,' he replies.

'And what was your reaction?'

'My reaction was I don't think it's particularly likely that the Spitfires have been buried in a beautiful, pristine condition and that you're going to be able to excavate them and rebuild them in any worthwhile fashion.'

'What do you think?' Mark asks:

I think if they buried the Spitfires, which I do think is possible, that they would have simply dug a hole and literally bulldozed the crates into the hole and covered it over. We looked in the contemporary RAF records to see if there was any reference to the fact that they were burying Spitfires or trying to dispose of surplus material in that way. But we found no record of them having done so.

'What does that mean?' Mark asks.

'It means they didn't record the fact that they did it if they did do it, or it means they didn't do it,' Sebastian replies with impeccable logic.

'The fact that there are no records is not significant?' Mark summarises:

Not necessarily, because units do not necessarily record every single thing that they do, and in a sense, because that is quite literally throwing something away, it may be that they simply didn't consider it particularly significant in the same way that most people don't really record what they throw away, because by the very act of throwing it away, you're saying it doesn't matter anymore.

Mark digests that for a moment, then says that according to the 1947 census, 'There were 60 to 120 planes that have no recorded service and then are suddenly struck off charge a year or two later. This means these planes were buried?' Mark asks, looking to Sebastian.

Sebastian does not take the bait and instead says levelly, 'I would say to you that you're making an inference that is not supported by the evidence, because you've gone from the fact that there is no recorded service for these aeroplanes to stating that that must mean that they were simply put in a hole in the ground.'

He adds:

And I am saying, not necessarily because we know, for example, that some aircraft, particularly in the Far East and the Middle East where the bureaucratic links back to the UK took time and were not as strong and they, the people in London, were not able to exercise the same degree of control as they might have been able to on units closer to home, that they simply didn't know where these aircraft had gone, and the inference that therefore they were never used is not necessarily accurate. It might be true. On the other hand, it might not.

One can almost hear the QED.

'What kind of paperwork would there be to indicate receipt of these planes,' Mark asks.

Well, one of the problems with records and paperwork is that government generates enormous amounts of paper. Just a simple squadron generates enormous amounts of paper, which is why you have someone in each squadron whose job is to deal with the paperwork. You do not keep every piece of paper of an organisation the size of the Royal Air Force during the Second World War, which at its peak strength, for example, was more than 1.2 million men and women. You do not keep every scrap of paper that's generated by that massive organisation. Generally speaking, only between about 5 and 10 per cent of government records are kept and considered worthy of retention and eventually will go into somewhere like the National Archives.

He pauses a moment, then continues:

If you kept everything, you would need several thousand hangars the size of the one we're sitting in just to keep the paper. And what's more, you would never be able to find anything because you'd have too much paper. So the sort of routine bills of landing, for example, for shipping spare parts or entire aircraft to and fro, across the globe, uh, and recording the fact that it's landed in Rangoon or wherever, are probably not kept.

'So again, the fact that there's no records might not be significant,' Mark sums up.

'The fact that there are no records for the shipment of all the aircraft that were ever sent to the Far East, that's not significant. It just means that those records were almost certainly destroyed.'

'How plausible is it that a hole would have been dug and the planes buried in their crates at Mingaladon?'

'I don't think it's beyond the bounds of probability that they buried some surplus aircraft,' Sebastian says.

'In their crates?' Mark prompts.

'I don't think it's beyond the realms of possibility that brand new, crated Spitfires would have been buried,' Sebastian says, choosing his words carefully.

Mark decides to end with another facet of David's story: the Karen.

'Tell us what the British–Karen relationship was during the war and then comment on the theory that the planes were meant as payment to the Karens,' Mark opens, to which Sebastian replies:

> The Karen were one of the indigenous populations within Burma who largely did not collaborate with the Japanese and indeed resisted the Japanese, and Force 136, which was the British covert operations force within Burma, Force 136 cooperated with the Karen, supplied them with arms, etc. in order to help them to resist the Japanese and act as guerrillas within occupied Burma. So the Karen were largely seen as friendly forces.
>
> But the idea that you're going to reward the Karen with highly sophisticated modern technological aircraft that require a sophisticated logistical and engineering system to support them is frankly preposterous.

On the train ride back to London, Mark and Anna and I discuss the day's shoot. Sebastian's allowance that the burials could have happened, and further that they could have happened either without being recorded or recorded but with the records subsequently discarded or lost, lends support to David's story.

But the softly spoken British historian has also completely demolished the idea that the planes had been buried to support the Karen. If the planes were buried, we believe, then most likely this would have happened as part of the post-war clean-up of the airfield, to prepare it for civilian use. In other words, if the planes are there, then they probably weren't buried, but they might very well have been dumped. David's own research report, which was apparently compiled by one of his partners or associates in the 1990s, makes the case 'there was a lot of kit to be cleared', and consequently 'a large hole was dug, and the lot shovelled into it'.

18

Tracy Spaight
The Holly Bush Public House
London
4 October 2012

Built as a house by the famous portrait painter George Romney in the 1790s, the Grade II listed Holly Bush Pub, with its etched-glass windows, hardwood floors, and cheerful fireplace, sits in the heart of the historic Hampstead district of north London. We take a seat at the bar and await the arrival of Stanley Coombe, who was stationed at Mingaladon in 1946. At this time we believe Stanley is the last living witness to the Spitfire burials and as such is key to David's story. All the other veterans whom David identified as witnesses to the burial have passed away.[*]

Stanley arrives right on time, wearing a cream-coloured blazer, chequered shirt, and beige slacks. Bright-eyed and with a twinkle in his eye and spryness that belies the fact he was a soldier in Bill Slim's 'forgotten 14th Army' almost seven decades ago, Stanley served first with the 9th Battalion, The Royal Sussex Regiment, later transferring to the Berkshire Regiment, and we understand it is while taking up a new posting with the Berkshires that he arrives in southern Burma after the Japanese surrender.

We shake hands. The film crew sets up their equipment, our sound engineer mics Stanley, and we begin the interview.

---

[*]   We later discovered that one of the other witnesses David identified was in fact still living, but he declined to be interviewed.

'How did you meet David?' Mark asks. He wants to establish how Stanley became involved in the story in the first place.

Stanley begins:

A friend of mine used to give me a magazine every month called *FlyPast*. He said, 'You might be interested in this one.' And there was a letter in there from a man named David Cundall, asking whether anybody had any information on Spitfires that were buried at Mingaladon! Well, I'd been telling people for years that I knew where there were Spitfires buried but nobody took any notice. So it took me about two or three weeks to make up my mind to reply. I eventually did and Mr Cundall got in touch with me. David came to visit me with Keith Win and another person called Jim Pearce. They asked if I would be willing to come to Burma and show them where the Spitfires were buried. I agreed and we went out in 1998.

'Can you tell us again about your service in the Far East?' Mark asks.

'I was there in 1944, and again in 1946, after postings in India and Singapore,' Stanley recounts. 'I was 19 years old when I was out there, and I was just a private in the army, that's all. Doing my little bit,' he says in a self-deprecating way:

We got off the boat at Rangoon – this would have been early 1946 – and we went to a base just outside of Mingaladon. I was with my mate in the back of a lorry, which was being driven by an Indian driver. We had to go across the end of the runway at Rangoon airport. While waiting to cross, we were told that later that day the road would be closed and the runway extended across the road. I remember there were some big crates along the side of this road, and they were being pushed down into a big, deep trench, down a ramp.

They were brand spanking new. I mean, they weren't dirty old crates; they were brand new, straight from the saw mill. I reckon there were six. And it seemed so curious, you know, that they were putting them in there. That's why I've always remembered it. The next day, we drove back to the airfield, to deliver something at married quarters. One of the airman was there helping us to unload, and I said to him, what was in the crates? He replied, 'Would you believe Spitfires?'

We exchange glances, as the interview draws to a close.

Stanley's testimony is compelling and believable. Maybe David is right, and something really is buried at Mingaladon. Stranger things have certainly happened in war, and military bureaucracies often do illogical things, as Joseph Heller satirised so brilliantly in his novel *Catch 22*.

Tracy Spaight
Home of Group Captain Maurice Short
London
4 October 2012

Group Captain Maurice Short's living room attests to a life well lived, with photos of children and grandchildren, commendations, and photos of him as an RAF pilot after the war. He served in the RAF for fifty-two years, joining up at age 16 and ending his career as a senior officer with NATO and holder of the MBE and Air Force Cross. Maurice served as a mechanic in the RAF at Mingaladon in 1945. He too has agreed to talk with us about his experiences.

Maurice tells us he remembers the outbreak of the war quite clearly: 'We had a festival in my hometown at Scarborough. And it was cancelled. And I remember kicking the wall and saying, "I'm going to kill Hitler," so I ran home and said to mother – I was 14 – I'm going to join up. "There, there son, what's the problem?" I said, "Hitler's just cancelled our cricket festival!"'

Two years later Maurice joined the RAF and was assigned to service the Bristol Hercules engines fitted to Halifax bombers. In 1945, he was posted to Burma and assigned to the 101 Repair and Salvage (101RS), first at Akyab, which was home to three squadrons of Dakota transport planes, and with the end of the war to Mingaladon, where he helped service and maintain aircraft for various units, particularly 267 Squadron.

Maurice recounted that in late 1945, Mingaladon became a centre for repatriation, with thousands of soldiers and former PoWs, many of them in shocking condition from years in captivity waiting for flights out on the overstretched RAF transports or for a berth on the crowded troop ships departing from Rangoon docks. There were also the tens of thousands of Japanese prisoners of war, the remnants of the Burma Area Army.

Amid this anthill of humanity vast quantities of war material is simply abandoned. To illustrate his point, Maurice tells us what happened when the American squadrons pulled out of Akyab (now called Sittwe) earlier in the year:

> I was servicing one of the Dakotas, up on the engine, and this huge fuel lorry came along, and with a hiss of the air brakes pulled up, out came one of your fine young [American] men and say[s], 'Hey, buddy, you got a bottle of whisky?'

And I am up on an engine in the heat of Burma. 'No, I'm sorry – why?' I say.

He replied, 'Well, if you had a bottle of whisky, you could have this god-damn lorry. We're leaving it!'

So I'm looking at this 40,000 gallon [lorry] and I'm thinking the guy is mad, but of course, we're at war. Well, he disappeared and I got on working and there was the sound of a motorbike and up came one of your magnificent, laid back – I've forgotten the name of them now, your well known ...

'Harley Davidson?' Mark suggests.

The very one! And another young American on it, and his call was, 'Have you got half a bottle of whisky?'

And I thought, 'These Americans love to have whisky.' I thought, 'I could do something with a motor bike.' But I said, 'No, I'm sorry,' so I lost a lorry and a Harley Davidson within half an hour. Isn't that a bad deal?

However, Maurice is on Mingaladon in autumn 1945 and while there he sees nothing like the crates Stanley has described seeing in spring 1946. Neither does he see aircraft going into the ground.

Rather, he recounts the story of an unorthodox disposal of Spitfires at Mingaladon that was picked up second-hand from his mates in late 1945.

As related to Maurice, the aircraft are not actually buried, but rather dumped in a marshy area near the airfield,

'And I just thought, "Oh boy, how can they get rid of such a lovely aeroplane?" His anger at the apparent waste of it still makes him indignant more than seventy years later. Then he adds some colour to the story of a shade that only an aircraft engineer could,

'And the thing that the lads around me said, "If only we could have got into them and taken the clock." They felt that the Spitfire clock was perhaps the most important and vital part of that aeroplane.'

Maurice describes his anger that the Air Force brass would discard perfectly good Spitfires:

They'd saved my country, they were beautiful aircraft ... how dare they? But was it true? And oddly enough, whether it was true or not did not cross our minds. It had happened. And when you take the case we'd been in Burma some time, we'd met some strange situations, pushing an aeroplane into a swamp, well, that was just another bit of a day.

Towards the end of the interview, Maurice grows philosophical. He talks about the terrible suffering and destruction in Burma – and the enormous task of caring for the liberated prisoners of war. This was, after all, the setting for Pierre Boulle's novel *The Bridge on the River Kwai*.

'People had been killed,' Maurice says, his voice thick with emotion. 'Much more awful ... We were seeing these poor souls coming out of PoW camps. What the hell did a Spitfire got to do with that? Nothing.' In the end, he says, taking care of people was more important than war material. As he puts it, 'Everybody had suffered by then and getting rid of aeroplanes was seemingly the order of the day.'

Stanley and Maurice had never met each other during their time in Burma, so we decide to bring Stanley to Maurice's house for a visit. Maurice greets him at the door.

'How do you do,' Stanley says in a cheerful voice, as he steps inside.

'Hello. Pleased to meet you, sir,' Maurice replies.

'And you sir, thank you,' Stanley says.

The two veterans shake hands and then Maurice leads him into the kitchen.

'You were out there, were you, as well?' Maurice asks.

'For my sins,' Stanley replies with a laugh.

'Were you 267, by any chance?' Maurice asks.

'No, no, I was in the army.'

'Oh, what an unlucky guy. Oh, bless you. That was a tough call.'

Stanley relates how he ended up in Singapore, in preparation for Operation Zipper, before being transferred to a new unit just outside Mingaladon.

'We were in the transit camp for a day or so and then we got on the truck to go to our battalion, which is the other side of Mingaladon, and it was when we were going [there] that we went across the little road that used to go at the end of the runway at Mingaladon. And that's when I saw the Spitfires being put in,' Stanley says.

'Where?' Maurice asks, leaning forward in his chair, his interest piqued.

'At Mingaladon,' Stanley answers.

'What were they doing, what, how do you mean put in? Were they ...' Maurice asks.

'Well, they were putting the crates in the ground, they were in their crates,' Stanley says.

'And whereabouts was it that you saw them put in the ground?' Maurice asks.

'Beside the runway, 'cause they were going to extend the runway, weren't they?' Stanley says.

'Had they dug the runway, a big hole for them to go into or ...' Maurice asks, his voice trailing off.

'They were using, you remember the bomb craters, yeah, well, what they did, they joined up all the bomb craters,' Stanley explains.

'Were they, were they still in their boxes?'

'Still in their crates,' Stanley confirms.

'Do you remember how many crates, could you guess?'

'I thought I saw six,' Stanley says.

'Good lord. Did anybody else say anything to you about these?' Maurice asks.

'Not that day, but the next day, we had to come down ... Well, we went round there and I saw, I said to these airmen, "What's in those crates down there?" 'cause you could see from there straight down the road to the airfield, you know, and he said, "Would you believe? Spitfires." Fair enough. Spitfire. Strange thing to do,' Stanley says.

'Give me your hand, sir. What a story,' Maurice says, extending his. 'So just going on a bit, did you actually see them, the side of the runway filled over after you'd seen the Spitfires laid there?' Maurice asks.

'Yeah, when we came back to Mingaladon,' Stanley says, 'it was all flattened again and the extension of the runway was finished.'

'You never heard they were dug up again, did you?' Maurice asks.

'No, not until. Not until now. Or going to be, should I say. But nobody ever believed me,' Stanley adds with a laugh.

'I do,' Maurice says.

'Ah, I mean when, you know, years ago I used to tell people. "I know where there's some Spitfires,"' Stanley says. He continues, adopting another person's sceptical tone of voice, 'Oh, yeah, you see him again telling his story.'

Maurice leans his chair back against the wall.

'Jiminy Cricket!' he exclaims, swearing without swearing in the polite way of a bygone era.

'I, we've just finished talking about whether it was real or whether it wasn't,' Maurice says, glancing at the film crew, who are huddled around the table. We are listening intently.

'I've never doubted it,' Stanley says.

'Well, you don't have any need to doubt it. You saw it,' Maurice says.

'Stanley never saw any planes,' Mark interjects.

'No, not as such,' Stanley concedes.

'You just saw crates,' Mark says.

'I saw crates. I had to ask an airman,' Stanley says.

'If you saw a crate, they're never empty,' Maurice says.

'No,' Stanley says, agreeing.

'A sealed crate is never empty. Now whether there were Spitfires or not is perhaps the only question we're left with,' Maurice concludes.

The two veterans move on to other topics, reminiscing about some of the more amusing experiences from their days in Burma.

Maurice asks Stanley if he remembers the fire that destroyed several Dakotas lined up by the taxiway, when an airman had the clever idea to make his morning rounds with a Tilley lamp rather than an electric torch.

Stanley lights up at the memory.

For our benefit Maurice explains what happened next.

'He puts his Tilley lamp down to check and tighten the taps, which are right at the bottom of the tank under the fuselage of the wing, when whoosh!, off it goes. He was all right as it happened, but the aeroplanes, of course ...'

Stanley interjects, 'Well, 'til the CO got hold of him.'

They laugh about it.

Maurice concludes: 'Oh, he's probably still in a Burmese jail.'

19

Tracy Spaight
Kumudra Hotel
Nay Pyi Taw, Myanmar
16 October 2012
1730 hours

I'm standing in the elegantly appointed conference room of the Kumudra Hotel in Myanmar's new capital, Nay Pyi Taw, facing an audience of fifty or so government officials resplendent in their black ceremonial jackets, along with their wives in colourful longyi. The most senior ministers sit in the front row in ornate gold chairs. There are also a dozen camera crews and photographers from various outlets in the Myanmar and international news media.

The UK Deputy Ambassador to Myanmar, Matthew Hedges, is also present, as is the Third Secretary, Fergus Eckersley, who is becoming the embassy's point man for matters buried Spitfire. They have all come to witness the signing ceremony. It is a solemn occasion.

I almost didn't make it. I'd gotten word that the ceremony was going forward barely a week before, while I was in the UK with the research team and Room 608. David and I had to hurry back to Myanmar, travelling via Amsterdam to Bangkok. I got stuck in Bangkok, since I didn't have enough time to secure a new Myanmar visa in advance. Worse, the airline wouldn't accept my letter of invitation from STP and consequently I missed the flight to Yangon. Fortunately, I was able to sort out my visa situation and arrived in Nay Pyi Taw on the eve of the ceremony.

David and I are both standing on the dais, dressed in black suits and ties. We are about to put our signatures to a contract granting David and Shwe Taung

Por the right to recover and repatriate any planes we find at former RAF airfields in Myanmar.

This moment has been a long time coming – for me, four months; for David, a quarter of his lifetime.

A Myanmar official welcomes the assembled guests and speaks of his hope that the project would bring the peoples of the United Kingdom and Myanmar closer together, a sentiment echoed by Deputy Ambassador Hedges, who speaks warmly about the project as a joint heritage venture.

The speeches finished, David and Htoo Htoo Zaw sign four copies of the contract, which are then countersigned by the ministers. I sign as a witness.

The audience applauds; cameras flash and officials shake our hands.

Then we all file to the other end of the hall for dinner. It is a convivial evening and a gratifying conclusion to months of hard work. News of the signing quickly circles the globe, in print and online, with articles appearing in the UK in *The Guardian*, *The Mirror*, and *The Telegraph*.

I'm elated, since we beat out David's rivals and secured the contract to seal the deal. But I can't help but wonder, what have I just won?

Could David be right, despite the lack of archival evidence?

Is it possible that the burial (or disposal job) wasn't recorded, or the records were simply lost or destroyed, as the head of the Air Historical Branch suggested?

Or are we chasing a wartime legend?

```
Tracy Spaight
Trader Hotel
Yangon
7-10 November
```

Just two weeks after we secure the contract I am in Myanmar once again, this time at the insistence of Shwe Taung Por, to work out the logistics and costs of the upcoming dig in January.

The government has asked Swe Taung Por to provide a detailed plan for the work – and so over the past few weeks, I've put together a fifty-page project design for the Mingaladon excavation, developed in consultation with David Cundall, the archaeology and geophysics teams, STP's engineer, and our digger driver/excavation expert, Manny Machado.

Soon after I arrive in Yangon, Htoo Htoo tells me that the government wants us to start our excavations not at Mingaladon, as we'd planned, but at Myitkyina, 1,000 miles to the north in the Kachin state!

David had mentioned the airfield as a possible burial site, but I hadn't taken this seriously, since Myitkyina was an American airfield from its capture in 1944 through 1945. It was used as a resupply airfield for advancing troops. No Spitfire squadrons were based there, just American P-47s and DC-3s. Moreover, none of the witnesses David says he interviewed were stationed at Myitkyina.

I tell them both that Wargaming is not willing to fund an exploratory excavation at Myitkyina, given the lack of evidence and high probability of failure, but if STP and David wish to go out there in December to have a look, before our planned January dig, then they are of course free to do so on their time.

In the end, we agree that David will fly over in December and they will do a test dig at Myitkyina using STP's funds. If they find Spitfires, then I promise them we will excavate the site and film it for the documentary. Otherwise, we will proceed as planned with the excavation at Mingaladon.

The British ambassador learns that David and I are in town and so he graciously invites us to attend the Remembrance Day ceremony at Taukkyan War Cemetery.

Taukkyan Cemetery
Mingaladon Township
11 November 2012

As she perches invisibly on the central rotunda that is the focus of the largest war cemetery in Myanmar, the Hintha remembers the men in jungle green with their notebooks, tents and typewriters.

She recalls also the men with shovels and sweat rags wrapped around their faces as they dug beneath the wooden crosses on the battlefields, by the prisoner of war camps and along the roadsides from the Admin Box to Rangoon.

She remembers the wooden trestle tables spread with the scatters of dirt-encrusted pay books and wallets, and the bottles, buried surreptitiously, containing the pencilled names and dates of death of the men who would never return to homes and families in Britain, Australia, the Netherlands or the United States.

In some cases those same written witness statements, deposited clandestinely often at great personal risk, contain the names of the Japanese soldiers and officials who wore the black chevron of the dreaded Kenpeitai military police and who had mistreated and killed their prisoners contrary to the rules of war. Dying declarations, buried in the hope that one day justice will be done.

And she remembers the bones, red brown from the earth of Burma, sometimes still shrouded in indecently small scraps of faded khaki drill, or jungle green uniform.

The typewriters clatter seven days a week: making ten copies of every form: location of burial, regiment, name, rank and number; date of death, cause of death (if known) and the comments that gave an individual back their identity, the scars, the freckles, the hair colour, the tattoos that were a tribal identity or the painful reminder of a drunken night out. And that is just the bureaucracy of exhumation.

Afterwards come the transport and concentration of the field burials into the new cemeteries, large and small, which can be maintained in perpetuity, and with that action comes a fresh set of records. The cemetery name, plot and row for each burial are entered on the register, and the headstone in standard form and inscribed using the unique standard upper case font designed by Leslie MacDonald Gillis is put in place.

It is right that the sun blazes overhead because the number of lost lives recorded here is searing. Taukkyan contains 6,374 Commonwealth burials of personnel who died in the Second World War, 867 of these remain 'Known unto God' in that simple phrase, of devastating meaning, created for the then Imperial War Graves Commission by poet and author Rudyard Kipling while mourning his own son Jack, missing in action at the Battle of Loos in 1915.

Rationalising the casualties of that earlier conflict, fifty-two Commonwealth servicemen of the First World War were reburied in the cemetery when it proved impossible to maintain their graves, which were spread across now independent Burma at Henzada, the Meiktila Cantonment, Thayetmyo, Thamakan, the Mandalay Military Cemetery, and the Maymyo Cantonment.

However, these corners of Rupert Brooke's foreign field are outnumbered vastly by the almost 27,000 names of the missing from the Commonwealth land forces, which is carried on the faces of the massive rotunda of the Rangoon Memorial, which forms the architectural centrepiece of the cemetery, and where the dedicatory inscription is carried with equal prominence in English, Urdu, Hindu, Gurmukhi and Burmese.

Adjacent is the Taukkyan Cremation Memorial with a further 1,000 names, recording casualties, mostly from the Indian subcontinent, who were cremated according to their religious preferences.

A final forty-six servicemen, casualties of both world wars, who died and were buried elsewhere in Burma are commemorated on the Taukkyan Memorial, because it was not possible to maintain their graves.[*]

Today bright sunshine bathes the landscape in warm browns and golds under a clear blue sky as David Cundall and Tracy Spaight stroll towards the memorial and are greeted by members of the British Royal Legion, who pin paper poppies onto their lapels – the symbol of remembrance and respect born in the fields of Flanders during the First World War.

```
Tracy Spaight
Taukkyan Cemetery
Mingaladon Township
11 November 2012
```

As ambassadors and military attachés, elderly veterans of the Burma campaign, their families, Anglican clergy, and others wishing to pay their respects gather, we take our own seats among the rows of white chairs that have been set out on the close-cropped lawn.

British Ambassador Andrew Heyn takes the podium and looks out at the small band of aging veterans, their chests proudly bedecked with medals – including the Burma Star, with its red, dark blue, and orange ribbon, representing the British and Commonwealth armed forces, the Royal Navy and the sun.

The medal is awarded to any member of the services who served on operations in the Burma campaign for one or more days between 11 December 1941 and 2 September 1945.

Ambassador Heyn speaks of comradeship and courage, as well as the sadness and brutal realities of war. He is followed by the Reverend Deacon David Judson Hogarth, who recites the Ode of Remembrance, from Laurence Binyon's poem, 'For the Fallen'.

Finally, one of the veterans recites the moving Kohima Epitaph. The words are attributed to the British Classicist John Maxwell Edmonds (1875–1958), who created a number of epitaphs for the war dead in 1916, and they were adopted for use in Burma at the suggestion of another classical scholar, Major John Etty-Leal, the GSO II (Intelligence Officer) of 2nd Division during the Burma campaign.

[*] Figures from the Commonwealth War Graves Commission, www.cwgc.org/find-a-cemetery/cemetery/92002/taukkyan-war-cemetery

When you go home
Tell them of us and say
For your tomorrow
We gave our today

That resonant request, with its deliberate echo of the epitaph to the 300 Spartans of Thermopylae written by Simonides of Ceos (556–468 BC), hangs in the air, as two members of the Tatmadaw play the haunting bugle cadences of the Last Post, followed by two minutes of almost physical silence.

The silence is sliced through by the Reveille, which symbolises the rising sun, hope, and renewal of a new day.

We watch as the ambassadors from twenty nations lay wreaths in the rotunda of the memorial. It is a poignant reminder of what happened here seventy years ago.

After the ceremony, I stroll alone along the cool green lawn, reading the names on the grave markers. So many young lives cut short. I choke up and sit by myself for a while, before heading back to the reception tent, where veterans and their families are drinking tea and chatting amiably with each other and various dignitaries. I talk with some of the veterans, thanking them for their service – including a member of the Burma Rifles, who is wearing his army uniform and still stands ram-rod straight even in his nineties.

As the crowd begins to disperse, I chance to meet another veteran, Major Roger Browning, who, I discover, commanded 652 Mechanical Equipment Company at Mingaladon Airfield in the autumn and winter of 1945. 652 MEC was an Indian Army engineering unit that was involved in building the runway extension that crossed the Old Prome Road. This is a remarkable stroke of luck because, if anyone would know about an operation to bury aeroplanes at the end of that same runway at that time, surely it would be Major Browning!

I motion for David to come join us. David cuts to the chase and asks him if he remembers seeing any crated Spitfires buried at Mingaladon at the end of the war.

Roger tells us that he has no recollection of any such operation, but that he had read about David's quest in the newspaper. He adds that since he commanded engineers involved directly in building the runway extension, he would surely have known about it.

At that comment David, who had been listening intently to Major Browning's account, suddenly loses interest in the conversation. After a moment he excuses himself and wanders off.

I'm shocked by his lack of interest in Major Browning's story, especially given how much weight he gives to the reported testimony of other veterans who were stationed at Mingaladon at this time. David seems to have no interest in evidence that fails to fit his secret burial theory.

Since Andy's desktop study, I've grown increasingly doubtful of David's version of events, but this encounter is the final nail in the coffin of his secret burial in 1945 thesis.

There's no way such an operation could have happened in autumn 1945 without Major Browning being aware of it. If they weren't deliberately buried, I ask him, could the planes have been dumped as part of the post-war clean-up?

He confirms that there was an operation to break up and recycle non-operational aircraft on the airfield, but he doesn't recall if any material was dumped and buried in situ. I take down his contact details so Andy and I can follow up with him when he returns to the UK and also hunt down his unit's war diaries if they still exist.

20

Andy Brockman
Shooters Hill, London
November 2012

Discussing the finer details of a possible public relations strategy for the Burma Project while sitting on my daughter's bed is an odd way to be making the acquaintance of Wargaming's head of PR for the project, Frazer Nash. But I need to take the call somewhere quiet and the rest of the house is occupied with a family enjoying its evening, and in any case I am discovering rapidly that nothing about this project is in any way ordinary.

Frazer tells me he has a problem. He says he needs to leave open the possibility that we might find buried, crated Spitfires, as David has been predicting in the media, and that I need to endorse that possibility.

I tell him that I cannot do that because all the evidence suggests that David's story of buried Spitfires at Mingaladon is almost certainly a myth and I recommend Wargaming position the company in a way that will preserve its credibility and give the project a soft landing in the likely event that no crated Spitfires are uncovered.

We talk around the issue, testing various wording until at some point we agree the public position we will take is that the expedition is setting out not to dig up Spitfires (though we would be equipped to do so if any are found) but to try to get to the bottom of a seventy-year-old mystery. With that understanding in place, the prefect framing device presents itself.

In an echo of the popular television series, the Burma Spitfire project will be presented as CSI Yangon with the Wargaming research team undertaking a very public due diligence that neither David Cameron's office nor the world's media seems to have seen fit to undertake thus far.

I am pleased that we seem to have resolved the situation without compromising our ethical code as archaeologists by endorsing what seems, at best, a misrepresentation of very thin evidence. While Frazer seems pleased since Wargaming will be covered whether the expedition turns up crated Spitfires, discarded airframes or nothing at all.

However, I am left with the disorientating thought that I have stepped through the fourth wall and am now involved in a real world episode of Armando Iannucci's *The Thick of It*.

By the end of the project my colleagues on the archaeology team will have nicknamed Frazer 'Malcolm' after the fictional Scottish spin doctor Malcolm Tucker, the 'Gorbals Goebbels', the anti-hero of Iannucci's vicious, bitingly funny political satire. As played by Peter Capaldi, the character is based allegedly on Tony Blair's spin doctor, the formidable and, like Malcolm Tucker, allegedly formidably foul-mouthed, Alistair Campbell.

I discover later that Frazer is not unflattered by the comparison.

Andy Brockman
The Union Jack Club
Waterloo
London
November 2012

Tucked away down a narrow side street opposite Waterloo East station on London's South Bank, from the outside the Union Jack Club (or UJC to its members) looks like a rather unprepossessing 1960s medium-rise block. However, inside, with its bars, restaurant and range of rooms it is a home away from home for serving and retired members of the British military who want reasonably priced food and a reasonably priced bed for the night close to the centre of town, and with it something of the reassuring ambience of an officers' mess, complete with paintings of military derring-do.

Rod Scott is a member, and now I have been allowed to bring him on board as a member of the research team we meet at the UJC to test David's evidence against that which we have unearthed from our visits to the National Archives at Kew and from our other sources.

Mostly we ensconce ourselves on the comfortable armchairs in the library with a laptop and coffee. Occasionally a curious member will wander past and ask what we are doing. Rod, who has worked on a number of clandestine projects for Her Majesty during his Army service, always manages to say something and nothing to put them off the scent.

Essentially we are trying to place David's theory about the burial of the aircraft in the context of what was actually going on in Rangoon and at RAF Mingaladon during the period David claims the Spitfires were buried.

To that end I have produced a set of images using tools in Google Earth to overlay air photographs from the 1940s on the modern Yangon International Airport.

These are not as accurate as the kind of geographic information system (GIS) used by photoanalysts in the intelligence community, or in commercial planning archaeology, but that does not matter for our purposes because we will be digging on locations that David has chosen anyway.

What they do offer is a snapshot of the kind of archaeology we can expect in the area David has identified for the excavation; archaeology that ranges from blast pens that protected parked aircraft in the dispersal area to the bomb craters left by the Japanese and Allied air forces that attempted to put the airfield out of action, and orientating everything is the arc of the old Prome No.1 Road.

However, it is the content of the RAF operations record books that is providing the most valuable evidence, not just because what we are discovering is fascinating in terms of providing historical colour, but disturbingly their content confirms we were right to question whether American personnel were ever present on Mingaladon in the autumn of 1945 into 1946 and whether the RAF was capable of burying aircraft and keeping such an operation secret. Indeed, we are seeing evidence in the documents that the service culture of the time meant that it was most likely that they could not.

One narrative in particular catches our eye and suggests that the RAF was not concerned about placing even sensitive and potentially embarrassing material about the capability and morale of its squadrons in the operations record books.

On 29 January 1946, the men of 194 (Transport) Squadron based at RAF Mingaladon came out on strike complaining about a newly instituted compulsory early morning work parade, poor food, poor living conditions, and the slow rate of demobilisation of RAF personnel, especially when compared with their comrades in the Army and Navy.

The strike was one of a number of such incidents that took place across the Middle East, India, Ceylon and Far East in early 1946. What precipitated the strike, its course and how it was dealt with by the RAF chain of command is the subject of a five-page narrative in the operations record book of Air Headquarters (AHQ) Burma. The narrative even admits that an investigation failed to identify the so called 'agitators' behind the strike who, it was believed, had also been involved in a 'Forces Parliament' held in the Rangoon YMCA.

AHQ Burma's narrative also includes accounts of the most sensitive political intelligence as it impacted on the operations of the Royal Air Force, including threats to the security of RAF material and personnel and uncomplimentary comments comparing the capabilities of ethnic Burmese workers versus their ethnic Indian counterparts.

However, nowhere in that narrative is there any mention of the presence of CBs, Seabees or any discussion of the burial of Spitfires.

In fact, the impression given by the response of 194 Transport Squadron to the order to undertake extra work is that, had the RAF erks been ordered to undertake the massively difficult and complex job of burying Spitfires for later retrieval, they would have downed tools immediately, held a strike meeting and voted with their feet not to do anything so stupid.

However, for Rod Scott the soldier, and a man used to filling in military paperwork and copying it up the chain of command, the stand-out event that throws all the assumptions David has brought to his version of the story into serious question is the simple story of Flying Officer Hughes of No. 41 Embarkation Unit and his missing sidearm.

On 21 June 1946, No. 41 EU's Form 540 operations record book records that the unfortunate junior officer was subjected to a formal investigation into the circumstances surrounding the loss of his service pistol.

To Rod the lesson is simple. If the loss of a single pistol could result in a formal investigation and an entry in the unit's official record, what would the chain of command do to you if you were not able to produce either the items themselves, or the orders and paperwork relating to the disposal, to account for even one, let alone thirty-six or more, brand new Spitfires, property of His Majesty the King?

Tracy Spaight
Imperial War Museum
London
30 November 2012

Originally, and ironically given its modern role, the Imperial War Museum was built as a psychiatric hospital in the nineteenth century.

Then the latest iteration of the famous Bethlehem Asylum, better known as Bedlam; now, instead of hosting afternoon outings for curious and wealthy voyeurs, the former wards tell the story of the conflicts of the twentieth and twenty-first centuries. Visitors to the imposing edifice of white stone, with its classical portico and a soaring copper-clad dome, are greeted not by wardens but by a pair of enormous 15in naval guns taken from the battleship HMS *Ramillies* and shore bombardment monitor HMS *Roberts*.

The unmistakable art deco shape of Spitfire Mark 1a R6915, which flew in the Battle of Britain with 608 Squadron, hangs from the ceiling of the atrium. It is about as fitting a backdrop as you could wish for the break-out interviews which follow our press conference.

Today, though, a different kind of battle will begin to unfold; a battle in search of a truth that promises to pit David Cundall's theory of buried Spitfires against what we expect to be a sceptical British press.

Leading reporters such as the BBC's Fergal Keane will be in the audience and David will be in the line of fire. Our task is complicated by David's past media statements, in which he has insisted more than once that he has actually *found* the planes themselves.

On one occasion, he has even gone so far as to claim that his team has lowered a camera down a borehole and identified the engine of one of the planes – but for some unaccountable reason has neglected to then take photos!*

We need to frame the expedition as an attempt to get to the bottom of a wartime legend rather than as a recovery operation – for the very simple and obvious reason that we don't know if the planes are actually there!

That means, most importantly, getting David to adopt a more qualified stance about what, exactly, we will find at Mingaladon airfield, and to back away from his speculative musings about the planes being buried as payment for the Karen, on the orders of Lord Louis Mountbatten – a theory that the Head of the RAF Historical Branch had already punctured with that zinger of a one-liner about the Karen having more use for the crate it came in than the Spitfire inside.

If there are any planes buried at Mingaladon, then it is far more likely that they ended up there as part of a post-war clean-up operation to prepare the airfield for civilian use. The airfield had, after all, been heavily bombed during the war and was cluttered with dozens of non-operational and discarded aircraft.

---

* www.telegraph.co.uk/news/worldnews/asia/burmamyanmar/9204921/British-farmers-quest-to-find-lost-Spitfires-in-Burma.html

As Andy discovered, repair and salvage units at Mingaladon were busy from May to November 1945 repairing or scrapping aircraft. In this context, it would not be impossible for parts of shot-up or discarded aircraft (even Spitfires) to have been bulldozed into pits.

Looked at objectively, even David's own 'dossier' leans towards this view and it's also consistent with the testimony of veterans Stanley Coombe, who thought it was a case of 'getting rid' of surplus equipment, and Maurice Short, who recalled being told of planes 'being pushed into a swamp' at the airfield.

The signing ceremony at Nay Pyi Taw presented me – and the Wargaming team – with a conundrum. Should we press on with the project, given the growing doubts about David's version of the story? Or should we withdraw from the project because we might very well be chasing a wartime legend?

I laid out the evidence for my colleagues. On the one hand, we had compelling and believable testimony from veterans Stanley and Maurice, who were stationed at Mingaladon during the war. They both recalled hearing or seeing things while stationed in the Far East that are compatible with the notion of Spitfires being buried or dumped.

Next, the head of the Air Historical Branch at the RAF, despite his scepticism about the Karen theory, nevertheless believed that it was not outside the realm of possibility that Spitfires could have been disposed of at Mingaladon.

And finally, we had recently interviewed Dr Adam Booth, who had accompanied David on his 2004 expedition to Myanmar and who reported hearing 'the crunch of wood' when they began digging at the spot David identified as the burial location.

On the other hand, Andy Brockman's desktop study, which I read while in transit to Myanmar for the signing ceremony, shows pretty clearly that David's story could not be true in the way he described it.

A closely related problem is whether to announce our sponsorship before the dig in order to benefit from the intense media interest in the story or to keep quiet until we actually find something. Initially, we decided to keep our participation secret. However, after watching the flood of global media coverage following the signing ceremony, we decide to announce our sponsorship before the dig, since if we don't – and nothing is found in January – then we wouldn't derive any media benefit.

To make this strategy work, we decide to adopt Andy's 'CSI Yangon' framing. The expedition will be an attempt to solve the mystery of what exactly happened at Mingaladon in 1945-46, through historical research and field archaeology. Even if the planes aren't there, we will still have a fascinating story playing out in the full glare of the media spotlight about the nature of memory and the enduring power of myth in the modern world.

I've come to trust Andy's judgement. He is a serious scholar and born researcher who sticks to the archival record, in addition helping us to assemble the right team of experts to make sure that the fieldwork in Mingaladon will be done to the highest professional standards.

We recognise too that the biggest risk factor is David Cundall himself. He has on numerous occasions appeared to conflate fact and speculation in ways that could damage the project, and so to prepare David, we hire Barbara Govan and Paul Bader from Screenhouse Media Training. The day before the press conference they join us in our hotel conference room in Shoreditch to prepare David for media questioning.

Also joining us are Andy Brockman and members of the Wargaming PR team.

21

Andy Brockman
Media Training Day
Shoreditch, East London
29 November 2012

It is the day before the scheduled press conference at the Imperial War Museum and this is my first meeting with David Cundall. I am nervous as to how he will react to an avowed sceptic suddenly being part of the team. We exchange greetings, shaking hands.

I see a tall, craggy man who seems somehow out of place in the glass-walled blandness of the conference room of a hipster boutique hotel, more usually geared to presenting spreadsheets and PowerPoint slides than exploring the mysteries of the Second World War.

I also remind myself that he is from Lincolnshire and Lincolnshire has always been a liminal place; a place that keeps its counsel and guards its secrets. A land where in winter the iron-grey fog shrouding the Lincolnshire flatlands meets the iron-grey North Sea, which in turn meets the iron-grey sky at the horizon.

Once part of the Danelaw, ruled by Norse Kings in York rather than the English Kings of Wessex, during the English Civil War the county was one of the principal recruiting grounds for Oliver Cromwell's New Model Army and meeting him it is easy to imagine David wearing the buff coat and lobsterpot helmet of a New Model cavalry trooper or leaning against the side rudder of a Norse drakkar, his weather-beaten features set against the spindrift as he steers for a safe harbour on the coast of the North Sea.

Wary, we circle each other metaphorically, making small talk.

David tells me that in the dry, hot summer of 1976 when archaeological crop marks began to appear all over England creating a life-size map of past land use he flew sorties as part of a pioneering photographic survey of his native county that is still discussed as a landmark project in archaeological circles. I am slightly reassured by this promising coming together of interests.

'David, three sentences,' Paul says, opening the training session. 'How did the story begin?'

'It came from a very good source,' David says. 'Jim Pearce. He was talking to eyewitnesses in America.'

'Why were they in America?' Barbara asks simply, probing the story.

David replies confidently.

'The American Seabees actually helped to bury them. They dug the hole.'

I close my eyes and shake my head in what I feel is quiet exasperation. Tracy later tells me that I looked set to explode.

'Seabees?' Barbara, asks, puzzled. David clarifies.

'Construction Battalion.'

'Can I just interject here?' I ask.

I am trying to be diplomatic, but I am also keen to stop David from plunging downhill, out of control, with no brakes on his imagination.

'There will be military historians and experts watching this who will point out very quickly that the Seabees were not active in Burma.'

This crunch point is the time to introduce the framing device I've discussed with Tracy, Frazer, and the film crew.

'I'd like to suggest that we approach the expedition as a police procedural.'

From the reactions around the table the idea is attractive. It's an analogy that the public can easily understand. Police procedural drama is popular all over the world, from the chilly Scandi noir tradition of *Martin Beck* and *Wallander* to the various glossy incarnations of CSI in the United States. However, crucially for the credibility of the Burma Spitfires project, it shifts focus away from David's assertions and instead focusses on our narrative and our systematic gathering, sifting and interpretation of the available evidence.

It's an analogy we will offer to the world's media at tomorrow's press conference.

Meanwhile, David rehearses his story and practices responding to hypothetical questions posed by the media trainers. He agrees to stick to the evidence for buried planes and not to speculate on why they might have been buried (if indeed any were) and by whom.

David further agrees not to state that he has found the planes but rather say he has identified a possible location for the burial, based on eyewitness reports. If David stays on message, the expedition will be covered, whatever we find in Burma.

22

Tracy Spaight
The Imperial War Museum
30 November 2012

Arriving at the Imperial War Museum, I spot Frazer Nash and, in our own version of the post-war cinema classic *Brief Encounter*, we meet under the Spitfire, which hangs from the ceiling like a life-size Airfix kit in a 1960s schoolboy's bedroom.

It's always easy to find Frazer. A mutual friend once described him as 'a shaken can of soda', as he is always bursting with energy. He has done PR for just about every major title in the video game universe since *Half-Life* and *Grand Theft Auto*, but today's event is terra nova for both of us and as if to mark the occasion he is wearing a sport coat over his black *World of Tanks* T-shirt.

'Are we ready for this?' I ask, shaking his hand in greeting.

'Yes. In any case, we'll soon find out,' he says with a laugh.

Complicating Frazer's task is the fact that we're not completely in control of the messaging, as we're co-hosting the press conference with the University of Leeds.

Isabel Hunt, the Director of Communications at the university, will be chairing the event and she insists we open with the geophysics, to highlight the university's contribution.

In Andy's view, this is backwards. He argues we should open instead with the CSI framing to make sure the press understands that this is an investigation to get to the bottom of a wartime legend – and only secondarily a recovery operation, if indeed there is anything to recover.

The events of the morning so far reinforce the need for this kind of framing. As we prepare for the platform event we are annoyed to discover that, without telling us, Leeds has already set up an interview with David on BBC Radio 4's agenda-setting Today news magazine programme.

The interview, carried out down the line to the studio from the BBC's radio car parked in front of the Imperial War Museum, is an unmoderated account of thirty-six buried Spitfires, in total opposition to the carefully nuanced messaging we have been trying to set up.

It's clear to all of us that we can't afford another incident like this where David is let loose without someone to provide covering fire for the expedition and – in mine and Andy's view – to protect David from himself.

Andy takes me aside to explain the reason he's so concerned about this and why, uncharacteristically, he is wearing a suit this morning. In the afternoon, he will attend a parliamentary debate at the House of Lords that will discuss the growing scandal of the gifting of the wreck of the 100-gun ship of the line, HMS *Victory*, sunk in October 1744 with the loss of more than 1,000 Royal Navy personnel, to a new charity that is widely regarded as a front operation for a Florida-based treasure hunting company, Odyssey Marine Exploration.

Andy doesn't want to see the UK Government become entangled in another case of the alleged commercial exploitation of an archaeological site. He is also concerned that the team must be seen to work within the terms and spirit of the British Protection of Military Remains Act, which came about because of the unethical and sometime downright dangerous practices of some self-styled aviation archaeologists in the 1970s and early '80s, particularly with regard to their handling of unexploded ordnance and human remains.

I have the same concerns for Wargaming. I too want to make sure our participation is in line with best archaeological practice.

Journalists begin to arrive and take their seats in the hall as the television crews set up cameras in the back row. Among the electronic media are BBC news, ITN, ZDF Television and CNN. Print is also well represented by reporters from Der Spiegel, Reuters, AFP, *The Guardian*, *Telegraph, Sunday Times, Financial Times,* and the *New York Times*, alongside many others.

We take our seats behind the table on the stage. Dr Booth, Dr Clark, and Isabel Clark (no relation) stage left, David Cundall and Victor Kislyi (CEO of Wargaming) in the centre, Andy Brockman and I stage right.

Facing us are more than fifty journalists and seven camera crews, including the BBC. One of the cameramen asks for a mic check, so I recite some lines of Tennyson's 'Lady of Shallot' from memory, which gets a laugh.

I'm feeling nervous, particularly in light of David's unscripted, off-the-cuff interview with Radio 4. I'm worried he might go off the rails once again. I read over my notes and wait.

We open with a short film about the recent signing ceremony in Nay Pyi Taw, which shows the British deputy ambassador to Myanmar, various Myanmar ministers, and David shaking hands and smiling for the cameras. Next each of us make brief introductory statements about our role in the project.

By prior arrangement, Adam and Roger go first. Adam introduces a PowerPoint slide showing a resistivity scan of Mingaladon airfield, which he made in 2004. Explaining that areas of high resistivity are suggestive of buried metal 'which could be associated with buried Spitfires', he points with a laser pointer to two large discrete red features, one of which looks like a letter 'L' and the other resembling a 'T'.

'Now, it's important to remember that on their own these data don't confirm the presence of Spitfires,' Adam cautions. 'What they are suggestive of is the presence of buried metal. The depth makes it difficult to constrain but it's around 10m, which is consistent with the reports of the burials.'

He changes slides, and a satellite image of the site, with the scanned area superimposed near the modern runway, appears.

'To put the scanned area back into the bigger picture of the site, you can see the two red blobs there, which are the areas that we'll be targeting for future investigation.'

Cameras flash and reporters scribble in their notebooks.

David speaks next, recounting his efforts to track down the missing Spitfires.

I started the project in 1996 when a friend of mine told me the story about the buried aeroplanes. It took me two years to research the story and also get a visa from the Myanmar government, which they granted to me in 1998. And I've been a total of sixteen times. Most of those visits have been to conduct surveys with either Leeds University or with commercial companies. The site we've identified is based on eight eyewitnesses telling us exactly the same story of what they saw, how many crates, how deep they were buried.

David thanks Leeds University and Wargaming for their support and leans back in his chair.

Wargaming's CEO Victor Kislyi slides the microphone closer and introduces himself. He explains that, while it may strike some people as odd for a video game company to get involved with an archaeological dig, history is at the core of what Wargaming does.

'The core value of all of our games is historical accuracy,' he says. 'That's what our customers really value and are looking for. So it's natural that we as a company extend this passion for history from the virtual to the real world.' He explains that whether we find aeroplanes or not, we are interested in the story.

He also expresses the hope that we can make a contribution to understanding the air campaign in Burma during the Second World War. I then say a few words about Wargaming's work with museums and non-profits, along with our support for historic preservation and educational outreach.

Finally, Andy Brockman addresses the room.

He tries to pitch the project in a way that maintains the thrill of the chase but includes enough clues and subtext to suggest there might be more, or rather more importantly, less, to the story of buried Spitfires than the media expects:

> I would like you please to consider this a police procedural. We've got a crime scene. We've got a missing person. We have got a lot of evidence. And we may even have one or two suspects. But at the moment we're deep in a very complex and difficult investigation. It's one of the most fascinating and complex projects I've ever been involved in.
>
> What we're actually interested in is converting the speculation, which I'm sure you're all aware that has been rife from the Internet and in the media, since the story broke really big in the spring of this year. Turning all of that speculation and the rumour into facts on the ground, which is what archaeology does. We take the evidence from our colleagues from Leeds, the documentary evidence, the witnesses that David quotes and so on, turning that into an evidence-based case.

That is the crucial point. It is all going to be about evidence and he explains that, like an investigating officer, we are embarking on this investigation with no assumptions.

'When the expedition ends,' Andy concludes, 'we'll have a cracking story to tell you. What that story is at the moment I don't know. You wouldn't ask the lead officer on a murder investigation who the murderer was on day one.'

To establish the seriousness with which Wargaming is taking the history and archaeology, Andy then introduces the project's archaeological team. Apologising that he cannot be here this morning, Andy explains Martin Brown of the international consultancy WYG and the Plug Street Project, formerly of the Defence Infrastructure Organisation Historic Environment Team, will run the site at Yangon International Airport and will be in charge of the digging and recording operation. Rod Scott, who will assist Martin and oversee our safety on site, is seated in the front row. The three men first met on Channel 4's archaeological programme *Time Team* in 2007 and when I offered Andy the job of lead archaeologist, he insisted we bring Martin and Rod onboard, as their expertise would be invaluable and he could not conceive of taking on this brief without them.

Andy concludes by thanking David for providing such a fascinating story to work with.

Isabel opens the floor to questions from the audience. Several hands shoot up.

Jonathan Beale of the BBC takes the roving mic, 'You say there's no physical evidence yet that you've seen that the Spitfires are there. I just wonder, is it possible that this is a wild goose chase? I thought you had put boreholes down and you had seen crates as well. Have you actually seen a Spitfire or any evidence of a Spitfire?'

I glance at David, wondering how he will answer.

'Yes, we did a borehole,' David says. 'We put a camera down. We didn't see an awful lot. We went into a crate. It was very … there was no real proper light there. The person who actually did it didn't really know what he was looking at but it was an object that looked like an aeroplane. I wasn't there at the time.'

Isabel asks me to comment, but I defer to Andy:

It's a very good question. It's a question that everybody is going to be asking very legitimately. I think the response to that is yes it could be [just a wild goose chase]. On the other hand, it could be one of the most fascinating discoveries in aviation archaeology. As I said, we don't know. The whole point about this exercise is to use the techniques of science and research and archaeology and historical document analysis to find out the truth behind this story. Where it's come from.

Prompted by Isabel, Roger weighs in from the perspective of the geophysics:

The geophysical results that you saw there on the screen are fairly striking to us as geophysicists. They certainly don't appear to be a geologically natural phenomenon. The electrical conductivities are too high. There's certainly something metallic there. So it's something that is consistent with but not necessarily conclusive proof of there being Spitfires there, sure. They could be reels of barbed wire or some old jeeps or something like that. But certainly we hope they're Spitfires. And as Andy's eloquently said, it's a story that needs investigating.

Once more, hands shoot up. The moderator chooses a reporter from the middle row.

'Peter Schwartzstein, I'm from Reuters. Has the thaw in the relationship with the Burmese government facilitated the digging process?' Isabel passes the question to me:

Most certainly. With the recent lifting of the sanctions that happened earlier this spring, both from the EU, the UK and more recently the United States, I think it's opened the door for this sort of joint heritage collaborative project. When David Cameron visited back in April, this was one of the things that he discussed with the Myanmar president. And I think they both saw this as a good way to bring the countries closer together.

William Green from MSN asks, 'Could you just give perhaps a little bit more detail about how these aircraft ended up there? And if you find them, what are you going to do with them? Are they going to fly over London?'

'How did the aircraft get there?' Andy asks rhetorically after Isabel throws the question to him:

Aircraft arrived in the China–India–Burma Theatre in a number of ways. They were flown in. They were crated in on ships. At the moment, we have no conclusive evidence of how the Spitfires that David is looking for arrived in Burma if they ever arrived at all.

As I said, this is an ongoing investigation where there is a lot of different evidence. And what we are here to do is to resolve that, hopefully to every-one's satisfaction. And as I said, at the end of it we'll have a story to tell you. What that story is and how it will involve aeroplanes arriving in Burma, moving around Burma, moving out of Burma I don't know.

Kate Ferguson from the National News Agency asks David to explain how he first became involved in the project. Isabel asks if David heard the ques-

tion; David is a bit hard of hearing on account of a hunting accident where a
friend discharged a shotgun next to his ear.

David nods that he understood.

A good friend of mine Jim Pearce, who recovers Second World War aeroplanes mainly out of Russia, told me the story and this was in 1996. I found
a total of eight eyewitnesses telling me the story, although some of them
got north/south mixed up but we sorted that out. They all pointed to the
same spot. They all said it was deep. It was around 8 to 10m deep. They
talked about [the burial] in a straight line forming a letter 'L' shape and
then later forming a letter 'T' shape, which we have on the survey. And
that's what we got. We also did ground-penetrating radar. And we do have
aeroplane shapes in this area. So I've got to the end of my survey. I can't
really do any more. We did do a borehole but we really need to dig and see
what's down there.*

The microphone reaches Sebastian DeLum from CNN, who asks, 'David,
were you the only person looking for these Spitfires? Or have there been
competing excavations as well? And one other question, could you confirm,
if you do manage to find them, who exactly will be able to keep them? How
much could they be worth? And how long will it take for them to get to their
final resting place?'

David plunges in:

There are three groups that have been allowed to look for these aeroplanes.
I was the first one allowed in in 1998. And in the year 2000 they gave the
contract to the Israeli group, who have surveyed the area. They didn't find
anything. No other group have found anything. So I think I'm the only
one. Regarding value, I don't know. We have to look at them. I haven't
done it for money. This is an exercise to preserve aeroplanes. And hopefully they will be restored and brought back to the UK and hopefully flying
at air shows.

I can sense Andy's growing discomfort over the discussion of commercial
value. He doesn't want the archaeological world to see the research team's

---

*   Direct quote from David, Room 608 footage. He conflates the red road survey by
      Malcom Weale ('aeroplane shapes') with Adam Booth's survey.

involvement in this expedition as somehow condoning and supporting a treasure hunt.

Martin is a long-standing and committed member of the UK-based Institute for Archaeologists (now the Chartered Institute for Archaeologists), the professional body set up to safeguard ethical and professional standards in archaeology. The organisation's code of conduct is very clear that members should not facilitate the excavation of item for sale, where the sale of the items may lead to the dispersal of the archive of finds or a denial of access to the public.

David pauses to catch his breath, and Andy takes the opportunity to interject.

'Can I make a point on behalf of the research team as well?' The silence gives him consent to continue, 'None of us have any influence or interest in any commercial activity around this story. We're treating it as a standard commercial archaeological excavation as will take place in the UK, which means we're doing it for a day rate. No percentages. No deals. Which hopefully means that we are entirely objective and independent.'

Andy doesn't add that the reason he and Martin are comfortable participating, despite David's intention to sell recovered planes, is that the issue will not arise because Andy's desktop study has led them both to believe that if we do find parts of any aircraft they will be worn out, shot up or junked pieces of airframe bulldozed into pits, not pristine Spitfires carefully buried in crates.

Victor also chimes in, to reiterate that Wargaming is motivated primarily by an interest in history and storytelling.

Isabel gives the floor back to David, who finishes explaining that his share is 30 per cent and that he plans to bring his share of the planes back to the UK for restoration. He does not explain how much this will cost or who will fund it, and perhaps fortunately nobody pitches that question.

Philip Whiteman, the editor of *Pilot* magazine, asks, 'Is this a story that originated from service personnel who saw these aircraft being destroyed or has the story come from local witnesses?'

'It was first told to me via some American service personnel who actually dug the hole,' David replies, seemingly forgetting his media training. He adds:

We've got UK eyewitnesses and also local Myanmar people who actually helped to bring the teak shuttering and teak beams. And on one of my trips to Myanmar I met the gentleman who was 15 at the time and he took me to the spot. He actually pointed to the spot and he said there were many,

many big boxes. And he and his father transported the teak timber to help to put the shuttering around the boxes.

We field a few more questions about how we will conduct the excavation, what condition the planes will be in if any are found, and how many planes we expect to find, then Isabel calls the press conference to a close and we adjourn to the mezzanine level for press photographs and one-to-one interviews.

Here David gives several interviews on camera, with the Battle of Britain Spitfire hanging from the ceiling behind him.

'I knew the aeroplanes were there,' Andy and I hear David say, as he speaks to a television reporter. 'I tracked down eight eyewitnesses who all reported seeing the same thing.' In the space of the next thirty minutes, David will claim – emphatically – on camera, that there are 'twelve crated Spitfires buried at the end of the runway', that he has 'radar images showing the shapes of thirty-six aeroplanes', that 'we may have found sixty', and finally, presumably in reference to the number of Spitfires apparently struck off charge at the end of the war in India, 'there are 124 Mark XIV Spitfires'.

All of the careful qualifications by the geophysicists and the CSI framing put in place by Wargaming and our archaeology team is going for nothing as the bulk of the media is gripped by Spitfire fever. It is a contagion that manifests itself with often breathless wall-to-wall coverage and speculative computer-generated graphics, embracing David's narrative and his dream of squadrons of new Spitfires springing from the earth of Mingaladon to grace the skies over London.

23

The Spitfires of Rangoon

A Novel of the Secret War in Burma

by Major William Wills DSO OBE

(a) Rumours must have specific objectives.
(b) Rumours must be easy to believe and difficult to dismiss.
(c) Rumours must be concrete and precise, never abstract or vague.

SOE Training Lecture Course C Propaganda, C6-C. Rumour

```
Singapore Cricket Club
Connaught Drive
Padang
October 1945
```

Two months on from the nuclear immolation of Hiroshima and Nagasaki by the B-29 Superfortress bombers of the 509th Composite Group and the end of the Second World War in Asia, the island state of Singapore, at the southern tip of the Malay peninsula, remained a giant military encampment. An encampment imposed on the island's long-suffering and sometimes angry civilian population of ethnic Malays and Chinese.

Rather, it was a series of camps, presided over by the British Military Administration (BMA) of Malaya, and the task that the BMA faced was Herculean in its demands.

For a start, after 1,297 days of occupation as part of Japan's Greater South-East Asia Co-Prosperity Sphere, Singapore City, the Emperor Hirohito's Syonan-to, the Star of the South, was no longer recognisable to the returning British authorities as Churchills 'Gibraltar of the East'.

To begin with the island's infrastructure had almost ceased to operate, with electricity and water in desperately short supply, the telephone system barely functioning and the docks, which were Singapore's lifeline and reason to be, severely damaged.

Meanwhile, more or less every open space in the once stylish city was either a dump of abandoned war material or had been put to use growing vegetables and rows of tapioca. The civilian population in particular had come to despise that plant, which the occupying Japanese authorities insisted could replace rice as the staple food of Singaporeans.

Worse to the local political and military intelligence officers and to the civil servants at the Colonial Office back in London, the Island of Singapore now represented a sensitive and potentially volatile heap of displaced humanity which had been deposited in a humid tropical petri dish, nurturing a viral brew of alternative political and economic cultures, most of them perceived as antithetical to the interests of the British Empire.

At the centre of the British attempt to bring some semblance of order to this chaos on Singapore Island and over the causeway in the post-conflict Malay peninsula itself, were eighty-eight officers of Force 136 of the Special Operations Executive and their Gurkha security force.

With the end of formal hostilities, Force 136 had turned its hand from attempting to create mayhem behind the Japanese lines to preventing the personnel of their wartime allies in the Malayan People's Anti-Japanese Army (MPAJA) and its leadership cadre of well-trained and indoctrinated members of the Malayan Communist Party from destabilising the delicate ceasefire. This was a particular concern because there were still 70,000 Japanese troops in Singapore alone, upon whom the British relied to maintain the peace on the streets.

Before the annoying interruption of the occupation, off-duty British Army officers in Singapore might have followed in the footsteps of Somerset Maugham, Rudyard Kipling and Noël Coward, adjourning to the bamboo chairs of the Long Bar of the Raffles Hotel on Beach Road to enjoy roast beef from the silver beef trolley and one or more of former bartender Ngiam Tong Boon's famous Singapore gin sling cocktails, with its foaming top.

However, in autumn 1945 the Raffles was also a wrecked shadow of its pre-war self and old Singapore hands were disgusted that its bedrooms, bars and famous white-painted Palm Court, with its electric fans and bamboo screens, were crowded with recently released civilian internees. Not only that, many of the new residents were wretched Dutch colonials, newly released from internment in the Dutch East Indies.

Instead the British Army requisitioned the facilities of one of Singapore's most elite institutions, the Singapore Cricket Club on the famous Padang playing fields opposite the Victoria Theatre and its distinctive clock tower.

This evening two officers sat in bamboo armchairs sipping another signature drink of colonial Singapore, the stengah. Gaining its name from the Malay word for 'half', the stengah is a measure of whisky topped off with soda and was beloved of the rubber planters visiting this outpost of European civilisation from up country.

Observant visitors to the club that night would also notice that while the two men wore badges of rank on their shoulder slides, the rings of a naval commander and the crowns of an army major to be exact, they wore no regimental, or branch of service, patches. It was as if they wished to retain an even greater anonymity among the mass of Naval tropical whites, Army jungle green and RAF khaki drill uniforms on the streets of Singapore.

'*Sehat selalu!*' said the major, giving the Malay toast to good health and chinking glasses with his companion.

'You know, Ian,' the major said with the conspiratorial nudge and wink of an inveterate gossip, 'Dickie Mountbatten was bloody lucky the war finished before he launched Zipper. If the Japs had decided to shoot back, Zipper would have made his excursion to Dieppe look like a bloody Roman Triumph.'

The commander grinned and invoked the spirit of Oscar Wilde.

'Well I was there at Dieppe and I can say that to launch one calamitous cock-up of a beach landing might be looked upon as a misfortune, to launch two looks very much like carelessness.'

'Precisely,' said the major. 'You would think that at least one of the desk drivers at SEAC would have thought to check that the sand on the landing beaches could support the weight of tanks.'

'Well, Dickie is not exactly a details man is he?' The men share the joke.

'No it is all "action this day" and damn the consequences, just like Winston. Do you know what the erks call SEAC?' asks the major.

'No pray tell.'

'**S**upreme **E**xample **A**llied **C**onfusion. Mind you I was talking to a colonel I know in OSS when I was up at Mykinya and he told me the Yanks, including the Department of State, call us '**S**ave **E**ngland's **A**sian **C**olonies, which is probably more to the point.'

'Anyway Bill,' said the commander. 'What brings you to Singapore? I thought you were stuck in Rangoon trying to persuade the Emperor's Sons of Heaven to be good chaps and give us a hand keeping law and order while we reinstate the Empire east of Suez.'

'Ah, things have moved on,' the major responded with a hint of mystery. 'This is a flying visit to give Dickie a verbal report on his secret operation to support the Karen.'

'Does that include that ridiculous Op at Mingaladon where the Yanks did us that favour by loaning us their Construction Battalion?'

'Oh yes,' said the major. 'As well as ensuring our esteemed supreme commander has the latest return on how many tons of clay have been moved from A to B and back again, I now have to make sure the security for the operation is up to scratch. Apparently, Dickie had to give a bollocking to an RAF pen-pusher in the control room at Mingaladon who was a bit windy about omitting certain particularly sensitive activities from the Form 541.'

He took another sip of his stengah, then added, 'It has got to the stage where some of the erks have been overheard spreading rumours about what was actually going on, so we are spreading a few, shall we say, alternative facts of our own.'

'So you are having fun making mischief as per usual?' suggested the commander.

'That is what SOE was created for isn't it? But I wouldn't say it's fun exactly, although it is a touch less dangerous than touring jungle villages up country avoiding Jap patrols and dishing out salt and longyis to the locals in return for the latest gen. Or your fun and games with 40 AU for that matter.'

The major thought for a moment then added,

'Of course it is all bloody pointless anyway. You would have to be completely pissed, or irredeemably doolally, to believe we would carry out an operation like that. That is one of the reasons it is such a good plan. And, of course, Winston was several sheets to the wind when he thought it up, but now Attlee is stuck with it.'

He snaps his fingers and in moments a Malay waiter dressed in immaculate whites appears at his shoulder. '*Dua stengah*.'

24

Tracy Spaight
16 Guild House, Rollins Street
London
2 December 2012

'Shall we begin,' I ask, looking around the large circular table at David, the geophysicists Roger and Adam, and Andy, Martin, and Rod from the archaeology team.

We are seated in a half-circle facing a large flat-screen monitor, upon which we'll display maps and other data to pinpoint where, exactly, David wants to dig – and how we'll go about doing the excavation, as we need to finalise the dig plan for the Myanmar authorities.

The room is located on the second floor of a nineteenth-century warehouse just off the Old Kent Road in south-east London. The floor has broad, planked boards and whitewashed, exposed brick walls. Natural light filters down through skylights 15ft overhead. Mark and Anna from Room 608 selected this location for its 'negative space', since they didn't want the environment to detract from the interactions of the key protagonists.

On this winter afternoon the atmosphere is distinctly chilly, and not just because the space heater is unequal to the task of heating the room. The filmmakers have put us in opposition, right down to the seating, to capture the tensions within the group – particularly between David and the archaeology team.

Andy begins by posing the question of how exactly the planes arrived at Mingaladon, since the available evidence suggests they were not brought in by ship and offloaded at Rangoon docks, as David has maintained.

'I can't comment on that because I haven't got my notes with me,' David says, looking a bit flustered, 'but we've got evidence that Mark XIVs went into India and at least 124 were struck off charge.'

'Yes,' agrees Andy, who has confirmed these facts.

'What I'm saying,' David continues, 'is that they could well have been transported via ship from India to Rangoon and not have the appropriate documentation to prove it. It is possible to support this, uh, theory that it is a political burial. They, somebody, the censor, would have removed this document,' David concludes.

Andy looks dubious.

David continues. 'The first story was very clear. They were crated. They arrived from the docks and they were buried on 17 August [1945]. So, I have to say that I do believe that. How they got there, I'm still maintaining by ship,' David says.

'Because you can't find any evidence of that,' he says, looking at Andy, 'it doesn't convince me that that never happened. So, I do believe somewhere along the line, and this happened, especially in Burma, where a lot of records got destroyed or lost.'

To be fair, David's assertion echoes the point made independently of David by Sebastian Cox.

'And that is a fact, as well. I was led to believe firmly by the – the Americans who saw them being buried. They arrive by train from the docks. And I'm still saying that that's what happened,' David concludes, sticking with his original story.

Andy considers this for a moment, then says, 'It's certainly the case that on the east side of Mingaladon there was a railway line that linked with the city of Rangoon. If it was serviceable, that would have been used for making deliveries.'

'Yeah,' David agrees. 'I was told that there was a crane. And they arrived at Mingaladon station and were lifted onto some kind of low-loaders. Low …'

'Queen Mary trailers,' Andy says, completing David's thought.

'Yeah,' David says. 'And they were towed to the burial spot. And they were pulled down by D3 digger and buried on or after 17 August, 1945, when it was very wet conditions. The second burial was in December when it was much drier.'

Martin Brown interjects:

Let's suppose they did bury the crates of Spitfires. And the only reason that we can really sensibly suggest for that, rather than just dropping a block of concrete on them, is for the Karen rebels to be able to recover them and – and use them. That doesn't stand up for me because what's going to happen with planes that have been buried – even in a box – in ground that we know is incredibly wet. You know, thinking about the stories of aircraft recovery from crash sites from the Vietnam War, there's nothing left because it's all just basically dissolved.

'But that would be on the surface mainly,' David asserts.

'No,' Martin replies. 'If you bury them in the ground, surely they're going to rot away.'

'Well, these are protected by a box,' David says.

'A wooden box,' Martin counters.

'Yes,' agrees David.

'It's going to leak,' Martin points out.

'Yes,' David concedes.

'And then it'll rot away,' Martin says, stating the obvious.

'I can't see that,' David says.

Andy spells it out. 'Wooden structures in tropical environments are constantly renewed because the timber – even the best building timbers like teak – only has a limited life. And so, you're constantly renewing.'

These facts hang in the air for a moment.

David isn't buying it. 'What I'm trying to say,' he says, speaking slowly for emphasis, 'is that these [crates] are buried. The joints are tarred. The contents are wrapped in grease paper. And I can't see where the oxygen is going to come in to start the corrosion process.'

Martin demurs, saying that there would be enough oxygen, particularly with ingress of water, but adds that we'll find out who's right when we find a crate and open it.

At this point, Mark steers the conversation back to the question of how the planes could have arrived at Mingaladon Airfield in the first place.

'If as you say, Andy, they didn't arrive by ship, could they have been flown in, disassembled at Mingaladon, packed into crates and buried that way?' Mark asks.

'Certainly, an aircraft like that can be disassembled,' Andy says, thinking through the logistics. 'Certainly, it can be put into a crate if you've got a transport crate for it or you can build a transport crate for it. And certainly, if you've got the time and the resources, you could dig a hole for it.'

'So, mystery solved, then, right?' Mark interjects. 'If you could have done all those things?'

'If you can do all those things, we've maybe solved the mystery. We've maybe explained how this could have happened. But can I look at something else with you?' Andy asks, as he pulls up an image on the monitor.

'This is an incoming cipher message to Air Headquarters Burma from Headquarters Air Command Southeast Asia,' Andy says, gesturing at the flat-screen monitor across the table.

'So, it's going further up the food chain from Burma to headquarters back in India. And it's a confidential message. It's [dated] 13 February, 1946. The chief engineer of Burma says that there is a serious shortage of sawn timber and lack of labour.'

'In other words, if you're wanting to build crates, you've got a shortage of people to do it and you've got a shortage of timber to do it,' Andy concludes.

'Yes,' David says, jumping in. 'But this is in February of, what, '46, is it?'

'Yeah,' Andy confirms.

'Well, this is after the burials when you would have a shortage if you'd used timber to make the boxes to bury the aeroplanes,' he says.

Andy's face betrays his surprise at this particular deduction.

Gathering his thoughts, Andy says:

It's throughout the period they're referring to shortages of timber. One of the priorities of the RAF is to get their personnel under a roof by the 1946 monsoon. Documents in this series [predominantly ciphered reports and messages passing between RAF staff in Rangoon and SEAC Headquarters] talk about prioritising RAF accommodation for construction. I think, again, it's stretching the point to suggest that they – in a way that's completely unrecorded – could divert what are clearly scarce resources in a very difficult situation to building crates for aeroplanes that they don't need to bury if they want to get rid of them.

Because they could just drop a concrete block on them. Which is what happened in India. So, there's this concept that we work with all the time called Occam's razor, which is basically the hypothesis with the fewest assumptions is likely to be the one that's most valid.

We've got this mystery. How do we set about solving it? I think that's what we need to move on to perhaps address next. But what do you think?

'So, they're not saying they haven't got any timber. They're saying that there's a shortage of it,' David says.

'Yes.' Andy says.

'But you only have a shortage when there is a higher demand. So, are people demanding wood to bury these aeroplanes causing that shortage,' David concludes.

Martin says:

I would suggest that they're causing a shortage by trying to build. Because there are – there are lots of good reasons for getting men out from under canvas. One is disease. The British Army learned something very serious at the end of the Boer War about not letting all your troops die of nasty things. The, the other one, though, is morale. And it's – it's after the war. And we know you've got problems with morale because everybody's sitting there going, 'I want to go home.'

Well, my point is this – that it's vital to use any timber you've got to build structures to get people out of the wet. To stop them, A, being miserable and, B, catching nasty things that are potentially going to kill them.

Andy tries to bring the meeting back to at least a semblance of cooperation. 'OK, I mean, I'm just going, just recapping for a second, David. I mean, I think it's really important to understand none of us are saying, and I'm certainly not saying ...'

David interjects, 'I understand that, fully. You have to find out the truth. I don't know the truth at the moment. I want to find out just as badly as you do.'

'Absolutely,' Andy says emphatically. It's a rare moment of agreement between them.

'We've got aeroplanes like that at Mingaladon being worked on,' Andy summarises, adding that the evidence suggests those aircraft were flown to Mingaladon, not brought there by ship in crates.

He also accepts that the fitters would have been perfectly capable, as well as keeping those aeroplanes in the air, of taking them apart and putting them in a box in a way that's going to maintain them as fit for purpose.

But, he adds, we must also bear in mind the practicalities of doing that in Mingaladon in the second half of 1945 with the prevailing ground conditions and availability of labour, equipment and construction timber recorded in the documents.

This context makes it very difficult to see how the story as David presents it works, Andy concludes.

'Is there a map?' asks Mark, trying to set up the scene for the documentary. 'Can you just show us ... where are we going to dig?'

'OK. There's the modern runway,' says Andy, using the mouse cursor to indicate the location.

We all look at the large flat-screen monitor, which shows an overlay of the 1945 airfield over a satellite image of Mingaladon airport. 'There's the modern air base up there and hangars and so on are all up there. The taxiway coming down from the military side of the airfield.'

'The first target is the area where the geophysics was done in 2004,' he continues. 'Which is this area here.' He traces a circle around this part of the airfield on the monitor. 'And then the second target is the area that you've indicated Stanley Coombe suggested was an area of importance, which is this area over here, towards the end of the extension of the 1945 runway. So, those are the two. We're not going to have time to do any more targets than that on this trip.'

'One of the reasons for working so closely with Roger and Adam,' Andy continues, 'and doing the geophysics in the kind of detail that we're talking about is so we don't spend time and resources digging in the wrong place.'

Martin Brown chimes in, 'If there is a hole full of crates, we will know.'

'Good,' says David.

'The question is, what happens if there isn't?' says Martin.

This question hangs over the group for several heartbeats.

'Well, immediately, someone's going to say, "They're just a few feet that way",' says Adam.

'Or, "You're digging in the wrong place",' Martin chimes in.

'Which is why you need to very specifically tell us this is exactly where you want the excavation. You have to be 100 per cent certain,' Rod concludes, looking at David.

'Right,' David says. 'When Adam and I did the survey, or rather Adam did the survey, we found a datum point. Didn't we?' he asks, looking across the table at Adam.

'Yes,' replies Adam.

'Good,' says Martin.

'If you look on the survey, if you can bring it back ...'

Andy brings up the 2004 survey map on the monitor.

'That datum point started at zero,' David says. 'That was calculated from eyewitness reports that we will find those aeroplanes.'

'Excellent,' Rod says.

'Great,' I add.

'Fabulous,' Martin says.

'It's the proverbial X marks the spot,' concludes Rod.

'Yeah, we've got it. We know it,' says David.

The meeting ends on a high note. We all agree we have to dig.

David says, 'I'm very happy. I'm very pleased I met you and it's been very interesting. I – I don't always agree with you, of course. And I think the only way to find out is to dig. And I'll see you gentlemen early in January.'

As the crew begins to pack away the kit and people grab a last slice of pizza, we say our goodbyes and go our separate ways into the darkness of a winter's night in south-east London.

```
Andy Brockman
16 Guild House, Rollins Street
London
2 December 2012
```

Like an army, a film crew (and archaeologists) march on their stomachs and when the battlefield is a disused warehouse on a freezing Sunday afternoon in December freshly delivered hot pizza and coffee take on an importance beyond the simple provision of nutrition.

As the crew and talent breaks from recording, director Mark Mannucci takes me to one side.

In his trademark emphatic, tell it like it is, New York way Mark tells me in a low voice that he wants me to challenge David more over his assertions about the burial of the Spitfires. The subtext is that so far the planning scene, as we call it, is all too nice and oh so British, and to make his film fly he needs that staple of drama, some conflict.

At one level I am sympathetic towards the predicament Mark faces. From a simple treasure hunt storyline ending with the big reveal of the Spitfires at Yangon, Mark and the team are now in for tens of thousands of dollars and he knows now that, far from there being a last real triumph for our most unlikely of heroes, we on the research team are of the firm belief that we are investigating an urban myth that is careering across the twenty-first-century media horizon completely out of control.

However, I am also aware that there is a concept in the media called 'muscular curiosity'. It is the opposite to the cooler, more process-based storylines nurtured on British programmes such as *Time Team*, instead relying on regular scenes of apparent conflict and jeopardy to keep the audience from switching channels. It is a style particularly prevalent in American documentary television and has reached its nadir in storylined documentaries dealing in pseudohistory such as Kaga 7 Production's *Hunting Hitler*, made for the History Channel.

If that is the route Mark wants to go down we have a problem because this is approach is not just temperamentally, even culturally, difficult for a group of UK archaeologists to adopt. I had hoped we had made it clear that, while we would do everything we could to facilitate the documentary, we would not take part in invented scenes that had no basis in the linear reality of the investigation.

Neither would we compromise our professional ethics just because it would make for a better TV scene in dramatic terms. In this case our rationale is that, contractually, David is our client and it is utterly unethical to act in a confrontational way with your client at a planning meeting like this, unless that is your client asks you to compromise your ethics.

So far, while he has said much that is questionable on historical grounds, David has not done so.

I respond to Mark's request with a form of words that I hope comes across as some sort of assent, while metaphorically crossing my fingers behind my back, which means I am not bound by the undertaking.

We resume the recording.

Later I learn from Rod that Adam and Roger think I was a bit hard on David during the recording.

What they do not yet know is that at the request of Room 608 I have also undertaken an analysis of the photograph apparently showing a Spitfire in a transport crate that was published in *The Telegraph* and other media outlets with a caption stating explicitly that it was one of the Spitfires of Mingaladon being prepared for burial.

However, I have discovered that the photograph, which is credited to a press agency in Hull, includes a box that carries a serial number consistent with a batch of Spitfire Mark V aircraft built at Castle Bromwich under Air Ministry Contract 981687 issued in August 1941, and far from being a Spitfire that was buried in Burma, the aircraft is almost certainly one of two. The first of these ended its career in Soviet Russia as part of the Lend–Lease supply of aircraft to the Red Air Force, while the second was written off in a landing accident in what was then the League of Nations mandate of Palestine in March 1945.

25

The Spitfires of Rangoon

A Novel of the Secret War in Burma

by Major William Wills DSO OBE

'Try never to talk more than once yourself. Make others talk. Arrange for innocent interception of your "sib"* on fertile ground, e.g. garrulous barber, gossipy barmaid, Spanish Ambassador.'

Special Operations Executive, Lecture Course C Propaganda

```
Lucy's Bar and House of Rest and Recreation
Singapore City
December 1945
```

For bored and lonely other ranks in liberated Singapore, Lucy's Bar was the kind of dive where relaxation or alcohol-induced oblivion could be had for a reasonable price and conversations had to be conducted at the level of a shout, such was the level of background noise and of the wind-up gramophone on the bar with its repertoire consisting entirely of scratched 78s by Vera Lynn and Bing Crosby. That was when the combined services 'Sods' Opera' was not on song, as it was tonight.

---

*   'Sib' Latin *Sibilare* to Hiss: in an echo of the serpent in the Garden of Eden whispering in the ear of Eve, the SOE code name for a rumour spread deliberately.

Accompanied by a Royal Engineers sergeant with a battered accordion slung across his chest, the inebriated choir launched into a rollocking rendition of a joyously rude military classic, with a few special adaptations to the lyrics made by the Royal Air Force erks from RAF Seletar.

For if ever the engine should stall
We're in for a heck of a fall
No roses or violets for flat-footed pilots
So cheer up my lads fuck 'em all

Cupping a hand to the ear of his companion across the table, the aircraftsman with the Brylcreemed hair and Cockney accent who introduced himself as Bill asked, 'So wot are you sayin'?'

The song continued in the background, the chorus growing still more raucous, as if it were possible,

Fuck 'em all,
Fuck 'em all.
The long and the short and the tall,
Fuck all those sergeants and WOIs,
Fuck all those corporals and their fuckin' sons,
Cos we're saying goodbye to 'em all.
And back to their billets they crawl,
You'll get no promotion this side of the ocean,
So cheer up my lads Fuck 'em all.

'I'm saying,' said the ginger-haired corporal, cupping his hands to his mouth and leaning back shouting into the aircraftsman's ear, 'I'm sayin' that my mate from 83 RSU, shipped in from Rangoon and he says that they've been burying brand new Spits at Mingaladon.'

'Burying the fuckers?'

Yeah, apparently it's all Mountbatten's idea,' said Ginger. 'It's a sort of stockpile, in case things go tits up again and the locals start having a go at us, or each other.'

'No, it's true,' Interjected a third airman with crooked teeth and acne, taking a swig from a bottle of local beer. 'They're gettin' rid of loads of Spits. My mate was with 316 MU an' says he heard they were pushing them into a swamp.'

'Don't be bloody stupid, why would they do that? I was at Mingaladon when they flogged knackered Mark VIIIs to the Frogs in Indochina,' said Bill, 'They all shipped out to Saigon.'

'Anyway,' he added, 'I know that 316 and the world and his wife was pushing everything off the back of the carriers in the bay. Why fuckin' bother burying a sodding great aircraft that has been SOC* when you can dump it, no questions asked?'

Lucy's had gone quiet, a solo Welsh voice taking up another song, set to the melody made famous on both sides of the line in North Africa as a simple yearning for love and human contact. The tune was 'Lily Marlene', but this time, with new lyrics, the effect was bitterly satirical.

> Soon we'll ship for Aussie, leaving old SEAC
> We're bloody sure that none of us are ever coming back.
> Farewell Chowringhee, Kidderpore,
> Your steamy shore
> We'll see no more.
> We're going round the corner, right round the fucking bend.

As the song ended the alcohol-fuelled frustration and the yearning for home in the room was palpable.

However, the moment of comradeship and silence was broken as an airman wearing the flashes of an RAF armourer swayed to his feet and motioned to the singer with his forefinger. The armourer placed a companionable arm around the singer's neck and said in a stage whisper and strong Birmingham accent,

'There's wun thing I 'ate more than Aussies, Japs an' officers, an' that's 'omesick fookin' Taffs.'

Unfortunately he telegraphed the punch and staggered off balance as the Welshman, clearly a rugby player as well as a singer, sidestepped the assault and, before he could recover his poise, a left uppercut deposited the Brummie on his back on a table, which collapsed and covered the dazed airman in a shower of bottles, beer and cigarette butts.

In moments the battle lines were drawn and it was hand-to-hand fighting, all against all, no holds barred.

The Cockney airman sank back into the shadows. The spectacle of flying chairs and crashing tables reminded him of a line from one of his favourite films, *The Prisoner of Zenda*, where, in the course of the climactic sabre duel, the villainous Prince Rupert, played by the suave Douglas Fairbanks Junior, pauses to quip, 'I cannot get used to fighting with furniture. Where did you learn it?'

---

*   SOC – Struck Off Charge, an RAF abbreviation indicating that former RAF property is now someone else's problem.

Stiff upper lip English hero Rudolph Rassendyll, played by Ronald Coleman, retorts, 'Coldstream Guards my boy!'

He ducked as a thrown bar stool crunched into the wall behind him, smashing the glass protecting the cheap portrait of the King. It was no loss to the world of art and had probably replaced an equally cheap portrait of Emperor Hirohito.

The sound of engines and the scream of brakes in the street was followed moments later by the crash of the door being kicked in to the accompaniment of service-issue whistles and shouted instructions to stay put.

Someone yelled, 'Out the back, it's the fuckin' Red Caps!'

As the staff and clients of Lucy's bar exited from every available door and window, not necessarily the open ones, and not all of them fully dressed, the airman called Bill found one of the few remaining unbroken chairs and, seated at a corner table, lit a cigarette, drawing on it slowly as the raid took its course.

'You're a fuckin' cool customer,' said the Military Police sergeant, reaching for his handcuffs. 'Breaking curfew in a brothel, don't you give a toss you're fucked?'

'No Sergeant, I don't,' said 'Bill', fishing a service identity card from the pocket of his jungle greens, his accent replaced by something closer to the quadrangle at Eton than the Bow Road. The MP scanned the lines, his mouth moving in disbelief as he read.

At length he said quietly, 'Right sir, I'd be getting along if I were you.' The sergeant saluted.

'No formalities please, Sergeant. I was never here,' Bill said airily, adding with a twang of menace, 'If you catch my drift.'

Major Bill Baron dropped his cigarette into an empty beer bottle, where it fizzed momentarily, and wandered away from the carnage of Lucy's, remembering the bottle of whisky he shared with Lieutenant Douglas Fairbanks Junior, United States Naval Reserve, in the autumn of 1942 while they were both attending the commando training course at Inverary Castle in the Highlands of Scotland.

Odd that the needs of operational security for Operation Merlin at Mingaladon had required him go into the acting business too.

26

Andy Brockman
Broadcasting House and the Heathrow Hilton
3 January 2013

An interview with Sky News over, I wander back into the Hilton, where the rest of the press pack is still seated around the perimeter of the meeting room firing questions at Tracy and Frazer. I join them and make another attempt to frame the expedition as Yangon CSI. Again the line is we are going to Myanmar with no preconceptions and with the intention of demonstrating the truth of the story by determining the facts in the ground.

David also gives interviews, each time seemingly ignoring our media training and managing to talk instead about secret burials ordered by Mountbatten in support of the Karen.

Speaking to *The Times*, he confidently predicts, 'We will have a box on the surface, you can open the doors, and you will see the aircraft inside. These are 100 per cent original Spitfires that have been buried for sixty-seven years, and they will still be shining.'*

As the press conference breaks up, Maeve Kennedy, the veteran Irish-born culture correspondent of *The Guardian* newspaper says to me words to the effect of, 'It's nonsense really isn't it?'

I repeat our agreed line, but I sense Maeve is too smart not to know she has called David's claims and my own scepticism correctly and all I can do is hope that, for now at least, there is not enough evidence for her to be able to stand up that version of the story.

---

*   www.thetimes.co.uk/tto/news/uk/defence/article3648836.ece

Another journalist with an interest in culture and heritage, and a properly questioning approach, is Robert Hall of the BBC.

I have worked with Robert already thanks to his involvement in covering a new heritage crime initiative from English Heritage with which I am also involved and today he offers to buys me lunch, so tuna sandwich and coffee in hand we find a quiet table off to the side of the hotel's ground-floor café.

We begin by talking around various potential stories, including the apparent ambivalence of the UK government in protecting its naval wrecks like HMS *Victory* 1744 from allegations of commercial exploitation and the difficulty of explaining to a general audience that treasure hunting might not be such a good thing when it comes to preserving archaeological sites. Then we move on to the Spitfires.

Robert also has good connections in the world of historic aircraft and knows Spitfire expert and Burma sceptic Andy Saunders of *Britain at War* magazine. Next week I will sit in my hotel room in Yangon and watch that connection in action as BBC World airs a package by Robert about the Spitfire mystery with Andy interviewed as the expert commentator.

Back in the Heathrow Hilton, Robert demonstrates the latest iPhone app, which the BBC uses and which allows its journalists in the field to record and upload interviews directly into the BBC newsroom. Unfortunately, I can't give him a scoop worthy of the technology.

In fact today is developing a worrying theme. Earlier, on the way to Heathrow, I stop off at Broadcasting House to record an interview for BBC World Service.

In a studio off the vast atrium that forms the BBC's news and programming hub I spend what is probably only around five minutes, but which seems like much more, frustrating the attempts of the interviewer to get me to admit to how exciting it will be when we find the Spitfires.

It is becoming a concern that this line of questioning is the norm. As was the case after the press conference at the Imperial War Museum a month ago, as we depart for Yangon the bulk of the coverage, in print and on television, is predicated on David's version being right, and on current showing the scepticism of Robert and Maeve is the exception, as few, if any, other journalists and news producers are asking the basic questions about David's claims that we hoped our framing had set them up to ask.

PART TWO
CSI YANGON

Burmese Daze

In which Sir Nöel Coward's 1932 satire on the
British Empire east of Suez, 'Mad Dogs and Englishmen',
begins to look like a documentary.

27

Andy Brockman
Qatar Airways Flight QR018
Saturday, 5 January 2013

On 13/14 August 1945 it took Admiral of the Fleet Lord Louis Mountbatten's personal RAF York transport MW102, with its distinctive duck egg green livery and blue and white SEAC roundels thirty hours forty-five minutes to travel from RAF Stoney Cross in the New Forest of Hampshire, close to Mountbatten's home at Broadlands, to SEAC Headquarters at Kandy, with refuelling stops at Cairo and Karachi. Mountbatten recorded in his diary that the time was a record. With a fair wind we will follow in MW102's slipstream and the journey begins smoothly as on time, at just after 8 a.m. on Saturday, 5 January 2013, the Qatar Airways Airbus A330 bursts through the ceiling of grey January cloud over London.

As our flightpath takes us out of Europe and into Asia, I fall to talking to my travelling companion, who it turns out is a quietly spoken, middle-aged family doctor who practices in the Home Counties north-west of London. He is Burmese and is returning to Yangon for a reunion with his university medical school contemporaries and their teachers.

Inadvertently he gives me a crash course in Burmese culture, explaining that, while in the consumer culture of the West a university reunion is seen as an excuse to party with added opportunities to assess one's own life, celebrate or revel in the successes and failures of contemporaries and rekindle old relationships, or at least they are according to Hollywood screenwriters, to a similarly educated Burmese a reunion is a chance to acknowledge and pay off a moral debt to one's teachers.

Later, when I hope we have built a level of trust, I carefully ask him if he is hopeful for the future of his country?

He replies that he thinks the release of Aung San Suu Kyi and the hesitant opening up of Myanmar is positive, but he hopes that Yangon will not go the way of Bangkok in neighbouring Thailand, which, he feels, has fallen victim to a headlong rush for high-rise modernity and the tourist dollar, and in so doing has lost its identity and its cultural soul.

Our conversation tails off and I doze as the aircraft flies south along the Euphrates valley.

Soon after, the aircraft turns to make its approach to Doha, where the horizon is softened by the sand hanging in the air, pinky grey in the sunset.

As we disembark and head for the bus that will take us to the transit lounge, I wish my companion a safe and happy trip and he reciprocates.

Then it is back to the transit bus and up the steps as we board a smaller Airbus A319 for the final long hop from Doha to Yangon.

As the twin International Aero Engines turbofans push the aircraft south-west into the night, we leave behind blankets of multicoloured lights in Abu Dhabi and Dubai, glittering and reflecting on the slick dark waters of the Gulf, and signalling to the world a region that can flaunt its economy founded on the twin blood supplies of oil and electricity.

Five hours later, as the nose of the aircraft swings south-east over the Bay of Bengal, I become conscious we are now flying in the wake of the aircrew of South East Asia Command, albeit flying in air-conditioned comfort in a God seat, rather than ploughing through the weather in an unpressurised Transport Command York, Expediter or Dakota.

However, looking down it is also as if we are flying decades back in time, because, as we descend towards Yangon in the watery light of early dawn, I register, as Tracy Spaight did also on his first visit, that, unlike most of the countries which lie behind us, the lights below are sparse and the ribbons of road are not lit up with processions of car headlights and neon advertising.

There is that sharp but reassuring thump as the landing gear of the Airbus drops and locks and the flaps and slats on the wings do their work. In retrospect I can observe that the wheels of Mountbatten's York last touched down here at 1440 hours on Tuesday, 9 October 1945 as his tenure at SEAC came to an end, but for now I am happy simply that a second thump and rapid braking marks our safe return to terra firma.

We pass through immigration, purchase our visas and reclaim our baggage complete and intact. There is also a brush by the waiting media, but my abiding memory of that arrival is the advertising billboard that I spot and photograph as our minibus pulls away from the terminal building.

In a symbol of just how different things might be to someone used to a European way of doing things, and to the consumer products advertised near major international airports in the First World, the product advertised outside Yangon International is a fertiliser manufactured by Vietnamese company Petrovietnam and the slogan reads in English, 'Phu My Urea for a bountiful harvest.'

I cannot help but think of that well-known English slang phrase about making fun of someone, 'Taking the piss', and I wonder if someone is?

Andy Brockman
The Burma Spitfire Project Offices
Yangon
7 January 2013

After a Sunday spent getting over the flights and orientating ourselves in the friendly and well-appointed Park Royal hotel, which sits as a capsule of international business class luxury, contrasting sharply with potholed side streets of downtown Yangon just around the corner and the narrow labyrinthine alleys of the Bog Yoke Aung Sen market a few hundred meters away across the main Yangon railway, this Monday morning the STP/Wargaming Burma Spitfires Excavation project is officially under way.

And Martin Rod and I commence our engagement as the STP Burma Spitfire Project's 'Historical Experts'.

The geophysics team are flying in later.

While it does not in any way effect the technical and ethical standards of what we will do, the fact that we will not be described as archaeologists by STP while we are in country is something of a diplomatic fix on their part, reducing the chance of any potential turf war between the Ministry of Transport, which is in control of the dig because it is taking place at Yangon Airport, and the Ministry of Religious Affairs and Culture, which oversees Myanmar's rich archaeology elsewhere.

Our first task is to venture out onto the streets of Yangon to visit the STP Spitfire project offices, which Tracy and Wargaming have just discovered they are renting.

Situated on the first floor of a small modern concrete office block, the suite of immaculate white-painted rooms with apple-green mouldings has the air of a doctor's surgery that wants to be a senior common room at a university, complete with new computers, leather armchairs and polished wooden desks.

However, the atmosphere is akin to that science fiction trope where an alien race creates an environment to facilitate every need of their abducted human guests without understanding fully what it is they are making. It is as if no one has ever been here before, certainly not to work.

The only personal touch is the small shrine to the Buddha, with its spray of fresh flowers high up on the wall of what appears to be the main office.

Nonetheless, Auntie Latt, a splash of vibrant colour in her bright orange sleeveless blouse, badged with the face of her guru, is beaming as she shows us around. Then cakes are produced in a generous gesture of hospitality and welcome.

As our hosts and the team mingle, David has occupied a sofa next to Stanley Coombe and has once again embarked on his well-rehearsed narrative of the burial, with Stanley chipping in from time to time and confirming again that the date he saw the crates on Mingaladon as March 1946, because he had just celebrated his birthday on the troop ship bringing him from Singapore to Rangoon.

Rod Scott and I are a few feet away at the side of the room and we are intrigued. We have not seen David talking with one of his witnesses before, and as we listen we begin to understand how this story has become established. We lean in to each other and begin our own commentary.

As David continues to talk, Mark Mannucci wanders over hoping to film some reaction, asking discreetly, 'How does it make you feel towards him, he's sitting right behind you?'

I do not want to have this conversation here and now, and fortunately Rod too is feeling the need to be diplomatically Sphinxlike.

'Feelings don't come into it,' Rod replies as Mark calls over Andreas.

Hoping to close down the conversation, I add, 'I think that question is best left for a situation that is less intense than this one where we are all on show for Swe Taung Por.'

'It's visually interesting,' Mark says.

It is.

Rod and I are at the edge of the room with our backs to David, who is still holding forth to Stanley and it is clear Mark can frame the shot to include David and Stanley, adding snippets of their conversation into the sound mix, presenting the audience with the key question of the whole expedition – who do you believe?

However, again I am mindful David is technically our client and it would not be appropriate to be seen to be offering a character study that inevitably frames our disagreements as personal, and I tell Mark that I would rather not provide that kind of visually loaded soundbite now, although I dress the refusal in the measured clothes of client/contractor etiquette.

'It's just that personally I would like to look at it in a situation where we are being more objective. Like that director's cut commentary to a video, I'd like to do it that way,' I say.

Understandably, as director, Mark wants his shot so he pushes back.

'As a filmmaker and investigator of this story I have a tremendous affection for David,' he tells us, 'but I also get frustrated because I sent my people on this long chase to find Seabees only to find there were no Seabees.'

Rod encapsulates our own frustration, 'Frustration it is absolutely.'

And he adds with a sense of resignation that we all feel, 'No matter how much work we do you know it's going to morph into something else. It's that belief almost that should we not find these items there, you know it will morph into the fact that we're in completely the wrong location …'

I finish the thought, '… and it has been covered up so effectively that the evidence has been taken away.'

I tell Mark:

What I will say is that from the point of view of an archaeological and historical investigator, OK, if you want to be pretentious about it, and taking personalities out of it completely, there is this fantastic forgotten story here about what was actually going on here in Rangoon and at Mingaladon, particularly in that incredibly intense period at the end of the war, and it's being lost because of the white noise this [the legend of the buried Spitfires] is generating.

Rod adds, 'Don't forget it's not only the war. It's after the war when you've got this political turmoil.'

I try to illustrate the point. 'We've just heard someone, Stanley earlier, say how we would wander up and look at the Japanese PoWs through the wire and there wasn't any animosity. "We were doing our job, they were doing theirs." Now that may be a perception now in 2013, but that's not what people are supposed to think.'

I explain to Mark that in Britain the treatment of Allied PoWs under the Japanese is still live, and I mention that on the farm where I grew up one of the farm workers had been a PoW in the Far East and even a quarter of a century later he would not contemplate buying a Japanese car, the memory of his treatment was that raw.

'There are all these wonderful complexities and narrative threads …'

But before we can reach a conclusion Mark apologises and breaks away because he has seen another shot he wants.

The research team will never visit these offices again.

Tracy Spaight
Park Royal hotel
Yangon
8 January 2013

There is a formality about conducting business in Myanmar that is all about showing appropriate respect, and today respect is being shown to our colleagues from STP as the Wargaming team gather around the large polished wooden table in the ornate conference room on the ground floor of the Park Royal and let Htoo Htoo and his senior managers describe the arrangements for the work at Mingaladon.

It feels like the photo opportunity at one of those international summits where the cameras will be kicked out after the opening platitudes. However, this time the cameras will stay.

For Andy, safety has been an overriding concern, ever since the fieldwork project was first mooted. Not discounting their experience and that fact that they have worked together before, it is the main reason why he has insisted on Martin Brown and Rod Scott joining the team and on Wargaming hiring a professional, English-speaking excavator driver, Manny Machado.

Andy's intention is to cover the team against any temptation to take potentially dangerous or unethical short cuts for financial or clock reasons, or to 'get the shot', by placing as many people as possible with knowledge, experience and, above all, the willingness to say 'no' between a request to do something questionable and that something actually happening.

With that in mind, the dig team are happy to be working with STP's general manager, Pe Win.

Pe Win is a man whose face betrays years of working outdoors and who is clearly experienced in a Western way of working. It turns out he has worked on large construction sites in Singapore and elsewhere where the health and safety regimes are similar to those in place in the UK and USA.

While the dig plan is agreed, we soon learn that we can't actually start digging, since the government has not yet issued the necessary permits – despite the fact we filed the excavation plan and requested permits several weeks before. Until the permits are in place, we can't take delivery of the JCB JS 220 and the backhoe at the airport to do the work.

I remind Htoo Htoo that we have a limited window to do the project, since Roger and Adam need to return to the UK for the start of the spring semester in two-and-a-half weeks. Martin and the film crew also face hard-stop dates.

The delays are not fatal, however, as we need to do the geophysics first, relocating the 2004 survey area and pinpointing the 'T' and 'L' sections David identified as the burial locations.

Fortunately, the geophysicists will be allowed to start the survey on Thursday.

The technical aspects of the meeting concluded, we pile into the minibus and head out to Yangon airport and the dig site, stopping at the main terminal to collect and model the new hard hats and branded hi-viz waistcoats that STP have supplied to the team.

As the bus leaves behind the ribbon development of roadside shops and houses and follows the Prome Road around the north-west end of the former runway 06, Andy is reconstructing the landscape of 1945 in his head and is beginning to be impressed at the number of clues to that landscape still present in January 2013, from the scarp leading up to the western end of runway where the runway was extended to the concrete hard top of the taxiway leading to the former engineering area and dispersal that appears still to be under the control of the Myanmar military, the Tatmadaw.

Seeing these survivals I am reminded that RAF Mingaladon had what is sometimes termed euphemistically 'an eventful war'.

For the British it was a war that began shortly after the attack on Pearl Harbour on 7 December 1941 with the shock and humiliation of the sinking by Japanese aircraft of the only major force of Royal Navy capital ships in the Far East, HMS *Prince of Wales* and HMS *Repulse*, off the coast of Malaya.

This catastrophe ushered in a new kind of fast-moving campaign, executed by highly trained personnel backed up by modern ships and aircraft for which the Royal Air Force in particular, with its order of battle in Burma hollowed out by the demands of home defence and the campaigns in the Mediterranean and the deserts of North Africa, was woefully ill-equipped to fight.

The north boundary of RAF Mingaladon
Close to the Prome Road
9 January 1942

Superintendent A.A. Donald, the District Superintendent of Police at Insein, has a major security headache that has lasted throughout December 1941. The problem is caused primarily by the fact that the main Prome Road crosses the north-west corner of RAF Mingaladon, which enables local people and refugees to shelter along the roadside and in the trees that encroach on the edges of the airfield, close to aircraft dispersal areas and engineering hangars.

By early January he has reached the end of his tether and in true British colonial service tradition he explains this in a report and memorandum to the station commander.

He describes how night after night he is forced to turn out every available policemen from a force already at full stretch, thanks to the combined threat of air raids and invasion, to try to stop people lighting fires around the RAF and Army lines which might attract the Japanese bombers.

Donald reports that in spite of many arrests the fires always return, often in a different place, so that, while he cannot tell if the firelighters are fifth columnists or what he describes simply as poor ignorant fools trying to keep warm and cook food, the risk to the vulnerable military targets is the same in either case.

The stress of the situation shows most clearly in the flippant, but bitter, final line of the memo as Donald writes, 'The one and only remedy against the lighting of fires at night is for the RAF to send up a plane and spray the fools or 5th Columnists with a machine gun as they take no notice of the friendly warnings or advice given to them.'*

On reading this, the RAF officer reviewing the memo marks Donald's comment with a large question mark in blue pencil.

However, on 17 January a notice is issued in Superintendent Donald's name that states that the decision has been taken to restrict access to the Prome Road between mile posts 8 and 18 to members of the military and civilians with a valid pass.

Andy Brockman
Yangon International Airport
Yangon
8 January 2013

Security on the north entrance to Yangon International Airport is provided by the paramilitary Yangon Police Battalion in their pressed grey shirts and sharply seamed dark blue trousers and, while few of its mostly young personnel appear to speak English, they are polite and professional, with what I feel is an underlying curiosity about their unusual visitors.

This part of the airport is a military zone and it is clear from the way we are being processed that we are there on sufferance, the result of careful negotiations and permissions granted at a high level within the Myanmar military.

---

*   TNA Air23/4651.

We sign in and are issued with airside passes on the kind of lanyard which now seems the ubiquitous badge of belonging in any professional situation anywhere in the world. We also familiarise ourselves with the rules we must observe on the site.

These involve primarily not wandering off on our own too far from the dig site and not pointing cameras in the wrong direction, which means in the direction of anything remotely military in nature.

In particular, we have been warned not to take photographs as we take the right-angled turn where the access road swings east, past the airport fire station.

It is not that the fire engines themselves are particularly secret. Neither are the small, well-tended vegetable gardens the members of the battalion use to augment their food supply, and probably to stave off boredom, a state secret.

The reason for the nervousness is the line of blue-painted, open-backed, police trucks, their sides lined with riot shields like a Viking battlefleet and the squadron of what look like French-built Panhard AML armoured cars, which share the fire station's hard standing alongside the more familiar and reassuring red airport fire tenders.

Subsequently I find out that the Tatmadaw obtained fifty rebuilt Panhards in one of its numerous arms deals with the Israeli government, but seeing them today I cannot help thinking that, while they are the kind of nimble, but heavily armed, vehicles that are very useful for patrolling the perimeters of airports, they are equally useful for providing a show of force during civil unrest, and they and the riot trucks are based just a short drive away from central Yangon, and Yangon University.

We are decanted from the minibus at the dig site and I get my first opportunity to translate what have hitherto been a mental collage of air photographs, maps, references in documents and the memories of David, Adam and Stanley Coombe into three-dimensional facts on the ground, and the result is fascinating.

David is in his element, walking Stanley Coombe across the site, accompanied by Room 608's cameras, confidently pointing to various places on the airfield, saying we believe (always the Royal 'we') that Spitfires are buried over here and over there and over there.

Mark Mannucci notices that I'm holding back, listening to David's performance, and in true reality TV style he asks, 'What do you think?'

My response is diplomatic, and therefore disappointing to Mark, who as ever wants some dramatic conflict he can use to drive the film, but his question and my response speak eloquently as to what is likely to happen over the next two weeks.

I tell him, 'I am not going to tell you what I think.'

I say this because I'm now convinced there will soon be a head-on collision between the documented history the team has already uncovered, the archaeology they are likely to uncover and David's burial theory.

28

Tracy Spaight
Park Royal Hotel
Yangon
9 January

After our visit to Mingaladon airfield, Shwe Taung Por informs us they are planning a press conference for the next morning, to announce the start of the dig. The plan catches me off guard. Frazer Nash isn't due to arrive until Saturday, as we hadn't planned on any media announcements until the end of next week, after we'd begun digging. I ask Htoo Htoo if we can postpone the event, but he says the media has already been invited.

More concerning, Htoo Htoo says that they plan to unveil their findings from the geophysics and test digs they undertook at Myitkyina in December. He asks that our team join him on stage.

After conferring with Andy, I tell Htoo Htoo that we can't do that, since our team wasn't there and didn't do the work – so we are unable to comment on it.

In fact, we cannot go on the record because if we did we would have to reveal the results of Andy and Rod's work on Myitkyina in the National Archives back in the autumn.

They have determined that, like Mingaladon, Myitkyina was a pre-war RAF station, but the team have also discovered that the airfield is not even listed as an active RAF station in the period 1944–48 when David alleges that Spitfires were buried.

Instead, the British military records confirm that, as a base for Japanese aircraft attempting to interdict the air route over the hump into China, Myitkyina was attacked frequently by USAAF aircraft of the 10th Air Force and by RAF bombers from as early as 1942. It remained a primary target for the RAF and USAAF until its capture by Chinese units and US special forces drawn from US Airborne and Merrill's Marauders on 18 May 1944. The adjacent Myitkyina town fell on 3 August 1944 after a bitterly fought siege.

For the remainder of the war in the Far East, Myitkyina was used to support the activities of the USAAF Combat Cargo Groups in the China–Burma–India Theatre, in particular during the effort to supply the Chinese 'over the Hump'.

The USAAF pulled out completely in December 1945.

Myitkyina was also used as a staging post in the demobilisation of US forces in the China–Burma–India Theatre.

An account from a memoir written by Walter Orey of the 1891st Engineer Aviation Battalion shows what the successful attackers had to contend with when the airfield area was finally secured:

Myitkyina and Bhamo
An advance party from the S-3 Section of Headquarters Co. was flown into Myitkyina in October 1944. Their mission was to prepare a site for the Myitkyina East airfield. Within a couple of weeks, A, B, and C Companies were flown into the Myitkyina area. The area was exceedingly difficult to clear because it was pitted with Japanese, Chinese, and American earthen fortifications, fox holes, and all the imaginable gear of battle.[*]

It follows that if David and the professor have found any conflict archaeology at Myitkyina it is most likely to be the material remains of the battle of 1944 and the subsequent occupation by the USAAF.

In short, Andy and the archaeological team do not believe there is any evidence that Spitfires were buried at Myitkyina, but that David and STP are singularly unprepared for the kind of conflict archaeology the documents suggests might well be present, including the presence of unexploded ordnance and human remains.

At 9.30 a.m., our team files into an upstairs meeting room, where dozens of journalists are already seated in chairs facing a table, behind which sit Htoo Htoo, Prof. Soe Thein, David, and Stanley Coombe.

A wartime map of Myitkyina airfield, some photographs and some geophysical plots have been tacked to a partition next to the top table.

Htoo Htoo opens the press conference, describing how STP has worked tirelessly with David to secure permission to excavate the planes. Next, Soe

[*]   www.cbi-theater.com/orey/orey.html

Thein describes their work at Myitkyina, including a geophysical survey he conducted and digging a test shaft. The shaft hit a wooden surface.

'We've found a wooden crate,' David says confidently, 'in the same area where the Americans buried the Spitfires.'

The team lowered a borehole camera inside the 'crate' and took photos, but the muddy water that soon flooded the shaft obscured the images.

'We'll have to pump the water out [of the shaft] before we can give you more information.'

I look at the photographs; the blurry, underwater images that could just as easily be photos from an underwater spelunking expedition. One of the images looks uncannily like a human face. Rod comments that the image reminds him of the 'face in a hole' puppet in David Bowie's new music video, 'Where are we now?'

However, unsurprisingly, several reporters ask why we don't travel first to Myitkyina, to excavate the Spitfire?

Htoo Htoo explains that the team will head there in a few weeks, after we've finished our work at Mingaladon. He then introduces Stanley Coombe, who talks about what he saw at Mingaladon airfield in 1946.

The formal element of the press conference over the event dissolves into an archaeological version of the spin room after a political debate.

Andy and I try to target key outlets such as the *Straits Time* and the BBC in order to try to damp down this latest bushfire of Spitfire-related speculation, while other members of the media make a beeline for David.

No surprise there. He is always good copy and seems to have an instinct for a sound bite.

After the press conference, I call Frazer in London (it's very early in the morning, but he's awake). I explain what Soe Thein told the press and the obvious problems this creates for our framing. He says simply, 'Leave it to me,' and rings off.

Frazer works overtime to kill the story in the UK press. He contacts the BBC, Reuters, AP, and others and explains that our research team was not part of STP's media event and was not involved in the work at Myitkyina. The background established, he asks that they not mention the Yangon project in relation to STP's Myitkyina dig. But Frazer is unable to canvas all the media outlets.

Ever fair and balanced, as its advertising tag line puts it, Fox News in the United States reports that, 'The Search for Missing WW2 Spitfire planes may have hit pay dirt in Burma.'*

---

*   www.foxnews.com/world/search-for-missing-wwii-spitfire-planes-may-have-hit-pay-dirt-in-burma

29

Andy Brockman
The Park Royal Hotel
Yangon
Friday, 11 January 2013

Because Stanley Coombe is the only alleged witness to anything like the burial of Spitfires who we are able to talk to in a way that enables us to frame our own questions, he takes on a key role in the research team's interpretation of the story.

Put simply, Stanley's testimony is Ground Zero. It is the bedrock of David's telling of the legend of Mingaladon. The telling that has convinced everyone from Prime Minister David Cameron to the Burmese government, STP and our own sponsors, Wargaming, that the post-war legend of buried Spitfires may just be true.

None of us doubt Stanley's essential honesty, particularly Rod Scott, who talks to Stanley at length. Thanks to their shared military service, the two men share a brotherhood and companionship that opens up topics and shared experiences the rest of us cannot share, and in the case of some of the things they talk about, memories and demons that we would not want to share.

However, Rod has also been trained in the dark arts of interviewing in a way that would make the interviews admissible in a court of law under the British Police and Criminal Evidence Act, and as a result of his conclusions, and our own research among the documents, much as we respect and like Stanley as an individual, we are beginning to form a picture that suggests his testimony is not all it seems.

Today the machines loaned by JCB have been delivered to the site, but we're still awaiting the digging permits from the government and this hiatus in our work at the airport means that, for the first time since we arrived in Yangon, Martin, Rod and I can put together these suspicions along with all the elements we need to build a picture of the story we now believe we are dealing with.

Rod suggests we adopt a police procedure in order to build and check our chain of evidence. Martin and I agree and we order up a white board and coloured marking pens from the Park Royal's conference support team, turning my hotel room into the CSI Yangon incident room I had talked about at the media call in the Imperial War Museum back in November.

In keeping with the sensitivity of what we are doing, and because we do not want to risk the distraction of the film crew asking us to repeat or rephrase the discussion, we don't tell anyone else what we are up to.

To frame our investigation, we begin by setting out a timeline indicating what the Royal Air Force was doing with its Spitfire squadrons in Southeast Asia during David's time frame of late 1945 to the summer of 1946, adding the three alleged burials, which we code name DC1, DC2 and DC3.

Next we add other documented events such as the dates of Operation Zipper and the movements of RAF squadrons as recorded in the various operations record books we consulted back in London at the National Archives.

These movements include twenty-six Spitfires sent from Rangoon to Seletar Airfield (Singapore) by aircraft carrier in August 1946 and twelve Mark VIIIs which were given to the French, who had just reoccupied French Indochina. More Spitfires left Mingaladon in September 1945 when 273 Squadron left for Saigon via Thailand, in a show of strength in support of the French colonial government.

We also note that the records of 41 Embarkation Unit – the unit that took delivery of all the RAF material arriving at Rangoon docks – show that no crated Spitfires were delivered to Rangoon between August 1945 and April 1946, the period of the alleged burials.

However, we can show thirty-seven Auster light cooperation aircraft shipped from Calcutta, which arrived in Rangoon in two shipments in December 1945 and April 1946 and were duly recorded by 41 EU's clerks, as well as twenty-five Harvard trainers. Both are single-engined aircraft of a similar size to a Spitfire.

Finally, we place this recorded activity against the experiences of Stanley Coombe and Group Captain Maurice Short as recorded in the interviews they gave to our colleagues at Room 608 Productions, including Maurice's observation that he never saw any crated aircraft delivered to RAF Mingaladon while he was on the airfield in the second half of 1945.

As we talk through the chain of evidence, I recall a line from one of the interviews Stanley gave to Room 608.

I take the transcript and I read it aloud to Martin and Rod. During the interview recorded on 2 August 2012, Stanley tells Mark and Anna, 'Well, no, I can't say that I'm actually convinced. I'm only going on another person's word that they were Spitfires in those crates.'[*]

This is our blinding light on the road to Damascus, our lightbulb moment. For anyone who still believes in the legend as David tells it, Stanley's testimony is fatal.

The evidence offered by the key witness, the person who David flew to Burma and who he produces or quotes at every press conference and during every interview, is no better than hearsay, which even Stanley himself does not find totally convincing.

The only secure witness testimony, the foundation of this whole story, is a single conversation between a young squaddie and an RAF erk, both a long way from home, where as Martin Brown now points out, 'The RAF guy might not have known what was in the crate either so he thinks what'll impress him. I know, Spitfires.'

As we work through the implications, things become worse for David's version of the story. Later in the same passage of the interview, Stanley tells the interviewers (our italics):

Um, apparently the records of the planes were all expunged uh, by, at the RAF records place. The English government, or the British government denied all knowledge of the planes themselves, and when, apparently, *I mean, this is only what I was told by David*, when they went to look in the archives at Kew Garden, the pages appertaining to those aircraft or the squadrons that they should have gone to, if they were going to RAF squadrons, had been torn out.[**]

In other words the entire story, from witnessing the actual burial to the conspiracy to cover it up, as reported to the world's media by the key living witness, is David Cundall's invention as told by David to that self-same witness.

---

[*]   Interview with Room 608 Productions, 2 August 2012, at 01:16:30.10
[**]   Interview with Room 608 Productions, 2 August 2012, at 01:24:14.19

Effectively, Stanley has unwittingly absorbed David's story as his own experience and has then repeated the construct in good faith, so that now, whenever an interviewer asks Stanley about what he saw on RAF Mingaladon in 1946, the answer comes not from his experience but we now believe from David Cundall's imagination.

30

Andy Brockman
Airside on the north boundary of Yangon International Airport
Saturday, 12 January 2013

The dragonflies hover over the griddle plate that is Mingaladon International Airport like so many six-legged predator drones.

They watch as Andy Merritt walks the expanse of grass between the runway and the perimeter road-recording line after line of data points at 50cm intervals for the digital terrain map that will be the basis of our research.

Meanwhile, Roger and Adam hammer the electrodes, which will measure electrical resistance in search of deeply buried objects, into the brick-hard earth, hoping the snakes have been scared off by the vibrations.

However, while the computerised map and three-dimensional envisioning of the space below the surface of the airport is taking shape slowly in the cyber world, Andy, Martin and Rod are having a more leisurely stroll across the site, getting their eye in on the real-world relief map of the airport itself – and a number of things are becoming clear.

Comparing the ground with the 1940s air photographs, which Rod has had printed out in the Park Royal and which Andy has on his Blackberry, it is clear David's idea that the 1945 ground surface was buried under 35ft of landfill with the Spitfires at the bottom is simply not the case. In fact, everywhere you look there are relics of RAF Mingaladon, including patches of what appears to be the post-war runway and taxiway visible, some close enough to the surface to trip over.

David Cameron meets Burma's president, Thein Sein, in Nay Pyi Taw. The UK Government has refused to release details of their discussions regarding the Spitfire excavations. (Photographer Soe Zeya Tun/Reuters)

The missing persons? An RAF Spitfire on display next to an Auster communications aircraft at the victory celebration in Rangoon in 1945. (The Imperial War Museum)

The crime scene. The alleged Spitfire burial site photographed by the RAF in spring 1945, with the runway extension already under construction by the Japanese. The Old Prome No. 1 Road curves from lower centre to upper right of frame. The visible blast pens, buildings and bomb damage show the potential for conflict archaeology, and unexploded munitions, on the site. RAF Air Photograph 1944. (The National Archive)

A watercolour by Thomas Hennell showing the extension works on the runway at RAF Mingaladon in autumn 1945. The picture depicts the graders and bulldozers of the Indian Engineers, not the US Seabees/CBs. (RAF Museum Collection)

Burma veterans soldier Stanley Coombe (L) and RAF engineer Maurice Short (R) meet for the first time in autumn 2012. Neither man saw Spitfires buried, but both reported hearing of the burial. (Room 608 Productions)

The press launch of the Burma Spitfires project at the Imperial Museum with Adam Booth's intriguing Red T-shaped anomaly from 2004 on the screen. L–R Andy Brockman, Tracy Spaight, Victor Kysli (CEO Wargaming), David Cundall, Isabel Hunt (Leeds University), Dr Roger Clark, Dr Adam Booth. (Room 608 Productions)

Field director Martin Brown (R), lead archaeologist Andy Brockman (C) and field archaeologist and military finds specialist Rod Scott (L) at the Yangon airport dig site. (Room 608 Productions)

David Cundall (L) and Tracy Spaight (R) talk Spitfires on the dig site at Mingaladon as STP translator Daw Tin Ma 'Auntie' Latt, looks on. (Courtesy of Gavin Longhurst)

Archaeologists Martin Brown (L) and Rod Scott (R) working on 'the whiteboard'. (Andy Brockman)

Spitfire expert Peter Arnold (L) and Dav Cundall (R) at Taukkyan Commonwealt Graves Commission cemetery in January (Andy Brockman)

David Cundall agreed trench locations with Field Director Martin Brown. (Andy Brockman)

Geophysicists Andy Merritt (L) and Dr Adam Booth (R) look at the latest data from the Spitfire dig site. (Andy Brockman)

JCB's big yellow trowel, operated by Manny Machado, begins the surface strip at Yangon airport under the supervision of Field Director Martin Brown. (Andy Brockman)

In addition to the layer of undisturbed alluvial clay, even in the dry season trenches in the area of Yangon Airport that David Cundall claimed in 2013 was the site of the Spitfire burial fill with ground water, both of which making it highly unlikely a deep burial was a practical proposition. (Andy Brockman)

David Cundall came to believe that the Spitfires lay under the 'Red Road'. (Gavin Longhurst)

Opposite page:
Top: 'The Last Supper' at the Park Royal Hotel. L–R: Frazer Nash, Tracy Spaight, Mark Mannucci, Anna Bowers, Gavin Longhurst.

Middle: After the Wargaming brief that their conclusion is that there is no evidence for buried Spitfires at Yangon airport, Frazer Nash (R) faces the media, including the BBC's Fergal Keane (blue shirt) at the Park Royal Hotel.

Bottom: The fateful meeting between Htoo Htoo Saw of STP and senior military and police officers that ended the 2013 Spitfire excavation. (All Room 608 Productions)

'You just have to dig deeper.' David Cundall's 2014 night-time excavations sponsored by the Clarendon Group. No Spitfires were found and none of the work was recorded archaeologically. (Courtesy of STP)

The three key elements of the 2013 buried Spitfires project come together on the dig site; David Cundall's dream, Tracy Spaight's project management for Wargaming and the ancient Buddhist culture of Myanmar embodied by STP's family monk, Poe Poe. (Gavin Longhurst)

Equally, while there are modern earthworks, such as a bank several metres high on the land side of the security fence, nowhere are there signs of the raised or sunken earthworks that would suggest a substantial excavation such as the burial of Spitfires had taken place in the past.

Most important of all, standing on the dig site and looking back to the east of the terminal building, there is a clearly visible gap in the trees leading to the active military section of the airport.

A quick reference to Google Earth and the plan of the 1945 airport shows that this has to be the surviving stub of RAF Mingaladon's Runway 24, the alignment of which was fixed by the British before the Second World War.

Confirming this identification, the taxiway lines up perfectly with the stub of the north-western end of the same runway and its associated taxiway, which can still be seen to either side of the modern Prome Road.

The conclusion of the ground truthing is clear.

While there were clearly earthworks undertaken by the Japanese and the British to extend the runway in the second half of the 1940s, David's contention that the ground surface of the airfield was raised by many feet is not supported by the evidence on the ground.

Certainly, close to the spot where he tells the team he wants to break ground on the site of Adam Booth's L- and T-shaped geophysics plots, the spot where we are told in 2004 the excavator hit timbers before the dig was stopped, there is clear evidence that the ground surface of 2013 is very close to that of 1945.

And there is another disturbing observation to be made.

David has claimed to have seen a photograph of the alleged burial provided to Jim Pearce by the retired Seabee in Florida, and as he describes it, in the photograph a Seabee stands next to a bulldozer while visible to the side of the frame are a row of large crates in a trench. There are hills in the background and the ground is dry.

However, as we can see, RAF Mingaladon, now Yangon International Airport, stands on a plateau with no surrounding hills, and in August 1945, when David claims the burial by the Seabees/CBs took place, other photographs in the Imperial War Museum archive show much of the airfield was ankle-deep in monsoon mud. It follows that, even if the photograph exists, it cannot have been taken at Mingaladon in August 1945.

Airside on the north boundary of Yangon International Airport
Yangon
Sunday, 13 January 2013

From his vantage point in the coarse grass next to the runway, the Nāga is curious. He is used to the passage of the fire engines on exercise and the four-wheel drives of the police battalion on patrol. He has even experienced construction crews, like that currently deployed on the opposite side of the airport near the secure military zone, at work, but these bipedal monkeys with the Western clothes taste different to Jacobson's organ, the astonishingly sensitive twin pits in the roof of each of his two mouths which process the minute molecular traces captured as his tongues flick and lick the air.

The newcomers sound different, too. The strangers speak a different language to the musical cadences of the Burmese with which he is familiar. Indeed, they do not seem to understand Burmese at all because the Burmese female seems to repeat everything said to her in the other tongue and turns the replies into Burmese. Even so the strangers are listening respectfully to the monk known as Poe Poe, as he improvises a shrine on a tree stump between the red road and the airport security fence.

Poe Poe blesses the site, enjoining the snakes not to bother the team. The Nāga agrees to this intercession, because he is curious to see what will happen.

31

Andy Brockman
The Commonwealth War Graves Commission Cemetery
Taukkyan
Monday, 14 January 2013

We are all conscious of the privilege and responsibility of sharing our expedition with a living comrade of the service personnel who are buried here.

Stanley Coombe's modest and genial presence offers us an unbreakable human connection with the comradeship, violence and loss that the Commonwealth War Graves Commission Cemetery at Taukkyan represents and, understandably, Mark wants to record our pilgrimage for the documentary.

For my own part I am happy to leave that side of the day to Martin Brown. Thanks to his own deeply moral outlook and his work with the No Man's Land and Plug Street Projects in France and Belgium, making the successful TV series *Finding the Fallen*, Martin has long experience of dealing with sensitive issues relating to discussing lost military personnel on camera.

I know also that as a soldier to whom such places and ceremonies have a particular and current resonance, Rod Scott too will not allow anything he feels in any way disrespectful to be recorded. Particularly so given the presence of Stanley Coombe.

The other reason for my absenting myself from this part of the shoot is the fact I also badly need some emotional downtime to process what has been happening.

For the sake of the project I want to try to connect with this piece of Myanmar's history at the interface of an Imperial past in physical and intellectual retreat and an unknown future.

I wander up and down the rows of bronze plaques set on coarse grey concrete markers, which seem to draw your eye down to the earth of Burma, noting names at random.

Private Christopher Anodebe of the Nigeria Regiment; Private Namo Dagarti of the Gold Coast Regiment; Sepoy Sardar Khan of the Royal Indian Army Service Corps; Naik Abdul Rakhman, 12th Frontier Force Regiment, aged just 17. Soldiers who died far from home, paying the ultimate price of retaining an Empire in the name of a King, Emperor and government even further away in London.

I note also the names of British-born personnel commemorated here, including members of the RAF. I stop by the grave of Squadron Leader Robert Dagnall, who worked his way through the ranks to become acting Commanding Officer of ground attack specialists 211 Squadron. Squadron Leader Dagnall was killed in action on 13 January 1945 along with his wireless operator/navigator, Flying Officer Ronald Stenning, flying a Beaufighter Mk X. The men were killed when their aircraft was hit by Japanese ground fire while making an attack on a gun position close to the railway junction at Prome. Buried initially close to the crash site, their resting place was located by a graves registration unit in 1953 and they were transferred to rest next to each other at Taukkyan.

Elsewhere, someone from John Hampden Grammar School in High Wycombe, Buckinghamshire, has left a memorial card and poppies to remember an old boy of the school; 24-year-old Derrick Darville of 2nd Battalion, King's Own Scottish Borderers. Derrick's grave is lost somewhere in the area of the Admin Box, where he was killed in action on 23 January 1944.

However, on the return journey the archaeologist in me notices it is not only the young servicemen whose remains lie in Myanmar who are a memorial to the Burma campaign. There are more material remains, too.

Entering the outskirts of Yangon, I photograph a long boundary fence where, instead of wooden planks, the horizontal bars consist of dozens of uncut sections of the same pierced steel plank that was laid by 14th Army's engineers in an effort to try to keep the roads, runways and taxiways of Mingaladon open in the monsoon season of 1945. It is the same PSP over which the wheels of 273 and 610 Squadron's Spitfire Mk VIIIs may have rolled during the monsoon of summer 1945, which forms another fence at the dig site at Mingaladon.

Closer to the centre of town, we pass a more substantial boundary from the colonial period. This is the red brick wall and watchtowers of the colonial-period infantry barracks, complete with its loopholes for rifles placed to ward off invasion from rival powers and from the local population in time of riot and unrest.

Video and Audio Recordings of Peter Arnold and David Cundall
The Commonwealth War Graves Commission Cemetery
Taukkyan
14 January 2013

While I am wandering and wondering among the line of grave markers and Martin Brown is discussing with Stanley Coombe whether Stanley will recite Laurence Binyon's 'For the Fallen' with its simple yet heartbreaking opening line, 'They shall not grow old as we that are left grow old', or the resonant Kohima Prayer, at our impromptu act of Remembrance, David Cundall is passing time with Spitfire historian and author Peter Arnold.

Peter has been very helpful to us in the past, in particular passing on a copy of an invaluable archive of air photographs of Mingaladon taken by the RAF to the research team. However, as the project has advanced, we have come to see him as a true believer in David's vision and as his outrider in social media, in particular on the Key Publications Historic Aviation Forum, where he posts regularly as an expert commentator on all things Spitfire and now all things buried Spitfire.

Later we will also come to see Peter as David's unofficial conduit to the media pack at the Park Royal. However, this afternoon the two aviation enthusiasts are on their own and the video and audio recordings made by cameraman Andreas and sound recordist Brian show that they are discussing the technicalities of landing a Spitfire, about which David seems somewhat unsure.

This leads to a discussion of Peter's sense of pride in being a member of one of the world's most elite groups, the Spitfire Owners' Club. Then to reminiscing about his first recovery of a Spitfire airframe, which he describes as a pile of scrap.

Peter demonstrates the cost of putting a Spitfire back into the air.

'Just the propeller hub, do you know what a propeller hub is worth? Fifty, sixty thousand pounds. Amazing.'

'And they cost a fraction of that in 19...' says David attempting to turn Peter's monologue into a conversation, but Peter is on a roll.

'You can't make a Spitfire propeller hub for sixty thousand pounds,' Peter says, recalling that twenty years earlier pioneer Spitfire collector Charles Church had been charged just twenty thousand pounds for the same item.

Peter explains how such parts can be re-made, sold on and re-used.

'There's just a level of corrosion you see, which says, yep, yep, that's OK and a bit more, no, that's scrap metal.'

Their conversation marks them out as being of the generation of young men who grew up post-war with a love of aviation in general and the Spitfire in particular.

It was a love born of the glamour of an aviation industry at the cutting edge of technology and basking in the heroic legacy embodied in the legend of 'the Few' of the Battle of Britain, and perhaps the frustration that they had no heroic crusade of their own. Instead Peter and David's generation inherited an Empire in retreat and the grubby, proxy wars of the Cold War where the sublimely functional AK-47 and unheroic improvised explosive device took the place of duels in the sky at the controls of a weapon of beauty, flown in a clean cause.

Mark Mannucci joins them, putting an opening question, 'Where are we guys? What is this place?'

Peter does not realise that Mark has not heard the conversation that has just ended and says they are describing his home where he kept his Spitfire projects.

David, however, is able to change gear and, with his habitual slow delivery giving a sense of gravitas, he says, 'We are at the Commonwealth War Graves Cemetery just north of Yangon and if you look up there it states that there are 27,000 soldiers buried here with no known grave, plus all the other ones out there with a gravestone.'

David expands on the theme, 'I've been here many times,' he says 'and every time I come here I get this feeling. It just sends a tingle down my spine to be honest, that all these people died for a cause.

'And when you actually ask the reason why they died nobody can tell you, because the borders really have not changed that much either in Europe or in Asia and the losers of the war seem to have done better than the winners. Like Japan and like Germany.'

'Have you been walking the grounds?' Mark asks.

'We've been walking the grounds looking at some of the names and some of the ages of these people, and they're 19, 20, 21 and these people have been deprived of their youth, and they have died for a cause that I can't really explain to be honest.'

'And you've been reflecting on that?' Mark questions.

'Oh yes,' David responds. 'These people ...'

'What have you been talking about?' Mark interrupts, as always wanting to focus his subject's remarks into something that might be usable in the editing suite.

'We've been talking about the war and why these people died, and …'

'How young they were,' offers Peter, picking up the theme.

'And how young they were,' David echoes, adding, 'and whether or not the youth of today would do the same things of the youth of 1940, 42, in that region. And I think they would.'

'I think they would too,' Peter overlaps.

'I think they would not let their colleagues down,' David concludes.

'Thank you,' Mark says. He has the material he wants.

'Thank you, pleasure,' David says in closure.

As Mark moves off the camera continues to record.

'I hope I've said that right?' David says.

There is a pause, then Peter ventures, 'I hadn't realised they had gathered all this stuff and I thought he was asking about what we had actually been talking about.' Meaning they had been talking about Spitfires.

As the crew moves elsewhere, Brian's radio microphones continue to record as Peter and David return to discussing Spitfires.

Peter explains that the Griffon-engined Spitfires such as the Mk XIVs alleged to be buried at Mingaladon are less desirable to warbird collectors, but he thinks there might be a conversion that the UK Civil Aviation Authority would accept that would return the Mk XIV Spitfire to the guise of its immediate ancestor, the more desirable Mk VIIIs, which were flown in combat in Burma.

Crucially the conversion might be viable financially as it would offer economies of scale.

'Well the only offer I've had is £6 million to restore twelve, as a squadron,' David says, 'which is not enough money. Not nearly enough money.'

Peter suggests some numbers based on a fixed price restoration contract, but David remains cautious.

'I haven't got that funding at the moment because I've got nothing to show.'

'You might have the equity in the aeroplanes,' Peter suggests.

David still resists seeing his project in terms of the hard figures that Peter is pitching.

He is also concerned that he risks his role in the project being diluted by the people who have access to the cash needed to undertake such an ambitious project. People such as Peter's former client, and David's near nemesis, Steve Brooks.

'Well what my dream is, is to have a flying squadron, but I don't want to lose control. I don't know how many aeroplanes I can sell to restore twelve. So if we are looking at £15 million and I've got twenty, I have got to sell eight for 15 million and that is way over the top.'

'It's not going to work,' David concludes, 'so I am doing nothing at the moment. Just getting it right and hopefully waiting for a few offers, which may or may not come.'

He adds reflectively, 'This is taking me back, Peter. I had no money in April. I told Brooks to clear off … I thought, "Well I've buggered it up." Then that fella [Tracy] phoned me. $750,000, who's got $750,000?'*

The unedited multi-channel sound recording shows that at the same moment that Peter and David are discussing the seven-figure value of restored Spitfires, Rod Scott is talking to Stanley Coombe, who has lived with memories no one should have to live with for almost six decades.

Rod indicates the graves.

'There's not enough Spitfires in the fucking world to justify one of these … I don't do this for money, I do this for them,' he says.

That evening back in the Park Royal, a rip-roaring argument takes place in the Room 608 production suite. Brian has played back the audio recording of Peter apparently discussing with David how to make the recovery of the buried Spitfires possible, even profitable, while they stood under the memorial to the missing at the largest British and Commonwealth military cemetery in Myanmar, and then appearing to lay down a smokescreen to obscure that discussion, with David claiming on camera that they were discussing the loss of too many young men.

The production team suggest confronting Peter and David with the evidence of what might be seen as, at best, poor taste and at worst crass insensitivity and a fixation with the financial rewards of finding the aircraft rather than their historical value.

However, the archaeology team will not compromise their objectivity by being seen to indulge in an ad hominem attack on Peter and on David, who is still their client, particularly as the bulk of the audio was recorded because the microphones were left open and not as part of a formal interview.

To their credit, Room 608 drop the idea. But that lies in the future.

This afternoon Stanley Coombe chooses to recite the Kohima prayer.

And as we are heading back to the hotel, Auntie Latt calls to say that the government has finally issued the permit, so we can begin the excavations in the morning.

---

*   By the terms of Wargaming's agreement with David Cundall, the bulk of the funds would only be released if the planes were actually found.

PART THREE

BURMESE DAZE

A Hole In The Ground

In which, as recounted by Bernard Cribbins,
a group of salt of the earth English workers set out
with the best of intentions to dig said hole
where instructed, only to be told repeatedly
that it is the wrong shape,
or is being dug in the wrong place.

32

Tracy Spaight
The Spitfire Dig Site
Airside on the north boundary of Yangon International
Airport (Formerly RAF Mingaladon)
15 January 2013

The geophysicists have a problem.

Over the past several days, they have resurveyed the entire 2004 grid, using differential GPS, electrical resistivity tomography, and magnetometry, but the geophysical responses have all flatlined.

The T and L-shaped sections David so confidently identified as the burial location have both disappeared!

'Whatever was causing the T section anomaly is now not there in the ground,' Adam explains to David, who is sitting beside the geophysicists under the gazebos STP's workers have erected for us.

'This is where all the eyewitnesses are pointing, from there, to there,' David says, indicating the area of the 2004 survey on Andy Merritt's laptop display.

'My advice at this point is fire up the JCB and let's dig some holes. We'll find out what it all means,' says Roger.

Manny climbs into the cab of the JCB and begins scraping the ground with the digger bucket, while the archaeology team monitors from a short distance away. They start the dig about 100ft from the runway, in a line with the 46-N landing light that marks the edge of the 2004 survey grid.

They soon hit a hard flat surface.

'Martin, I've got an edge here mate,' says Rod, as he uses a trowel to scrape dirt from the surface Manny has just exposed.

'First moment of breaking ground, and we're potentially getting a really important feature that relates to the whole story, the whole narrative, the whole theory,' Martin says.

The Burmese workers use shovels to clear off more of the topsoil and vegetation, revealing a broad flat surface.

'The whole of this here is the tarmac surface. Welcome to the 1945 runway!' Rod announces like a tour guide.

'Yeah look at that, tarmac. Red crushed brick that's your hardcore layer and then you're on to sand,' Martin says, describing the layers underneath.

'They're digging in a place of interest,' concedes David, who is standing nearby. 'But they're doing it their way. The archaeological way. They're taking it layer after layer. After two hours we've found a piece of concrete,' he says dismissively. 'What I'd like them to do is dig down, break into a box, and show the world an aeroplane.'

'We've discovered where the 1940s are, David,' Rod says cheerfully, when David walks over to look.

'That means we can discount this bit of the area,' Martin says, indicating the tarmac. 'Because you're not going to bury stuff under a runway.'

'No, we want to be looking over there,' David says, pointing towards the perimeter fence.

'If I carry on the strip ...' Martin begins.

'Back that way,' he and David say together, both pointing towards the perimeter fence.

'Then you may find something thing 50 yards over there,' David finishes.

'Well ...' Martin says, calculating that 50 yards will take us well outside the area of the T and L-shaped sections David had indicated as the burial locations.

'At least 50 yards.'

Manny fires up the JCB excavator again and begins extending the trench towards the red road and the perimeter fence.

Earth begins to pile up along the side of the trench. Suddenly, Martin's voice rings out excitedly.

'Look at that fucker!'

We all run over to take a look. A crowd of Burmese diggers, the monk Poe Poe, Stanley Coombe, and others gather by the side of the trench to peer into the deepening hole.

There's a large structural timber in the digger bucket. Manny deposits the timber on the ground and Andy comes over to examine it.

'The actual box is under 25ft of soil,' David says to the cameras, with the trench and the timber as the backdrop to the shot.

'That's a lot of weight for a box to carry. They put some sort of wooden roof over it to support it,' David says.

'What we've got here is a very strong structural timber that was loose in the topsoil, in the overburden,' Andy says.

'Or is a used timber that they've borrowed from something else?' David suggests.

'It's a structural timber of some kind from a very strong structure. Our guess would be it's from some sort of bunker or something like that,' Andy says.

'What the eyewitnesses said,' David says, trying to tie the timbers to his secret burial thesis. 'They brought some big square teak timbers to put the boxes on. This could be a broken piece, I don't know, that's actually under the boxes.'

Andy is in the back of the shot, shaking his head.

'Or it could be some sort of structure, to hold the shuttering, to stop it from collapsing. But it is consistent with what I found before,' David says.

Manny deepens the hole for a while and then stops. Martin and Rod climb down into the trench to explain what we're looking at.

'What we've got, if we've taken off the top foot, we've got loads of stuff, there's brick, there's coke for fuel, that's all human action that's deposited all of this, right down to our lovely brick here, underneath it, where the natural subsoil kicks in — there it is, it's blue, it's sticky, it's plastic. You can make a pot from that. And that's geology!' says Martin.

'Geologists, how old is blue clay?' Rod asks, although he knows the answer already.

'It could be anything from a few hundred years to 20,000,' says Roger Clark, looking down into the trench at Martin and Rod.

'So if that's an undisturbed layer of this stuff and even if it's the newest stuff, that's only a few hundred years old,' Martin says, pointing at the ground for emphasis, 'there cannot be anything from World War II buried underneath.'

The words hang in the air. There's nothing buried here.

'What's interesting about this soil though,' Martin continues, 'It's fairly heterogeneous. It's all different. And that's consistent with it's come out, it sat around for not very long, and it's gone back in again.'

Manny, who is wearing his 'just dig it' T-shirt, weighs in on what he's seeing from the JCB cab.

'See it in the slope going up right through there,' he says, pointing at the trench wall.

'Someone has dug off in that direction, as far as I can tell.'

With the archaeologists and the expert machine operator in full agreement, the conclusion is inescapable.

Someone excavated here during or after Adam Booth's 2004 survey.

'Martin, get out!' Rod Scott shouts urgently.

Martin scrambles out of the trench as the rest of us see with horror the slight but gathering movement which Rod's experienced eye has already picked up, prompting the warning.

In the way of the nāga snake shedding his skin, a slab of soil and clay on the west face of the trench sloughs off in an awful slow-motion collapse, smothering the spot where Martin had stood moments before.

33

Tracy Spaight
The Spitfire Dig Site
Airside on the north boundary of Yangon International
Airport (Formerly RAF Mingaladon)
16 January 2013

It is only 9 a.m. but it is already baking hot.

'Yesterday we had a very good day,' Martin begins, addressing our Burmese workforce, the geophysicists and the archaeologists gathered together in the shade of the gazebos that have been erected by STP next to the shipping container and which now form our base of operations at the airport.

'As you know we opened a big hole, having spoken to Adam and David, and they confirmed that that was a good place to start. The results of yesterday were interesting. We've got areas where we know there were no burials. We made enormous progress. Thank you all. If we have another good day, we'll be a long way down the road.'

Martin asks if David would like to add anything but he shakes his head.

Everyone disperses to begin the day's work. The geologists head up the field to extend their survey another 100m beyond the 2004 grid. Manny fires up the JCB to extend the trench in the direction that Martin and David had agreed to yesterday afternoon. The archaeologists gather by the trench to monitor the digging. By mid-morning the trench is a good 50ft long and 10ft deep.

There is still no sign of boxes or aeroplanes.

David sits by himself under the gazebos. He strikes up a conversation with Adam, who has returned for water.

'I think if we want to have a Spitfire up to tell people before Sunday, we have to dig along this red road,' David says.

'Do you know where they are along the red road?' Adam asks.

'No, not accurately,' David replies.

'Well, that's the problem isn't it, it's a long road,' Adam says, shading his eyes and looking off into the distance. The road extends as far as the eye can see, east and west.

'Where along here do you think it is,' asks Adam.

'Just come here please,' David says.

They walk a short way up the road to the east and stop.

'Maybe in this area,' David says. 'This side of the fence.'

'Or maybe that side of the fence,' he says, turning and pointing beyond the perimeter fence. This area falls outside the dig plan we'd submitted to the government in the autumn.

'We could dig down and if we hit a box that's fine,' he says, and then vents his frustration with the archaeologists.

'I want to make one point clear. Yesterday we found some pieces of wood, we found some concrete, and we found a nail,' he says dismissively.

'Well, you OK'd this,' Adam reminds him.

'I OK'd it because the archaeologists wanted to do that,' he says, forgetting all his previous assertions that his eyewitnesses all indicated that location.

'I just want them to dig in the right area,' he says.

'I know there's pressures to find Spitfires, but we have to adopt the right approach,' Adam says, a note of exasperation creeping into his voice.

David thanks him and then wanders off to find Stanley.

'We have to make progress,' David says to the camera. 'We can't rely on one site. If they're not there, for any reason, we have to have plan B.'

He finds Stanley and they walk back to the area David has just showed to Adam. Stanley recounts what he remembers from 1946.

'This is the road,' Stanley says, gesturing towards the gap in the trees beyond the fence. 'We were going in a lorry, up here. In the V, over there, I would say just on the other side of those trees, that's where I saw the crates,' Stanley says.

I join David and Stanley, to see what they're discussing. David begins pitching me the new location.

'There's every evidence to prove that there's something under this area here,' he says. 'We carried out some ground-penetrating radar over this "red road", as we call it. We found some very interesting images – they are aeroplane shapes, even to a point, in some sort of container,' David says.

I don't put much credence in his new location, since up until now he has been emphatic about the T- and L-shaped sections in the 2004 survey.

'Whereabouts?' I ask, shading my eyes and gazing down the airfield.

'Along the red road, and on the other side of the fence,' he says, sweeping his arm over a stretch of ground large enough to bury all the aircraft on the inventory of SEAC in 1945.

'Do we know what infrastructure is under here,' I ask, worried that if we dig in this area we may inadvertently knock out the power for the runway lights.

'No we don't. We just dig down where we find some anomalies,' David says. 'It's hit or miss.'

I'm stunned for a moment.

David's throwaway comment seems to pretty much sum up his whole approach to the excavation.

At around two o'clock in the afternoon, a convoy of black SUVs with tinted windows, and an escort of trucks full of armed military police, pull up to our dig site trailing red dust. Auntie Latt tells us that it is the local chief of police and the head of the Yangon district government.

The police jump from their trucks and tell us to stop working. Manny shuts down the JCB and we file off the dig site. We take shelter under the gazebos, wondering what's happening and whispering in worried undertones.

Wearing immaculately pressed dark green military fatigues, the commander of Yangon district approaches Htoo Htoo, who then walks with the official around the site, gesturing to the earthworks. They confer in Burmese while an aide shades the official from the intense sun with an umbrella.

Auntie Latt explains to us that the reason for the unannounced visit is that local papers have reported that we are digging too close to the runway, or even tunnelling underneath it.

We watch as one of the uniformed men measures from the edge of the runway to our trench. The officials discuss amongst themselves and with Htoo Htoo and then everyone piles back into their vehicles, disappearing back down the road in further clouds of red dust.

Htoo Htoo tells us that the dig is over for the day, so we pack up our gear and head back to the hotel.

Had we but known it, as we travel the 8 miles back to the Park Royal through the Yangon rush hour, beaten by Burmese bureaucracy, we are also replicating the travails of another archaeological expedition a century and a half earlier.

Jerusalem
1867

Captain Montagu Brownlow Parker is not the first British officer to attempt to excavate the remains of Biblical Jerusalem. In fact, he intends to continue where one of his most illustrious predecessors left off.

General Sir Charles Warren, GCMG, KCB, FRS, Royal Engineers (1840–1927) is possibly most famous for failing to stop the nocturnal activities of Jack the Ripper in the autumn of 1888 while Commissioner of the Metropolitan Police, but less well known is his role as a pioneering archaeologist in the Holy Land of Palestine twenty years earlier.

Then simply Lieutenant Warren Royal Engineers, Charles Warren travels to Jerusalem in 1867 at the behest of the newly constituted Palestine Exploration Fund (PEF).

Educated at Cheltenham College, Sandhurst, and 'the Shop' – the Royal Military Academy, Woolwich – Warren is chosen for the task mostly on account of his recent perilous survey of the Rock of Gibraltar, much of which is carried out with the young officer dangling high above the port on the end of a rope, notebook in hand.

In 1867 the skills and equipment of a military engineer and those of an archaeologist are so similar as to be interchangeable, although whether this is down to the nature of the standard archaeological methodology of the period, or the number of military officers who take up archaeology as a pastime befitting an officer and a gentleman, is a matter for debate.

Certainly, the input of military men is bringing a new discipline and organisation to the world of archaeology, with an archaeological expedition now resembling nothing so much as a campaign by one of the many expeditionary forces that London dispatches around the globe to bring 'civilisation' to the natives and marketing opportunities to the entrepreneurs of London, Manchester, Liverpool and Glasgow.

In those terms Warren's expedition is a small one, but it is funded to the tune of £300 by the private Palestine Exploration Fund, with the promise of further regular payments to follow. The money will fund Warren's fieldwork team, including an expedition photographer, a surveyor and, as befits an officer who knows that the British Army is actually run by its cadre of seasoned non-commissioned officers, a trusted NCO from his work on Gibraltar, Sergeant Birtles.

The task that the PEF has set Warren and his team is no less than to assess the authenticity of the traditional site of the Resurrection in the Church of the Holy Sepulchre and to investigate the site of the Temple of Solomon and the location and topography of the ancient City of David. However, the expedition does not get off to the easiest of starts.

Unlike the British Embassy in Yangon in 2013, Noel Temple Moore, the British consul in Jerusalem, has not been let in on the plans for Warren's expedition. This is an oversight because the consul is acutely conscious of the strategic importance of Palestine as the northern half of the hinge between Egypt and the rest of the Middle East, dividing along the new Suez Canal that is about to open. Consequently, Moore refuses to intervene when, in the absence of permission to excavate from Constantinople, the Ottoman governor receives complaints that the British intend to excavate the third holiest site in Islam, the Haram al-Sharif, which the Christian and Jewish inhabitants of Jerusalem call Temple Mount.

Undismayed, Warren, with the confidence of one trained to arbitrate between anyone from tribal elders to heads of state, and in the expectation that Her Majesty's uniform will be respected, suggests to the governor that the instructions from Constantinople must have been merely delayed, so where is the harm in anticipating the wishes of the Sultan and allowing the expedition to proceed?

To Moore's surprise, the tactic works and the Ottoman Governor of Jerusalem, Izzet Pasha, gives the British team permission to excavate anywhere in the immediate vicinity of the monumental retaining walls of Temple Mount.

Hiring a gang of local workers to undertake the hard labour, Warren orders an excavation hard against the southern wall of the sacred site.

Soon Warren's digging crew uncover a passage that appears to lead under the Haram al-Sharif itself. However, the clang of sledgehammers on crowbars has been noticed by worshippers in the al-Aqsa mosque, who fear their sanctuary is about to be invaded by the infidels, and Warren's team are forced to halt their work and retreat in the face of a shower of stones.

As a soldier, Warren knows it is futile to try to continue an attack when your enemy is well supplied with ammunition, has high morale and holds the high ground.

In response, Governor Izzet Pasha calls out the city garrison to calm the situation, at the same time rescinding the permission to excavate that he had granted just days earlier.

Warren's plan has not survived first contact with Ottoman bureaucracy and the religious sensibilities of Jerusalemites.

Within days the Sultan's firman (decree) arrives, presenting Warren with yet another dilemma. The wording of the document has been drafted in

Constantinople by people who clearly have no idea of how Warren intends
to achieve his aims, and very little idea of the geography of the Province
of Palestine. The document manages to confuse the mosque in Hebron
with the Haram al-Sharif. Worse, the firman appears to actually forbid
excavations anywhere near any religious shrine. Clearly, if it is published
or circulated the Imperial firman would have the effect of closing down
Warren's expedition permanently.

Warren's solution is another diplomatic masterpiece. He announces that
the firman, which everyone expects will grant him permission to excavate,
has arrived, but he does not publish the text. He then begins work close to
the church of the Holy Sepulchre.

This time the opposition comes from the commander of the Jerusalem garrison. Ottoman troops close the excavation at gunpoint.

Undaunted, Warren shifts his operation to the southern slopes of the city,
which in 1867 at least have the advantage of not being occupied by any of
Jerusalem's rival religious groupings. The new location will also allow Warren
to test the extent of the boundaries of Jerusalem in previous eras.

However, having been faced with this succession of diplomatic head-
aches, Consul Moore withdraws support, leaving the young officer to his
own devices.

By now everyone knows that if people in the coffee shops of Jerusalem
start talking about the latest activities of 'the mole', they are talking about
the British Army officer called Warren and he is the centre of some
disturbing rumours.

Warren has been using small gunpowder charges to help sink shafts more
than 130ft to the bedrock beneath the accumulated walls, roads, rubble and
water cisterns of the city. The entrance of the first shaft is camouflaged by a
large cactus and this element of subterfuge adds to the innate suspicion of any
such activity on the part of foreigners. The word on the streets of the Old
City is that the Englishman is storing barrels of gunpowder under the Haram
al-Sharif and that one day the shafts and vaults will be blown up, taking the
third most sacred site in Islam with them.

With the need for security now paramount, Warren and his faithful companion, Sergeant Birtles, take to working alone, guarded by a small group of
Muslim friends whose task is to distract anyone who takes too close an interest in the sounds coming from the shafts and passages under the city.

Warren records the archaeology they discover, 'It was very exciting; we had
visions of wonderful vaults beyond us with sculpture and what not, but, when

we had got through the wall, we only found earth against it with rough face, or rather no face.'

Expressing disappointment at the negative result, Warren describes how he and Birtles were also forced to escape the sticks and stones of another suspicious group of men, whom he had earlier persuaded to set off on the hunt for a large, but factitious, edible lizard.

'As soon as we had done the work, we got our tools out of the passage in the same secret manner we had brought them in and appeared under the clear winter sky – two very grubby-looking mortals, for we had been groping head foremost in the earth,' Warren records.

Knowing that their state would arouse suspicion, Warren and Birtles next attempted to clean themselves up, only to discover that the men who had been sent after the lizard had realised they had been duped and had returned to hunt their original quarry, the two archaeologists.

'It was very exciting.' Warren writes of the narrow escape with classic *Boy's Own* British understatement. 'But we had completed our work and were not to be torn in pieces on this occasion.'

He adds that were he on active service, Sergeant Birtles would win the Albert Medal or even the Victoria Cross for courage in the face of the enemy above and beyond the call of duty.

But this level of work and risk cannot be maintained. There are constant problems with funding and even Warren's return to London to try to wring more money out of the Honourable Secretary of the Palestine Exploration Fund, George Grove, only results in an intermittently adequate flow of cash to Jerusalem.

Warren is also desperately short of timber to prop up the increasingly complex series of old and new tunnels and shafts that now honeycomb the Old City. He fears that any accident undermining a building, or worse, taking life and limb, will give the new Ottoman Governor, Nazif Pasha, the perfect excuse to shut down his operation permanently.

Adding to the difficulties, the faithful and brave Sergeant Birtles becomes ill and is invalided back to Britain to convalesce.

Ultimately the decision regarding how to continue is taken out of Warren's hands. A new firman arrives from Constantinople banning all excavations in Jerusalem and this time Warren is not able to keep the content secret.

Warren returns finally to England, his work in Jerusalem at an end. It is not before time. According to the foreword to the first publication of his results in November 1870, he too is exhausted by his efforts and wracked by fever.

His achievement is to have dug, mapped and drawn dozens of shafts and tunnels that are effectively an archaeological biopsy of the 4,000-year history of Jerusalem and, while he has not found any of the rumoured lost treasure of the Temple, he has found some pottery handles upon which are painted the words 'Property of the King' in Biblical Hebrew. They are the first genuine finds from the Biblical period ever to be excavated and reported scientifically anywhere in the lands of the Book.

Warren has also seen the Palestine Exploration Fund transform itself from an enthusiasts' club, reliant on philanthropic donations, to a professionally run operation drawing on regular funding derived from selling subscriptions.

Like the 2013 Burma Spitfires project, the fund is assisted in this endeavour by an increasing amount of coverage in the popular press, including an article by one of the greatest journalists of the nineteenth century, William Howard Russell. The pen pictures of Warren's work by journalists such as Russell are partnered by the sketches and engravings of the artist William Simpson, working for the *Illustrated London News*.

And Warren has achieved this archaeological milestone without loss of life or causing a religious riot.

It is one of the foundations of professional Biblical archaeology, a cause that will remain dear to British hearts for the next eighty years.

In August 1909 Captain Parker begins his own campaign of excavations on the slopes of Mount Ophel by ordering his work gang to reopen a shaft first dug by Sir Charles in 1867.

However, Captain Parker has not just learned to make use of Warren's archaeology. He has learned from the way Warren handled his relations with the Ottoman bureaucrats and that a successful outcome to his own expedition will entail a generous helping of what the new Jewish immigrants to Palestine from poverty and pogroms in Poland and the Russian Pale would call 'chutzpah'.

Of course, a sense of self-confidence bordering on entitlement comes naturally to an aristocratic British officer such as Captain Parker. After all, even in a city as steeped in religion as Jerusalem, his presence should bring to mind the words of the Reverend John Aylmer, who wrote in 1559, 'God is English.'

34

```
Tracy Spaight
'Basecamp'
The Room 608 Productions Suite
Park Royal Hotel
Yangon
16 January 2012
```

We gather at 'basecamp' – Room 608's production suite at the Park Royal Hotel. Today's surprise visit by the military police rattled us all. We're getting a first-hand glimpse of how the Burmese political and economic system actually works.

As Carmen Martinez of the US Embassy in Yangon wrote in 2004, in a leaked confidential assessment that is both concise and brutally frank:

> Burma's military leadership thrives atop a flourishing patronage system that dates back hundreds of years. The junta holds the key to huge success or crushing failure for those in business, the military, or civil service, but only rewards the most loyal and pliable. Such an environment breeds fear, suspicion, and above all begrudging support for the status quo. Unfortunately, this climate makes it very difficult to expect that the generals will be challenged by disgruntled members of the military or business community. After all, who will be the first to risk his position and family's future welfare by taking a stand?*

---

*   US Embassy Yangon intelligence Report dated 25 February 2004.

Our colleagues at STP are dependent on that system and are now utterly exposed by the fact of their accepting everything David has claimed at face value.

This presents Wargaming as the project sponsor, Room 608 Productions and the archaeological team with a sharp ethical dilemma, and it is a dilemma compounded by the potential for our participation to be perceived as a throwback to the colonial period, where the local economy and the local people who make it function are exploited for the primary benefit of foreigners.

Htoo Htoo calls us at around 5.30 p.m. to tell us that the dig has been suspended while the government confers. Htoo Htoo tells us that he is driving to Nay Pyi Taw now to meet with the Minister of Transportation and the other members of the Spitfire committee about how and when we can proceed. He confirms that we won't be allowed to dig tomorrow.

I have the unenviable task of breaking the news to David.

I decide to tell him in person, so I head down to his room on the fourth floor. He answers the door and we chat briefly in the hall. I can see Peter Arnold and David Rose (a reporter from *The Telegraph*) sitting in chairs in the room. I'm annoyed about this private briefing since David is supposed to coordinate all media interviews with us, as the project sponsors.

I tell David that the dig has been suspended and Htoo Htoo is in discussions with the government about whether and when we can continue. David's face grows red with anger. He blames me for blowing his big chance and slams the door in my face. I can hear him tell Peter and David Rose in a loud voice, 'We've lost it!'

My immediate reaction is, 'This is my thanks for all my efforts over the past year?'

I re-join Mark, Anna, Gavin and Chloe at basecamp and recount David's outburst. I'm not in the mood to talk with him, but I agree that it has to be done. Anna rings David's room and asks him to come down to join us at dinner at the hotel restaurant.

Fifteen minutes later he does so. He apologises to me, but it is perfunctory.

'Basecamp'
The Room 608 Productions Suite
Park Royal Hotel
Yangon
17 January 2012

Since we're not allowed to dig today Andy, Martin and Rod hunker down in Andy's hotel room to continue their whiteboard analysis of the events of 1945–46. The rest of us head out to shoot some B-roll for the film.

We also arrange for the expensive geophysics equipment we brought from the UK to be quietly removed from the dig site in case we are not allowed back.

Htoo Htoo arrives at the hotel around 5 p.m. looking tired. He has just returned from Nay Pyi Taw, where he worked late into the night with the Ministry of Transport to hammer out a new agreement on how to conduct the dig going forward. He is joined by Auntie Latt, who translates for us.

Htoo Htoo tells us that the government will allow us to resume digging on Friday. That's the good news. The bad news is that we can only dig with shovels! They will allow us to use also the JCB excavator and backhoe, but with another catch. They can be deployed only at night, between 10 p.m. and 4 a.m. (when the airport is closed).

The archaeology team is understandably not keen on the new restrictions. Digging in the dark is difficult and dangerous, not to mention borderline unethical as the conditions would make it more likely that we might fail to spot, and thus destroy, important archaeology. Not that archaeological ethics are the biggest issue when we might also miss unexploded ordnance and blow ourselves up.

At the same time, we recognise that we won't have another opportunity to complete the fieldwork. It's now or never. We discuss whether we can illuminate the site sufficiently to continue without compromising safety.

Htoo Htoo speaks for a while and Auntie Latt translates. She tells us that in addition to the runway proximity issue, the government is concerned about the scale of the excavation.

'They don't want you to make many trenches but to have the most possible spot and only when we are sure that something is there then we excavate. Because making trenches here and there and everywhere with all the mounds of dirt it doesn't look good,' she says.

Htoo Htoo and Auntie Latt depart and the archaeology team heads off to dinner in the Park Royal's Japanese restaurent, while the rest of us debate how to manage David, who the team perceives as becoming increasingly erratic in the wake of our discovering the previous excavation at the 2004 survey location where he had told us to dig.

Predictably, David doesn't agree with Andy's whiteboard findings, which we've shared with him, and since Tuesday he and Peter Arnold have effectively formed their own distinct cabal. They remain convinced that the crated Spitfires are buried at Mingaladon, if not at the T and L-shaped section then perhaps beyond the perimeter fence or somewhere along the dirt road that runs parallel to the runway.

Adam Docker takes a photograph of us at that moment. We're all sitting on one side of the conference table, which is draped with a white tablecloth and covered with dishes. Even the film crew is at the table, since they have been pulled unwittingly into the swirling maelstrom threatening to overwhelm the project. There are no observers any longer. We are all participants and players.

Adam looks at the image on his camera for a moment, laughs out loud, and then shows it to the group.

'Does this remind you of anything?' he asks.

'It's da Vinci's *Last Supper*!' several of us exclaim at once. We wonder if we're all about to be crucified by the media pack.

The dark humour has a serious point. For the UK press, the story is about David and his quest. They are prepared for a tale of triumph if he finds planes and tragedy if he turns up empty-handed. While understandable in journalistic terms, this framing completely misses how Wargaming and the research team has approached the expedition.

In December, the British press decided they would send reporters to Myanmar to cover the story, whether we wanted them there or not, so we'd scheduled a press conference to announce our preliminary findings on 20 January. But now the press knows as well as we do that we haven't found any planes and that we're not digging on the airfield.

They know because long lenses have been observing our progress from the airport terminal, which has a clear view of the dig site, and for the same reason they know we haven't been on site today. Consequently they are clammering for answers.

Frazer tells us that we have to tell the media what Andy and the research team have figured out on the whiteboard. We cannot sit on this information or the press will indeed crucify us. Moreover, the information has to come from David, as the project leader. We call him and ask him to join us.

When David arrives, we explain the situation.

'We have a firefight problem,' Frazer says.

'We need to control the story, so it's good for us, good for them and good for you,' he continues, looking at David.

'I don't want to be made a fool of,' David says, expressing a rare vulnerability.

'It doesn't help us to have anybody made a fool of,' Gavin reassures him.

'Let's find out what Htoo Htoo has to say,' David suggests.

'We are giving him a head's up, so he's informed on the narrative we're beginning tomorrow. Nobody loses face,' Gavin says.

'If you have a prepared statement, give it to them, so there's no misunder- standing,' David suggests.

'You still have to read it,' Gavin tells David.

'Can someone write it down and I'll do it,' David says.

He then stands up and leaves.

'Huh,' Mark says, summing up our surprise at David's sudden departure.

We had planned to draft the statement as a group, so we'd all be on the same page.

The Key Aviation Forum
Burma Spitfires Thread
17 January 2013

At 22.44 GMT on 17 January 2013 the well-informed and well-connected former Foreign Office diplomat Derek Tonkin posts on the Burma Spitfires thread on the Key Historic Aviation Forum.

'I gather tomorrow's media will carry an initial report about the results of the dig at Mingaladon. I also gather that the reports will say that no Spitfires have yet been found.

'There has been intense media coverage. I expect all sorts of excuses. Source: gossip at a party in London this evening. But my source is reliable.'

Burma sceptic Andy Saunders, the editor of *Britain at War* magazine, who has good connections with the BBC among others, replies in a similar vein, 'Indeed … My reliable sources have been giving similar indications all day and are at odds with the "information" posted on the Facebook page main- tained by David's supporters.

'Perhaps tomorrow we will have some answers.'

35

Tracy Spaight
Park Royal Hotel
Yangon
18 January 2013

Good morning Myanmar!

Over the last few days, the atmosphere in the Park Royal hotel has become something like a more peaceful version of Saigon's famous Rex Hotel on the eve of the Tet offensive, with an increasingly bored, frustrated and distrustful media pack trying to pry information out of any passing individual who might know anything at all about what is going on up at Mingaladon, meanwhile waiting for Wargaming's promised briefing about the Spitfires excavation and hoping it will not be a modern-day version of the Joint US Public Affairs Office's infamous Five O-Clock Follies. Indeed, adding to the sense of history repeating itself as farce, the one time the archaeology team leave their habitual haunt in the Park Royal's Lobby Bar to venture down to the hotel's dimly lit basement nightclub, Park 5, with its tables ripe for a quiet assignation disappearing into the shadows, they emerge with the distinct impression that the establishment might have slipped through a tear in the space-time continuum from Tu Do street Saigon *c.* 1968, complete with a Filipino covers band.

Against this background, over an early breakfast, Gavin, Frazer and I meet with Andy, Martin and Rod to discuss the situation and the latest stories being published on UK news websites.

It has become apparent to all of us that the media story is getting out of control and from the quotes which are appearing, David and his supporters, principally Peter Arnold, seem to be briefing against the research team and, by association, Wargaming.

Finally we conclude that the current three-way standoff between the assembled media pack camped out in the foyer and at the airport, Wargaming and the research team, and David Cundall cannot hold.

Like a faulty boiler driving a Victorian paddle steamer up the Irrawaddy, the pressure is building to a dangerous level and people could get hurt in the inevitable explosion. This means that, while noisy and dangerous in its own right, there is no alternative. The safety valve must be released and it looks as if Andy is going to be the engineer wielding the monkey wrench of documented history.

We also agree that David and his supporters have already abandoned ship and are paddling up a creek of their own digging, but the troubling fact is that David seems so immersed in his own bubble of perception that he has not told Htoo Htoo that the ship is even in trouble.

Perhaps not surprisingly, David fails to materialise this morning. Nonetheless, we call him and knock on his door, but we can't find him anywhere. He's disappeared, and 10 a.m. local time – the appointed hour for the press announcement – passes without any sign of David.

Frazer, Gavin, Gavin's wife Chloe and I gather again at basecamp to discuss what to do. We make phone calls, including to a local hospital (just in case David has been injured or taken ill), search the ground floor of the hotel and ask hotel staff if they saw David get into a taxi.

Htoo Htoo arrives a short time later. He takes a seat at the conference table where we are all huddled. He looks around expectantly.

'As of this morning, David is missing,' Gavin tells him.

'Where?' Htoo Htoo asks, in his broken English.

'We don't know,' Gavin and I answer in unison.

Htoo Htoo cocks his head and then smiles at the absurdity of the situation. Auntie Latt enters the room, with her cell phone to her ear.

'I've been trying to call him, but he doesn't answer his phone.'

'Who?' Mark asks.

'David.'

'We don't know where he is,' Mark says.

'Oh my God, this is bad!' she exclaims.

The hotel room phone rings. It's Frazer calling from the lobby. The press are demanding answers, since David didn't show up for the scheduled announcement. Frazer says we have to tell them our spokesperson is not available and that we'll have to postpone.

Anna goes downstairs and knocks on David's door again.

'David, it's Anna. Are you in there?'

She is about to give up when, to her surprise, David opens the door.

'Come in, I'm not feeling very well,' he says. 'I'm very dizzy.'

Anna asks if she should call a doctor, but he demurs.

'David, you disappeared.'

'I'm sorry, I don't want to be made a fool of. I just want to walk away.'

Gavin and I come down, but David tells Anna he doesn't want to talk to us. Anna promises to convey that we want to make sure he is OK.

She goes back in the room to talk to David.

'We've got to stop this archaeology,' he says. 'We've got to concentrate on Spitfires.'

'Uh huh,' she agrees without agreeing, trying to calm him down.

'We've spent twelve days and what the hell have they done?' he asks.

The doctor arrives a short time later. He checks David's blood pressure and concludes that he's fine, but suggests David go to a hospital as a precaution.

Anna and Mark sneak him out the back of the hotel, so he can dodge the press.

With all this chasing up and down corridors and escaping down the back stairs it is impossible not to conclude that the whole situation is beginning to resemble the plot of a classic French farce, particularly as the archaeologists were forced to employ the same approach when they returned from their efforts to rescue the geophysics kit.

36

Andy Brockman
The Park Royal Hotel
Yangon
18 January 2013

As a self-confessed news addict with a serious Radio 4 habit, I have been watching and listening to Fergal Keane's work on the BBC for most of my adult life, so it is just the latest surreal turn in the Burma Spitfires story that finds me in one of the Park Royal's private dining rooms high above Alan Pya Pagoda Street with Fergal Keane himself, and his BBC producer, Nick Springate, who I had first met in London at the Imperial War Museum.

As Fergal, Nick and I talk over coffee it feels like one of those back channel meetings during the Cold War where the Circus met with the Cousins or a representative from Moscow Centre in a brush past in the Rathauspark in Vienna, or for a discrete dinner at the Mayflower Hotel in Washington, the objective being to pass on the authorised leaks of gossip and information that stop politicians making the kind of mistake that could turn the planet into a rotisserie.

We are not playing for such stakes here thankfully, but I am about to offer the BBC the Crown Jewels of our own intelligence about the lost squadron of what we have come to call 'Operation Unicorn' and it is being done very deliberately to ensure our story goes out on an international cross-media platform that is respected all over the world for its integrity and objectivity.

Crucially for this strategy, Keane has the kind of background and familiarity with historical research and documents that means he will understand the nuances of the story I am about to reveal.

Born, as I was, in 1961, the Irish-educated and Irish-speaking Fergal Patrick Murphy Keane OBE is one of the BBC's most senior, best known and most respected foreign correspondents and one of its most distinctive voices. His warm Irish tones are unmistakable to anyone who has watched or listened to the BBC's news and current affairs output at any time in the past quarter century.

Starting his career with Irish State Broadcaster RTE, he moved to the BBC in 1989 and since then has filed reports from most of the world's troublespots from Northern Ireland to South Africa, including most famously the horrors of the Rwandan genocide. He owns a BAFTA, Sony Radio Awards and the George Orwell and James Cameron prizes to show how well his work is regarded by his peers.

Like Nick Springate, Keane is also an old Burma hand with a historian's interest in the region during the Second World War. The author and presenter of a television documentary about the still murky involvement of British intelligence and the Foreign Office in the 1947 assassination of General Aung San, in 2010 he publishes *Road of Bones*, a well-received account of the epic siege of Kohima in 1944. The battle to take Kohima, a small town in the Naga Hills of north-east India, rivalled the deadly close-quarters fighting on the Eastern Front for sheer ferocity and saw the turning of the tide of the Burma campaign.

Defeat at Kohima led to a Via Dolorosa for General Kotuku Sato's 31 Dai-sanjūichi Shidan (31st Infantry Division, the ferocious division), which had attacked Kohima; and the Japanese Fifteenth Army, with so many Japanese soldiers dying of hunger, wounds, disease and exhaustion on the muddy jungle tracks of the Naga country and north-west Burma that the trek took on the macabre title Keane gave to his book.

Keane is also one of those reporters for whom humanity sits at the centre of his work. Perhaps his most famous broadcast is still his 'Letter to Daniel', written when he was based in Hong Kong and first broadcast in the long-running 'From Our Own Correspondent' (FOOC to its fans) strand on Radio 4 in February 1996. In the course of thirteen short paragraphs Keane manages to convey the disbelieving joy of finding yourself, for the first time, the parent of a healthy child, while at the same time using his experiences of reporting the suffering of other children, injured, abused and even killed in Eritrea, Angola, Afghanistan and Rwanda, to visit the gnawing fears that every new parent has for the precious life they are now responsible for and the injustice of a world that can betray and destroy such a wonder.

Now, with the authorisation of Wargaming's onsite senior management, Tracy and Gavin and PR manager Frazer, I offer the BBC a full background briefing, on the record, to do with as they see fit.

Keane and Springate accept the invitation and we reconvene in my hotel room in front of the whiteboard. This will be a solo performance as Martin and Rod are up at the dig site on Mingaladon trying to wrestle some more archaeological data out of the regulatory impasse.

As I talk the pair through the chain of evidence laid out on the whiteboard I hold nothing back, and I sense that the two journalists are both fascinated by the story I am telling, but also possessed by a rising anger.

Keane has also been awarded the Index on Censorship prize for journalistic integrity and as I conclude it must be that which prompts him to say something I recall as, 'If you knew all this, how could you keep it quiet?'

Inside I feel sick because I agree with him.

With the briefing completed and Fergal and Nick now free to fly to London, I am happy that the full story and its context are now in the public domain, but I also feel I have let down the objective truth we are supposed to stand for as independent archaeologists and academics.

In future years I will regret, even more than I did at that moment of accusation, that I did not insist on facing the entire press corps camped out in the foyer and bar of the Park Royal, laying out the evidence and taking questions.

We had a good story to tell about the need to test David Cundall's account of what happened to the Mingaladon Spitfires on the ground, and although it would have been bruising for the dig team and Wargaming and brutal as far as David was concerned, the result would have been cleaner.

The media pack would have been able to justify the expense of sending reporters to Yangon with a story about how the British Prime Minister had been taken in by a Lincolnshire farmer with a dream, but with what also appears to be an utter inability, or unwillingness, to hear, let alone properly assess, historical evidence.

It would also have taught the media and the public another lesson in plain sight about fact checking, about the need to talk to the right experts and about cutting through the hype of trigger words like 'Treasure' to tell the actual story and not the one they, the newspaper circulation managers and the television channel controllers, want to be true.

Not that it would have done much good in the long term in all likelihood.

After the publication of the fake Hitler Diaries on 23 April 1983, Rupert Murdoch, the owner of the *Sunday Times*, which published them, commented that 'circulation went up and it stayed up. We didn't lose money or anything like that.'*

---

*   Robert Harris, *Selling Hitler*, p.368, and Linklater 'Murdoch's bravado forced through the publication of the Hitler Diaries' *The Guardian*, 25 April 2012.

In fact, the newspaper added 20,000 new readers when the diaries were published and kept them even after they were unmasked as crude forgeries dreamed up by a bent dealer in Nazi-era memorabilia, Konrad Kujau, to dupe a motley collection of former Nazis, nostalgic for the good old days, and their media groupies.

For now I am just happy that the evidence-based truth, as we see it, is about to be broadcast by an impeccable, internationally respected source, undercutting the misinformation and innuendo that is being put out by David's supporters on the Key Historic Aviation Forum and elsewhere.

```
Temple Mount
Jerusalem
17-19 April 1911
```

Thanks to his archaeologist Pére Vincent, after three seasons of digging the Parker expedition has produced the most detailed plans of the underground works of the Old City of Jerusalem yet created.

However, for Parker, academic archaeology's gain is his investor's loss, because there is no sign of treasure of any kind in the tunnel of Hezekiah or beneath the Spring of Gihon, let alone the fabled lost Ark of the Covenant.

As a result, Captain Parker is losing faith in Dr Juvelius and his somewhat individual interpretations of the Book of Ezekiel. Fortunately for Parker, a Jerusalemite mosquito intervenes and solves Parker's problem of how to sideline his inconvenient esoteric expert and free the expedition to simply dig. In autumn 1910 the Finn is taken ill with malaria and returns to Europe to convalesce.

Freed from the impediment of Dr Juvelius and his theories, Parker knows he must also make progress before the following November, when the excavation permit granted by the Turkish authorities expires, and he has a plan.

In early April 1911, as it is every year in the week following the Paschal Full Moon, Jerusalem is thronged with pilgrims of all faiths because at this holiday, the Jewish Passover, the Greek Orthodox Easter and the Islamic festival of Nabi Musa coincide to bring about a volatile combination of religious observance, wild party and powder keg.

Captain Parker reckons that with the population of the Holy City and its police distracted by the three-way festivities, there will never be a better opportunity to go for broke and dig beneath Temple Mount itself.

However, to make sure he will not be disturbed he takes the precaution of using $25,000 of his investor's cash to bribe Sheikh Halil, the hereditary Guardian of the Haram al-Sarif (the Noble Sanctuary), which contains the Al-Aqsa

Mosque, the third holiest site in Islam and the unmistakable visual signature of the City of Jerusalem herself and better known as the Dome of the Rock.

On the night of 17–18 April, as Jerusalem celebrates and then sleeps off the celebration, Captain Parker and his digging crew, dressed in Arab clothing, enter Temple Mount and rope down into the cavern that lies beneath the sanctuary of the Dome of the Rock.

Legend has it that the cavern leads directly into the bowels of the earth and to a great treasure, guarded by the mighty and terrible Jinn.

This is not the first night Parker has dug under the sanctuary. On the previous occasions the team has managed to accomplish its work and steal away into the early morning as the city begins to stir. However, tonight, with the festivities at their height and his house full of guests, one of the keepers of the Mosque seeks his own sanctuary by sleeping on Temple Mount itself.

It is the early hours of the morning when the keeper hears the metallic clang of hammers on cold chisels. On investigation, he sees shadowy figures, contorted grotesquely as they work in the sickly yellow light of oil lamps, but as he listens and watches he realises that these Jinn speak English.

His cry of anger at the sacrilege and fear of who the Jinn might be tears the cool quiet of the Haram al-Sarīf. As Captain Parker and his crew bundle up their tools and scramble to escape, the keeper runs screaming into the darkened streets, raising a hue and cry at the unforgivable desecration.

The news spreads rapidly through the Old City as angry citizens fill the labyrinth of streets, crying for the return of the Crown, the ring of King Solomon himself, the Sword of Mohammed and even the fabled Ark of the Covenant, all of which are now rumoured to have been taken by the Englishman, in what is rapidly turning into the biggest public relations debacle for Europeans in Jerusalem since the sack of the city by troops of the First Crusade.

By 19 April the Ottoman Police are facing down the mob that has gathered at the gate of the government citadel over the iron sights of their Mauser rifles. They are defending the honour of Islam and the Holy Places, good civic order, and governor Azmey Bey Pasha's job.

Meanwhile, Captain Parker, his associates and their luggage are heading for the port of Jaffa and Clarence Wilson's yacht, as fast as they possibly can.

However, the captain cannot travel faster than a message in Morse code carried along a telegraph wire.

As Azmey Bey Pasha is spat upon by an angry cross-section of the citizens of Jerusalem, Captain Parker is invited to submit his baggage for inspection by forewarned Ottoman customs officials in Jaffa.

37

Tracy Spaight
Park Royal Hotel
Yangon
18 January 2013

As morning breaks in the UK, the British media begin to post and print stories about the Spitfire expedition. The BBC summarises Andy's assessment that there are no buried crated Spitfires at Mingaladon but also quote David, who accuses the archaeology team of digging in the wrong place. David's accusation is repeated in the *Daily Mail* and *The Guardian*.

The *Daily Mail* article is typical of the coverage telling the paper's readers: 'Although he is the brains behind the project, the excavation work and archaeologists are being funded by wargaming.net, a video games company. "The archaeologists weren't digging in the area we believe holds the Spitfires," Mr Cundall says. "Instead, they wanted to see what sort of war remains were buried."'

The Wargaming team are livid.

The archaeologists broke ground at precisely the location David identified as the burial site on three occasions: at the IWM press conference, at the pre-dig planning meetings and on site at the airfield. It only became 'the wrong place' *after* we dug and didn't find anything.

The article goes on to say that David is making plans to dig at Myitkyina, 'where a submerged crate has already been discovered'.*

---

*   www.dailymail.co.uk/news/article-2264361/No-Spitfires-buried-Burma-decades-long-hunt.html

In the British media, David is a sympathetic, salt of the earth guy ploughing ahead whatever the odds. But after the past few days on site, and his allegation in the press that we're 'digging in the wrong place', it's become clear to the team that what they see as David's determination seems to have shaded over into obstinacy and close to a destructive obsession. They suspect that, if unchecked, he would happily turn Mingaladon airfield into a gigantic open cast mine.

In one of those moments when a remembered event makes a synaptic connection with the perception of the present, I realise that David is not an affable Don Quixote figure tilting at windmills. He is more like Lope de Aguirre, the protagonist of Werner Herzog's 1972 film *Aguirre, Wrath of God*.

In the film, which is based loosely on fact, Aguirre leads a group of conquistadores down the Amazon River in search of the legendary city of gold, El Dorado. However, the men who follow Lope fall prey to starvation, sickness and the arrows of angry local people.

It doesn't end well.

Our Lope de Aguirre, David, has rebelled against the members of the expedition who want to turn back and convinces his followers (led by Peter Arnold) that the mother lode of el fierabrás (Spitfires) lies just a little further upstream.

It is time for the rest of us to abandon the raft.

```
Spitfire Dig Site
Airside on the north boundary of Yangon International
Airport (Formerly RAF Mingaladon)
19 January 2013
```

Thanks to Htoo Htoo's tireless efforts with the airport bureaucracy, our team is allowed back on the dig site today, so all of us board our chartered bus and trek over to the airfield after breakfast. David sits by himself at the front of the bus, cradling his antiquated metal detector like some kind of electronic talisman.

Our goal is to find the Old Prome Road so we can place Stanley's journey securely in the 1945–46 landscape. The geophysicists plan to finish their expanded survey today, in this same area. The geophysics survey will help direct the placement of trenches for the nocturnal excavation work.

We have to address the tensions between David and the research team, so we can maintain at least a semblance of cooperation for long enough to finish the surveys and fieldwork that are essential if we are to offer a reasoned conclusion based on evidence. With this aim in mind, as the minibus takes the now familiar route out to the dig site, Mark Mannucci quietly asks Gavin Longhurst if he will address the troops and try to bring everyone together.

Gavin agrees to be Henry V on the eve of our archaeological Agincourt.

'We are a family,' Gavin begins, speaking to the team in the wooden pavilion that STP has built adjacent to David's favoured burial site. 'And this family has come under fire in the past few days. We've got external pressure in the form of the press. But that shouldn't stop us from being a family.'

Gavin turns to David and Auntie Latt.

'I need you both to say a couple of words to keep up our spirits,' he says.

David is having none of it.

'Htoo Htoo is my agent. He has worked incredibly hard. Auntie Latt and Htoo Htoo are my friends, and you people are not,' he says, glaring at the rest of us.

Unsurprisingly, David's comments fail to bring the desired unity. In fact, Andy is livid to the extent that Martin Brown feels the need to put his hand on his arm in a gesture of 'not now'.

'We all thought that we'd find Spitfires in a few days and we haven't,' David continues. He includes the whole team in this belief, though the rest of us were not so sanguine about the chances of finding buried, crated Spitfires.

'The Burmese are not happy with us and we have to repair the damage,' he says.

Gavin asks if Auntie Latt has some 'words of positivity' for us.

'We have responsibility to make the project a success,' Auntie Latt says.

'Can I just say,' Andy interjects. 'I said, when we started this project that we were going into it with no assumptions and we would test everything. We're still in the position of doing that. Whatever the press ends up reporting, we're going to do the best possible job that we can for you, for STP, for David and the people of Myanmar,' Andy says, with complete sincerity.

'Please work together with us,' Auntie Latt pleads.

We promise to do so.

The meeting breaks up, and David wanders off with Soe Thein to survey along the red road. He has broken with our team completely, both intellectually and physically, and is now running what is, to all intents and purposes, a parallel operation.

Since our last site visit, a guard tower has also been erected next to the dig site and teenage guards, cradling M16 assault rifles, monitor our activities, although there is a sense that they are not quite sure why.

However, in spite of the strained circumstances, by the end of the afternoon the geophysicists have completed their survey.

Using multiple methods capable of seeing both near surface and more deeply buried artefacts and geology, Roger, Adam and Andy have surveyed more than 52,000 sq.m of the airport, including a huge area near the end of the 1945 runway where Stanley Coombe reported seeing crates.

What is clear is that the anomalies Adam recorded in 2004 are no longer present, although there is evidence of an excavation in the area in which they were located, and there are no identifiable anomalies remaining that are suggestive in any way of the presence of buried aircraft.

With the technical and documentary lines of enquiry at the Yangon crime scene exhausted there remains one final throw of the dice, and it is the ambition shared by both the archaeologists and by David.

The ambition to dig.

38

Andy Brockman
Spitfire Dig Site
Airside on the north boundary of Yangon International
Airport (Formerly RAF Mingaladon)
20 January 2013

If one metaphor for archaeology is that it is like exploratory surgery on a landscape, then the work of Manny and Rod overnight was a paramedic's heroic intervention at the roadside to save the patient in a car crash from certain death.

This open site surgery came about because, given the ban on using machines in daylight, the team were faced with a difficult set of choices, ethical and practical. Could we base the final report and conclusions on the relatively small sample we have already excavated, albeit that sample includes the place David identified as his primary target for the dig, or could we, should we, try to sample a wider area, even though that would mean Manny digging by the machine's floodlights?

Martin Brown can only recall one previous occasion when he has excavated by floodlights and that was because a clear and present threat to human remains on the site rendered that the ethical thing to do.

Like Martin, the rest of the archaeological team are uncomfortable with the idea he has outlined on practical and ethical grounds. However, Manny as the machine operator and Rod as health and safety and UXO monitor, also say that, if they are given the go-ahead, they find the risks acceptable and controllable.

After an impassioned discussion, we reach a compromise. In the way that a TV surgeon sometimes breaks the rules to save the patient, Martin makes it clear that, while whatever happened overnight could not be considered archaeology, if more areas were to be opened up then the team would record them archaeologically to the best of our ability in the morning.

As a result, Manny and Rod have been able to open three additional trenches in the dark, and of these Trench 2 proves to be the most important.

Trench 2 is a giant east–west incision across what we suspect is the course of the Old Prome Road upon which Stanley Coombe's truck was travelling when he witnessed whatever it was he witnessed in the early spring of 1946.

Standing at the western end of Trench 2, Martin Brown is in his element, engaged on the detailed microsurgery that will restore quality and meaning to the experience. However, this is not surgery in the viscera of the ground by microscope and computer-controlled manipulators. This kind of archaeology is a sensory experience where the story is revealed through a combination of eye and touch, where the most subtle changes of soil colour can have a meaning, and where grain and texture can tell tales about how a soil was created and when.

Standing on the lip of the trench looking down, the most obvious fact about Trench 2 is that water is filling the eastern end of the trench, confirming once again that, even in the dry season, the water table on this part of the Mingaladon plateau lies within 2m of the surface. But as you get your eye in you see something else.

Towards the western end of the trench is a thick reddish-orange strip of material, some 4m wide, which lies 30cm below the topsoil and is clearly visible in both east and west sections ('section' being the archaeological jargon for the side of the trench).

The compacted mass of coarse material is some 30 to 40cm thick, and the archaeologists have seen this kind of feature many times before. It looks like the foundations of a path or road and Martin thinks this may be either the remains of a dirt road that once crossed the plateau, or even of a metalled road where the top layers have been planed off by the various phases of airfield development that took place following the RAF reoccupying the site in 1945.

But there is something else.

As Martin's trowel works the trench section either side of the road feature the soil gives to reveal large, well-defined lumps within the soil matrix. Martin has seen this feature before, not in the excavations here at Mingaladon, but in the trenches of the Western Front near Ypres in Belgium, which he has excavated as the director of the Plug Street Project.

The lumps are the remains of sandbags.

RAF Mingaladon
Thursday, 25 December 1941

It is Christmas Day, but the only gifts the Japanese 7th and 10th Flying Battalions intend leaving for the RAF at Mingaladon are in the form of high explosives, and the Japanese flyers begin with a considerable advantage.

The RAF's defence is improvised and hamstrung by the lack of an adequate early warning system, of enough anti-aircraft guns and, following its destruction in an air raid two days earlier, of a functioning operations room to coordinate such defensive resources as do exist.

It is probably inevitable then that at around noon, in spite of combat air patrols set up by the RAF's own Brewster Buffalo fighters and the P-40s of the American Volunteer Group (AVG), around fifty Ki-21 and Ki-30 bombers are able to sweep across the airfield in waves dropping sticks of high-explosive and anti-personnel fragmentation bombs, just as British Commander in Chief General Wavell and his colleague, General George H. Brett, the Commander in Chief of the USAAF in Asia, land in their unarmed Chinese National Aircraft Corporation DC-2 transport.

As the first bombs explode, too close for comfort, the VIP passengers are hustled unceremoniously into the relative safety of a nearby slit trench by Oley Olsen, the CO of the 3rd Squadron of the AVG.

As the men dive for cover, Olsen hopes that none of the local snakes have chosen to take up residence in the sandbags and duckboards.

In under ten minutes it is all over.

Wavell, Brett and Olsen emerge from the trench to find their own aircraft has survived the onslaught. However, RAF Mingaladon is a butcher's shambles.

As 4,000 gallons of aviation fuel burns, forming a black shroud over the airfield, three of the precious Buffalo fighters lie shattered and on fire in their dispersal pens, destroyed before they could even be scrambled. A further five, which have not even been uncrated by the engineers, lie smashed and burnt in the wreckage of a bombed-out hangar.

Mingaladon's runways too are almost unusable, so pitted by bomb craters that the act of landing an aircraft is a game of 1,000hp Russian Roulette for the returning aviators.

The human cost of the raid has also been high. A number of the Bofors anti-aircraft gun pits crewed by the Indian Army have been hit and the remains of the gunners lie uncollected, while in Rangoon and the surrounding villages the total civilian casualties of the Japanese air raids is estimated to have passed 5,000.

There are also casualties among the RAF pilots. As the clear up begins, Flight Lieutenant Jack Brandt of 67 Squadron's B Flight has the melancholy task of organising the burial of three of his comrades who have been shot down in the chaotic dogfights over Rangoon and Mingaladon; Flying Officer John Lambert RAF was lost flying Buffalo W8220 (RD-V), with its distinctive nose art of the Devil grasping a globe painted by one of the ground crew, and two New Zealanders, Flight Sergeants Ted Hewitt and Ron MacNabb.

Brandt records that the three airmen do not even have the dignity of their own shroud as they are laid to rest. All the available blankets are needed in the local hospital.

Neither are 67 Squadron's weary pilots and ground crews allowed even a small Christmas luxury. On 25 December 1941 Christmas dinner at RAF Mingaladon is hardtack and a mug of water because the cook house has also been destroyed in the bombing, which here inflicted perhaps the most bitter material loss of the day for the RAF.

The 50-gallon barrel of beer that was being kept back for 67's Christmas party lies smashed, its precious contents drained and soaking into the dust and blood.

Tracy Spaight
Spitfire Dig Site
Airside on the north boundary of Yangon International
Airport (Formerly RAF Mingaladon)
Sunday, 20 January 2013

As the dig team work against the clock to complete the excavation, photography and recording in Trenches 2, 3 and 4, we are joined once again by a convoy of dark blue Police SUV's which that loom out of the cloud of red dust carrying Home Affairs Minister, Lieutenant General Ko Ko, and his entourage, including the aide de camp, who records everything on the camera of his top-of-the-range iPad.

As the fieldwork team disperses for the last time, we leave behind Htoo Htoo, who is briefing the general in the guest pavilion which has been built beside the red road opposite the team's original dig site. It is the place where David told them he was convinced that the Spitfires were buried, but where the team discovered only post-war tarmac, broken timbers and ground which had already been disturbed down to the natural blue clay.

The senior officers of the Tatmadaw have a reputation for brutality, but here it is not the bullet, bayonet and combat boot but the general's cold professionalism that brutalises David and the unfortunate Htoo Htoo Zaw, because David's

entire construct around the buried Spitifres has collided head on with unsenti-
mental military logic that demands written orders from the chain of command
before anything happens. As a result, that construct lies in ruins.

Worse, the ruin has led to David's business partner's patriotism being
impugned by a senior member of the Government.

'How is it he can say all this for certain?' the general asks Htoo Htoo of
David's story. 'Does he have documentation? How reliable is he?'

Taken aback, Htoo Htoo mouths a few words that do not come out properly. Then he offers to fetch David, who is standing next to Htoo Htoo's sister
just outside the pavilion, watching the car crash of a meeting, but the general
has not finished.

'You are a Burmese national. Don't be dumb! They will think Burmese
people are stupid and laugh at you on the inside! I am saying this so we won't
be embarrassed and our country won't be embarrassed.'

Htoo Htoo is reduced to silence.

'OK, so that's it,' says the general matter of factly and he stands to leave, followed swiftly by his entourage.

The 2013 Burma Spitfire dig at Yangon International Airport is over in
every sense. Perhaps remarkably, the general has allowed the cameras of Room
608 to remain to record the meeting.

The final shots show Auntie Latt almost in tears.

We come to understand this is more than just an immediate emotional
reaction to the tension of the meeting.

Earlier, as we waited for the general's arrival, she tried to lift our spirits, and
her own, by singing in tuneful accapella the Connie Francis Country music
classic, 'Too Many Rules', with its hauntingly apt lines praying to the stars that
the singer has not lost the love of their partner.

As she knows only too well, and we later discover, in a political system
where love is in short supply, the general is one of the most powerful members of the cabinet and is not a person to cross.

Close to Than Shwe, in 2014 the International Human Rights Clinic at
the Harvard Law School published a legal memorandum accusing Lieutenant
General Ko Ko of responsibility for multiple war crimes while serving as
commander of the Tatmadaw's Southern Command during operations against
Karen and other independence fighters between 2005 and 2006.*

In 2015, he was selected by the Government to defend Myanmar's human
rights record at the United Nations.**

* hrp.law.harvard.edu/wp-content/uploads/2014/11/2014.11.05-IHRC-Legal-Memo-
randum.pdf
** hrp.law.harvard.edu/student-perspectives/government-official-suspected-of-war-
crimes-put-in-charge-of-human-rights-review-for-myanmar/

39

Tracy Spaight
Debrief with STP
Spitfire Dig Site
Airside on the north boundary of Yangon International
Airport (Formerly RAF Mingaladon)
20 January 2012

As the last spill of the setting sun catches the wispy cirrus clouds high above the airfield, I sit opposite David and STP under the roof of the now somewhat forlorn pavilion, while Room 608's cameras continue to record.

Htoo Htoo is still shaken from his encounter with the general and now he needs answers from David.

Auntie Latt, her tone uncharacteristically business-like and direct, asks David pointedly, 'Who did the burials? Is it the Air Force or who?'

'The British did it,' David answers, discarding his long-held contention that American CBs or Seabees undertook the burials.

'The British?' she asks.

'Yeah,' David confirms.

'But British Air Force or Army?' she asks.

'I think it was British Army, really,' he replies, seemingly spinning a new narrative out of thin air.

'If the British Army did the burying, since it is an army, there would be a record of the process. Don't you have the evidence of the burial?' Htoo Htoo asks. Even though he is speaking in Burmese, his frustration and exasperation with David needs no translation.

'There is no evidence. There was no evidence. It was a political burial. By the British to support the Karens for their support of the British in the Second World War,' David says.

'So it was …' Auntie Latt begins.

'A political burial,' David says, completing her sentence.

'Burial meaning what?' she says, confused.

'Well, it was payment to the Karen …' David says.

'The Spitfires?' she asks, surprised.

I realise that this is the first time she's hearing the story.

'Yes,' David says. 'It was for their effort in the Second World War.'

Auntie Latt looks dubious. She translates for Htoo Htoo, 'He said, the British Army did the burying. But the evidence you asked for is not there. The reason there is no evidence is that the planes were left as souvenirs for the Karen.'

Htoo Htoo listens, then casts a surprised glance at David. He starts shaking his head as Auntie Latt finishes speaking.

'That's what he's saying, but maybe it's not true. Probably it's not true,' Auntie Latt says in Burmese.

David continues, 'I have no evidence other than what I've told you. But the evidence is in the surveys that we've done at Myitkyina. And I'm very, very satisfied that we've found something of great interest,' then he adds, 'And, um – I've been told there is a file, uh, but they say it's still classified.

Not registering that the promise of such an unobtainable secret held by the deep state is a device used frequently by conspiracy theorists, Htoo Htoo latches on to this suggestion, hopeful that perhaps the British government might be persuaded to open the 'secret file' to assist the dig.

'This minister reads everything, he reads every article and we are in a lot of trouble,' says Auntie Latt.

However, David's first concern is still his contract.

'We have a contract,' he protests, and asks, 'They can break it anytime?'

'Anytime,' says Auntie Latt flatly.

As the sun sets, David is left hunched, isolated. But, as has always been the case, David can fly home any time he chooses, while Htoo Htoo, Auntie Latt, and STP have to carry the memory of this and the accompanying damage to their reputation and loss of face in all their social and business interactions.

It is impossible not to see the scene as a metaphor for the end of colonial rule and a reminder of the damage done to the individuals and ethnic groups who were seen to have sided too closely with the departing colonial power.

Earlier, at the round table in Andy's room back at the Park Royal, the archaeologists and the Wargaming team had expressed concern for STP.

Indeed, Rod Scott felt that in some of their recent conversations Auntie Latt had seemed scared of the direction the dig had taken, while Andy made clear that he felt we all had a duty not to leave STP to, as he put it, 'twist in the wind'.

There seems to be no point in mentioning another key fact that came out of the research among the documents at Kew.

While they found no corroboration for the Spitfire burials, the team did discover a significant entry regarding the RAF's involvement with the Karen tribes. It is an entry that proved Sebastian Cox was perhaps more correct than he knew when he told Room 608 that, offered a Spitfire in a crate, a Karen would dump the Spitfire and live in the crate.

During January 1946 the Dakotas and Liberators of 232 Group airdropped some 250 tons of rice to the Karen tribes in the lower Shan State because damage and neglect of their paddy fields during the fighting of the previous two years had led to the Karen facing famine during the 1946 monsoon.

In other words, had David and the other researchers investigating the buried Spitfires story actually looked at these records, they would have seen that the last thing the Karen needed in 1946 was Spitfires buried at Mingaladon miles from their heartland. What they did need was rice simply to stay alive and the British Government, in the shape of the Royal Air Force, provided it.

STP office
Yangon
21 January 2013

After the events of yesterday afternoon, and in light of David's ever-changing story, I decide that we need to limit the damage to everyone, which means closing down the dig and withdrawing Wargaming's support.

As a result, I take a taxi to STP's office to meet with Htoo Htoo Zaw. Despite our differences, and our repeated clashes over project costs and logistics, I've come to like and respect him.

'*Mingalaba*,' I say, using the formal greeting of the Burmese. It means something akin to 'auspiciousness' or 'we are blessed'.

He smiles and says hello in English. We both know this will be a hard conversation. We take seats in his office and Auntie Latt translates for us.

'I came here today to tell you in person that Wargaming is going to withdraw from the project,' I tell them. 'I haven't told David yet, but I will do so today.'

'I want to speak with you first, because I have come to respect you both these past several months. I want to share with you what we've learned, so you can make an informed decision about whether to continue working with David.'

'Yesterday the general asked for documentary evidence that the planes were buried. Our researchers, who are experts at working in archives, couldn't find any documentation to support David's story. Moreover, there are no secret files, as David alleges. All the wartime materials on Burma have been declassified.'

I tell them that, despite this, we decided to come to Myanmar because we thought planes might have been dumped as part of a post-war disposal job. I tell them about the negative results from the geophysical survey, and Dr Booth's conclusion that the site has been disturbed since the 2004 survey.

'We looked where David told us to look. It's on camera. We asked him very clearly, David, right here? By landing light 46-N?'

'Yes,' Auntie Latt says.

'In the L-shaped and T-shaped sections,' I say.

'Yeah, yeah, yeah,' Auntie Latt says, confirming she remembers.

'And he said, yes, right here. We dug there, and we didn't find anything. We extended the trench 50ft out and dug down to the undisturbed alluvial soil. There's nothing there.'

'Yes,' Auntie Latt says, agreeing to these facts. She translates into Burmese for Htoo Htoo.

'Each time we dug, David would change his mind and tell us we're digging in the wrong place. After he confirmed that is where we should dig,' I say, a note of exasperation creeping into my voice.

'Yeah,' Auntie Latt says, and then translates for Htoo Htoo.

'David doesn't respect our research team, because their results are not confirming his vision. He does not respect the facts from the documentary record or the field archaeology. He is disparaging Wargaming and our research team in the press. We can't have that, so we're withdrawing from the project.'

'I came here today out of respect, to tell you that I am prepared to do anything I can to help you have a soft landing,' I tell them both, thinking about the events of the previous day. I don't want any harm to come to them over what can now be argued to be David's Spitfire delusion.

Htoo Htoo listens to the translation and then tells me that it is their duty, as a Myanmar company, to continue with the excavations. He says that his contract is with David, so whatever Wargaming decides to do on the sponsorship side is between me and David. He tells me that STP has its own financial resources and will continue the work, since they believe David.

'Prime Minister David Cameron came to Myanmar and talked to our President Sein Thein about the Spitfires for forty-five minutes,' Htoo Htoo says, through Auntie Latt.

'Both leaders agreed they wanted to do this, so it is our duty to do it to the end. We believe that he [Cameron] must have proof or evidence. There must be something that has prompted him to tell our president that he wants to do this project. There must be something behind David Cameron's words, which makes it worthy for us to do the project.'

They believe both Davids, the farmer and the Prime Minister. There's nothing more I can say. I have discharged my ethical obligation.

I tell them I respect their decision. To help them save face with the government, I promise to provide enough funds to close down the dig and remediate the site at Mingaladon. I promise to confer with them about any future media announcements on the project, including a planned press release that we will be withdrawing support for David Cundall. Ultimately, we delay our presentation on the excavation findings until June, to give STP time to finish.

'Even though we're at this point,' I tell them both, 'I've enjoyed the opportunity to get to know you and see your beautiful country. It's been an honour.'

We shake hands.

'If we find a Spitfire at Myitkyina,' he tells me through Auntie Latt, 'you will be the first person to know about it.'

I wish them luck and promise to fly over to see it if they do.

The phone call never comes.

40

Tracy Spaight
Pavement café in Yangon
22 January 2013

I am sitting on a red plastic milk crate on a busy pavement, watching the traffic and sipping something called 'pearl milk tea' from a chipped china cup. It is an indescribable blend of tea, milk, and tapioca. Mark and Anna are sitting on the other side of our makeshift table, with tea cups crowded on top. We're all physically and emotionally drained from the past two weeks. We're in a reflective mood.

Joining us is our translator and fixer Shwe Win, who has shared our surreal adventure. Shwe is a bespeckled, soft-spoken guy. He has a friendly smile and a sunny disposition. We've got to know him over the past two weeks, as we've driven around the city in taxis or the minibus. He has been invaluable in helping us get around and communicate with locals.

The one place he wasn't allowed to accompany us was inside the secure perimeter of the airport, access to which is controlled by the military police. The reason, as we soon discovered, is that he spent seven years in jail as a political prisoner of the regime.

In 1998, shortly after enrolling in college to study English literature, Shwe was arrested for participating in an anti-government demonstration and distributing pro-democracy pamphlets. I note that this was during the same time period that David was currying favour with the military junta for permission to excavate at Mingaladon.

Shwe tells us:

I was taken at 10 o'clock at night. The military police and intelligence officers came to my house. I was taken to an interrogation prison. They asked me, 'Where did you get these subversive pamphlets?' I was tortured. No water. No food. No sleep. They put me in a cell. I had no contact with my family. My mother tried to find me. She visited the police station but they told her they don't know where I am. Finally, I had a trial. No lawyer, but there was no point in hiring one. There is no proper judiciary. Everything is controlled by the military.

He was sentenced to twenty years in prison.

Shwe tells us about the hunger he and his fellow prisoners endured:

You cannot imagine. We were provided with rice. But it is not the kind of rice you can buy in the store. Our country was socialist before 1988. We had to wait in a long queue to buy rice at the state cooperative. You had to bring a plastic bag with you. Some rice would spill over on the floor. They would sweep this up and feed it to pigs. It would be full of dirt and small pebbles. That is the rice we had to eat in prison. We had no choice. We had to eat it for our survival. So what we did was process it. We put water in a plastic bowl. We put three handfuls in it to get rid of the dirt and small stones. After we processed, we were left with two fists of rice.

He tells us about the labour they forced him to do in prison:

Labour is no problem for me, as long as it is meaningful. You know the story of the British and Australian PoWs who built the bridge over the River Kwai? At least that railroad could be used by civilians in the future. But when you have to do something that is totally meaningless, something that is designed to torture you, then that is different. Every day, at 7 a.m., we had to polish the prison floors. We had to shine the ground like a mirror.

He mimics polishing the floor.

'Rub it. Illuminate it. Until you can see your image.'

Shwe explains how he managed to keep his sanity. His family finally learned his whereabouts and his father came to visit him in prison. Shwe asked his father to buy an English language dictionary for him, so he could keep his mind busy. His father did so and left it with the prison authorities – but they refused to give it to Shwe, and they forbade his father to mention the dictionary during his visits:

When I asked my father, he said, 'Don't ask me about the dictionary.' So I knew they had it. I didn't want to risk confrontation, so I waited until the ICRC [International Red Cross and Red Crescent] visited, I shouted, 'I want my dictionary.' Finally, an official visited my cell and gave me the dictionary. He said, 'Don't ask for anything more.' But soon I asked for Dickens!

Shwe tells us he learned entire chapters of *Nicholas Nickleby* by heart.

He grows philosophical. 'Life is so fragile. So unpredictable,' he tells us. 'I understood [in prison] that tragedy is part of human life.'

When he got out of prison, Shwe struggled to find his identity. 'I was like a ghost, searching for my previous human existence,' he says. He recounts how he went to the home of a close friend. 'I knocked on the door. His mother came out. She knew me well, but treated me like a complete stranger. I was very surprised. I didn't realise she was afraid, because of my prison background,' Shwe says, remembering.

The regime did not break his spirit. After his early release in 2005, Shwe pursued his dream to become a journalist, writing under various pseudonyms for international audiences about life in Myanmar. His work was eventually picked up by the *New York Times*. He now writes under his own name.

Shwe tells us that he believes things will get better in his country. 'If we can be positive, things will improve bit by bit. We need patience for real changes to come.'

In his unassuming way, he tells us that he has forgiven those who imprisoned him. 'I have no anger in my heart,' he tells us and smiles.

Shwe's ability to forgive, and his hope for the future, make a deep and lasting impression on me. We all want this to be the real Myanmar. A country poised between dictatorship and democracy, where aging generals cling to power and a new generation will risk all for a free and open society.

25 January 2013
Waikzawtayon Monastery
Mayangon

On my last day in Myanmar, the film crew and I accompany Tin Ma Latt to the Waikzawtayon Monastery, in the township of Mayangon, which is on the northern edge of Yangon. Tin Ma Latt explains that her family has supported the monastery since the 1970s. There are about 150 monks here. Most of them are young boys.

We watch them shuffle quietly into the stone courtyard in single file. They are wearing maroon robes. They remove their straw rope sandals and place them in neat rows in front of the temple door, and go inside to pray. Soon the sound of chanting echoes through the compound. It is beautiful and otherworldly.

When they finish, the monks collect their alms bowls and prepare to leave through the ornate gate to the city streets beyond. Auntie Latt explains that they are going out to collect alms from lay supporters. Today she has brought croissants and coffee packets, which we distribute in their alms bowls as they file past. I follow her example.

Afterwards, we talk with Auntie Latt about the Spitfire project, against the backdrop of the monastery. She says that she is disappointed about how things turned out at Mingaladon but hopeful they may still find something at Myitkyina. David has already departed to begin the work:

If by some chance, we don't have any Spitfires. Then I will say, 'The world is like that.' As a Buddhist, we believe it is not up to our wants and desires. Our Buddha has said, you cannot always get what you want. If it is not there, it's not there. I don't know what David will do. But I do wish that David can take both good news and the bad news, in equal state of mind, because I like him very much.

Rangoon
1930 Hours
7 March 1942

The makeshift column of jeeps and trucks carrying the last of Rangoon's British military garrison, the Gloucesters, set off up the Prome Road, passing the still smoking wreck that is RAF Mingaladon.

With them go the last semblance of the authority of King George VI, King and Emperor in Lower Burma, Lieutenant Colonel Tony Main's Field Security Force.

Behind them, like the broken legs of a giant millipede, the cranes of Rangoon docks have been blown up and toppled into the river, while the remaining warehouses have been dynamited by the last ditchers, teams of military engineers who have then been evacuated by boat.

Rangoon is now a city of looters, patients released from the city's mental asylum, scavenging dogs and the dead, all of them lying under the billowing funereal blanket of black smoke rising from the burning tank farms of the Syriam oil refineries.

Even Rangoon Zoo does not escape this desperate twilight of Empire. In an echo of that literary metaphor illustrating the collapse of British colonial authority, George Orwell's 'Shooting An Elephant', the more dangerous animals are shot to prevent their becoming a danger to the public, while their herbivorous brothers and sisters are released to take their chance in whatever is to come.

41

Tracy Spaight
Myanmar
Spring 2013

David leaves Yangon for Myitkyina on 24 January, shortly after the
Mingaladon surveys and excavation failed to find any Spitfires. He plans
to excavate the 'crate' that his Burmese partner, geophysicist Professor Soe
Thein, and his team had located in December 2012 and announced at a press
conference on 9 January 2013. David is confident that this time he will find
the planes and return in triumph.

A few weeks earlier, over the Christmas Holidays, he communicated to
me that Soe Thein's team had found a pile of white stones at the Myitkyina
burial location, a discovery that David claims Jim Pearce back in Sussex has
confirmed is consistent with what the American witnesses had told him.

Neither David, nor Jim, have mentioned this crucial fact in any of the previous descriptions of the alleged burial at Myitikyina.

The fact that Myitkyina served as an American airbase after its capture from
the Japanese in 1944, as our team found, and that no British squadrons were
based there between 1945 and 1948, does not faze David.

On the aviation forum, Peter Arnold opines that David should 'expand
the hand-dug hole' and 'expose more of the crate, if that is what it is, cut a
substantial hole in it ... and record what is there.'*

---

* Peter Arnold, Key Historic Aviation Forum, The Burma Spitfire thread, post 1500,
20 January 2013.

David does dig and after two weeks of work in late January and early February 2013, David and his team have recovered several pieces of what appears to be old fencing material – but in spite of news reports to the contrary there are no signs of any crates, let alone of any aircraft.*

The team soon lose interest in the professor's site at Myitkyina and abandon the dig.

With this site now also a bust, David and his supporters turn their attention back to Mingaladon, which at least has the virtue of having been an RAF airfield at the end of the war in Burma and a base where Spitfire squadrons actually operated.

David will spend the next four months (March to June 2013) surveying and excavating at Mingaladon once again – funding these speculative excavations in part with Wargaming funds, which the company claim he is legally obligated to return.

Aviation historian and Burma Spitfires sceptic Andy Saunders reports in the aviation forums in March 2013 that 'extensive excavations have been observed a short distance away from the original trenches dug by the archaeologists (in January 2013).

'My own "spy" tells me that a large area over 100ft x 100ft appears to have been excavated down to "around 20ft or so".'**

The Google Earth satellite images recorded on 13 March 2013 seem to confirm this report.

Peter Arnold reports on 16 March that the team has found 'interesting conflict archaeology'*** and that 'this location just happens to be where two of the independent eyewitnesses said there were crates and burial activity in the 1945/46 period.'

Andy Brockman is amused that Peter has used the term 'conflict archaeology', because, as recorded by the film crew, archaeology, in any sense that the rest of the world recognises, is the last thing David and Peter seem to be interested in.

---

*   uk.businessinsider.com/man-who-tried-to-dig-up-140-spitfires-in-burma-2015-9. And also: www.telegraph.co.uk/history/world-war-two/9880471/Burma-Spitfire-hunter-David-Cundall-vows-to-continue-search-despite-loss-of-sponsor.html

**   Andy Saunders, Key Historic Aviation Forum, The Burma Spitfire thread, post 2522, 20 March 2013.

*** Peter Arnold, Key Historic Aviation Forum, The Burma Spitfire thread, post 2532, 26 March 2013.

However, with the dog whistle blown to attract the attention of the Key Historic Aviation Forum, if not the attention of the media, who by now are justifiably sceptical about the whole enterprise, David's team switches to silent running from mid-March until mid-June 2013.

In broad outline, it appears that David is excavating in March in the vicinity of the January 2013 excavation site, before shifting his focus to a second location close to the landing lights and the Old Prome Road, where he digs further deep exploratory trenches in May/June.

He also commissions a survey by Tin Htut of Electrum Services Co. Ltd, which is reported to have revealed an electrical anomaly at a depth of about 11m. David's team digs at this location in June 2013 and uncovers a brick wall of unknown height at a depth of about 3m.

According to Peter, at this point David writes to Jim Pearce asking if Pearce has any information about a brick wall, and claiming that Jim then replies that one of the alleged Seabee witnesses, who he calls 'Tom', described to him how the crated Spitfires were deeply buried in a complex structure involving, shingle, large timbers and brick uprights.

Although apparently contradicting David's 20 January statement that the British Army carried out the burials, it is clearly fortunate for David that Jim is able to recall these crucial details confirming the manner of burial after the discovery was described to him – just as he had also recalled the previously overlooked white stone markers at Myitkyina after they were allegedly discovered and reported to him in December 2012.

Pooling this new series of recollections, the Burma Spitfire Facebook page, which seems to be maintained as a semi-official voice of David's quest by someone in close contact with David himself, reports on 17 June 2013 that:

the team have tried boreholing down to confirm what these anomalies actually are, but have hit thick concrete after 1–2 meters. This was too thick to be broken by the digger shovel. This is actually in line with eyewitness accounts that claim two layers of concrete were laid over the boxes (one immediately above the boxes, and one at the surface), along with brick pillars and teak timber, in order to support the weight of the soil over the boxes. We have also found spare teak timbers that were buried in the hole, seemingly unused.

The anonymous author adds that, 'the site is also in line with where our eye-witnesses claim the aircraft were buried.'*

The monsoon rains soon make further excavation impossible. The resolution of what precisely David and his team had found – if anything – will have to wait until the next digging season begins in early 2014.

```
The Port of Jaffa
Ottoman-ruled Palestine
April 1911
```

In spite of the protests on the part of Captain Parker, the Ottoman customs officer is insistent. His men must take apart, open and inspect all of the Parker party's baggage.

They find nothing illegal. However, the officer remains suspicious and orders Captain Parker and his companions to remain in Jaffa until fresh instructions have been received from Azmey Bey Pasha in Jerusalem.

'But we gentlemen can solve this misunderstanding,' soothes Captain Parker. He invites the customs officer to visit Clarence Wilson's steam yacht, which still rides at anchor out in the harbour, there to discuss the matter over coffee, or maybe something stronger.

All Captain Parker asks is that he and his men are allowed to go ahead and make arrangements appropriate to the comfort of his honour the Sultan's representative and the other honoured guests. The customs officer remains suspicious, but he agrees and soon he is reassured as, looking across the gentle evening swell, he sees the yacht lit up overall.

Then he sees steam belching from the funnel and the waters of the harbour begin to boil as the screw churns under the yacht's stern, the bow pointing at the open sea.

The customs officer swears, calling down the wrath of God on the perfidious Englishman.

He then wonders how he is going to explain Parker absconding to Azmey Bey Pasha and what it is like to be posted to supervise the flies and scorpions in the furthermost desert outpost on the new Hijaz railway.

---

*   The Burma Spitfires Facebook page was active October 2012–June 2013 (the last post).
     www.facebook.com/BurmaSpitfires?fref=ts

PART FOUR
A FINDING OF FACT

Truth is ever to be found in simplicity,
and not in the multiplicity and confusion of things.

Sir Isaac Newton

42

Andy Brockman
RAF Museum
London
19 June 2013
2000 Hours

From the start of the project, Wargaming's archaeology team have agreed that, in contrast to David's secretive approach, they will make the findings of the project and the supporting evidence available as fully as possible, as soon as possible, in an open and accessible way. Tonight is the first stage in that process, with the team presenting what the English courts call a 'Finding of Fact'. That is a finding made by a judge on the basis of probabilities.

Appropriately, the venue for this reveal is the RAF Museum Hendon, located at the famous former RAF aerodrome in north London. The museum boasts an impressive collection of First and Second World War aircraft, at this time including an entire hall devoted to the Spitfire's finest hour, the Battle of Britain.

By 8 p.m., about 100 people have taken their seats in the lecture theatre, including buried Spitfires sceptic Andy Saunders and historian and writer Joshua Levine. Stanley Coombe is also present at our invitation.

However, David has not been invited to join, on the grounds that his views are well known, particularly as he has repeatedly disparaged the team in the press. Tracy wonders if he will try to attend the talk anyway and perhaps make a scene – but he fails to show up.

Nonetheless, as is only right, his views will be represented, both in the presentations and, we suspect, by the brooding figure of David's most vocal supporter, Peter Arnold, who is seated to the far left of the auditorium just out of the eye line of the speakers.

In an attempt to make sure the team's conclusions are shared as widely as possible, the whole session is to be recorded and posted on YouTube.

The camera crew signals that they are ready.

'Our story this evening is about a legendary and iconic plane, the Spitfire,' Tracy begins.

The room grows quiet. He explains that Wargaming became involved in the project because the company is passionate about history, an ethos that has led to partnerships with museums around the world, including the non-profit Pacific Battleship Centre (USS *Iowa*) and the Tank Museum in Bovington, Dorset, with its recently opened Wargaming Education Centre.

Next he shows a photo of a Dornier Do 17 bomber being raised from the bottom of the English Channel. The story is front-page news across the country and he announces that Wargaming has partnered with the RAF Museum to create the Wargaming Interpretation Zone to help tell the story of the Battle of Britain.

With that background in place, he describes how Wargaming became involved in the Burma project following Prime Minister David Cameron's announcement of the British Government's support for the search and the subsequent media reports.

However, he adds that by August 2012 it was becoming clear that there were gaps in the Spitfire story as presented by David Cundall and the British media, which led him to engage a team of researchers and archaeologists to undertake an independent desktop study of the documentary sources and to manage the field archaeology at Mingaladon.

'To explain what we learned, I'll now hand it over to Andy Brockman,' Tracy says.

I take to the podium.

Once more adopting the familiar framework of the police procedural, I introduce the 'scene of the crime' air photographs of RAF Mingaladon airfield from 1944 to 1946, to show the orientation of the runways and how the site changed in the post-war period.

The geography established, I then explain that, just as with a crime, a historian faced with a theory such as the burial of Spitfires must establish means, motive and opportunity.

The opportunity certainly existed, because the RAF was in possession of RAF Mingaladon from May 1945 until the end of British colonial rule in early 1947.

'The motive is a different matter,' I say, theatrically pushing the button on the projector remote.

A blank slide appears.

'That's the motive.'

A few chuckles can be heard from the audience.

I explain that the team scoured hundreds of pages originated by the units based in Rangoon and at Mingaladon, finding nothing to suggest that any of David's three burials had occurred.

I add that the team looked also at British Cabinet papers, secret reports to the Cabinet on the security situation in Burma and reports from the SOE, as well as files from Southeast Asia Command, and in all that material found no evidence of a motive of any kind that would lead the RAF to decide to bury Spitfires.

In fact, 'There is no evidence that such an action was contemplated or discussed, let alone undertaken, by anybody in South East Asia Command.'*

As to the means, if one wanted to bury aeroplanes at Mingaladon, the first requirement is to be able to excavate an enormous amount of earth – and then put it back again, as well as lift and move the heavy crates without damaging the crates or their contents.

'Could they do it?' I ask.

I show a slide taken from the operations record book of 132 Repair and Salvage Unit, the unit most likely to be involved in any burial of RAF aircraft that was operating out of Mingaladon at this period, showing it had just three cranes to undertake its routine work across two airfields.

In fact, the operations record books of this period are a story of shortages of everything, from skilled personnel (because of the number of people being demobilised and repatriated at the end of the war) to timber, local labour and heavy equipment. However, there is graphic evidence of what the RAF and Royal Engineers were actually doing.

I show an entry from an operations record book that details the ongoing problems with weather and damage to the taxi tracks and the runway, which necessitate them being under almost continuous repair at the time David suggests his first burial was taking place.

Finally, I show two contemporary watercolour paintings by British war artist Thomas Hennell, who visited Mingaladon in the summer and autumn

---

*   A video of the Hendon presentation is available at www.youtube.com/watch?v= 7UpAxEJMT6g

of 1945, just as the RAF was extending the runway and repairing the taxiways in the monsoon mud.

Pointing to the paintings, I observe that the RAF have bulldozers (but you can't dig a hole easily with a bulldozer) and graders for levelling, but that the principal tool is the pick and shovel in the hands of labourers, some of whom are Japanese PoWs.

In the absence of any evidence for the burial of aircraft, the next question has to be: is there contemporary evidence for what actually happened to surplus aircraft at Mingaladon?

David and his supporters have never addressed this issue, but I do so now. 'Yes there is,' I say. 'A lot of it.'

Starting at the top of the chain, with Sir Keith Park, I quote Park's postwar report that states between May and August 1945, repair and salvage units returned to service 830 aircraft and dismantled a further 420 that had been written off.[*]

I add that AHQ Burma reported that, in November 1945, 100 aircraft were scrapped at Mingaladon by the Supplies and Industries Branch.

In a moment of humour that sometimes illuminates these dry bureaucratic documents, the officer writing the report observed, 'The aircraft scrap was being put to good account. Local "cottage" industries were making cooking utensils and many other articles which were in short supply in Burma.'[**]

This gives me the cue to introduce the tag line of our whole presentation, 'The salvage operation was not a case of beating swords into ploughshares, but rather warbirds into woks.'

'What about the witnesses?' I ask, before explaining that the witness material as presented by David is extremely problematic, with statements that were uncontextualised, showing evidence of leading questioning, and some others suggesting witnesses were believed without checking, simply because they claimed to be veterans from a particular unit.

I add that there is also no evidence whatsoever that any significant numbers of American personnel, let alone CBs/SeaBees, were transiting through Rangoon with their heavy equipment in August 1945 as the legend alleges, and their alleged witness statements simply have to be discounted.

However, I continue, there is compelling witness evidence, and I reference Group Captain Maurice Short, who saw no Americans or crated aircraft

---

*   Sir Keith Park, Supplement to *The London Gazette*, 19 April 1951, p. 2165.

** Ahq Burma Orb, November 1945 (UK National Archives Air 24/359).

while stationed on Mingaladon, but did recount hearing rumours of odd things happening to aircraft at Mingaladon after December 1945.

'We also had the pleasure of interviewing Stanley Coombe, who has an honest and truthful testimony, once you strip off the other things that other people have laid on top of it,' I add pointedly.

That leaves the alleged cover-up.

'What if there really was a top-secret operation, executed on Mountbatten's orders, and which left no paper trail in the archives?' I ask, before explaining that the only way to be sure that the legend was just that – a legend – was to go to Mingaladon and use all the techniques of field archaeology to ground truth the story.

'Wargaming, to their credit, backed us on this. They said they wanted the best practice, they wanted something that was professional, ethical, produced good science and would be published – which is one of the reasons we're all standing before you tonight.'

Rod Scott takes the podium. Using the bomb assessment of photographs of Mingaladon airfields throughout the period of Japanese occupation Rod explains how our team was prepared to work with the Commonwealth War Graves Commission and other relevant authorities had we discovered human remains.

Dr Roger Clark is the next speaker. He recounts his first phone conversation with David, which led to a twenty-year association scanning for crashed Second World War aircraft in the UK, and explains how geophysics can help in finding buried metallic objects.

As he puts it, an EM survey can exclude the possibility of buried aircraft or provide evidence that is 'necessary but not sufficient' for buried aircraft – nothing more.

Roger is followed by Adam Booth, who explains how he, Andy Merritt and Roger Clark resurveyed the 2004 site (and extended it another 100m, to encompass the area of Old Prome Road). They used differential GPS for mapping and two separate geophysical techniques, but were forced to conclude that the anomalies seemed to have disappeared, a fact the geophysicists found 'puzzling'.

The team concluded that the ground had been disturbed and that some metallic material had been removed in a subsequent excavation.

Martin Brown begins his contribution by underlining the fact that the positions for trenching were agreed collaboratively. He explains this was because the team needed a buy-in from everyone on site, whether it was the airport manager, the STP site manager (an 'absolute star' he says), the geophysics team, David as project initiator, and machine operator Manny Machado.

Next he addresses the excavation on the 2004 anomalies that had promised so much. Posting a slide, Martin shows the audience that the trench revealed a good 2m of disturbed earth, overlying blue clay.

'The blue clay is where we stopped,' he says.

'That blue clay is geological. That's been there for some thousands of years. And there can be nothing of interest below this to anyone looking at the mid-twentieth century.'

Martin's conclusion based on the evidence in the ground alone is that the area had been 'significantly disturbed'.

He ends his segment by describing the archaeology found in the trenches, including wooden beams and sandbags, and the remnants of a road, which is on the right alignment to be the Old Prome Road, and then passes the baton (or rather, the projector remote) back to me, to whom it has fallen to tie everything together.

I walk the audience through the same sequence of documentary evidence the team explored first on the white board in Yangon and then describe how Stanley Coombe arrived in Rangoon in the spring of 1946 soon after his birthday; recounting the now familiar story of how he travelled in the back of an army lorry up the Old Prome Road and reached a point close to the old maintenance and dispersal on the south-west side of the 2013 dig area, and how he then looked out of the left side of the lorry and saw crates and what appeared to be construction activity.

The next day he is back on Mingaladon and asks an RAF man, 'What's in those crates over there?'

He asks because he is still curious and can see them across the airfield, and the RAF man says, 'Would you believe it mate, they're Spitfires.'

Again I suggest that, while it is not conclusive, what Stanley sees is consistent with a delivery of Auster aircraft to Rangoon that is recorded by 41 EU in April 1946.

'At the same time,' I add, 'we also have evidence for what's really going on with Spitfires at Mingaladon,' and describe the aircraft that were forwarded to other stations by the RAF, or handed over to the French Air Force in French Indochina.

'The evidence-based case is that while the opportunity existed for the RAF to bury aircraft at what was then RAF Mingaladon – the means and motive just did not exist.' I conclude, 'The shortages of labour, of heavy equipment, of timber, coupled with the monsoon weather, make it physically, virtually impossible that the burial could have happened as David described it.'

'However, there is ample evidence Spitfires and other aircraft – many hundreds of other aircraft – were disposed of by the RAF in ways that are attested all over the world; by sale, by being flown elsewhere and by scrapping.'

Equally importantly, the archaeological evidence from the 'crime scene' that Martin describes entirely backs up the picture presented by the documentary work to the extent that the team can conclude 'beyond a reasonable doubt' that there are no buried Spitfires on RAF Mingaladon, and by extension any of the other sites that have been mentioned in Burma.

But there is one last question the team wants to answer.

Why did the legend of the buried Spitfires of Burma become so widely believed?

I suggest that for the press and broadcast media, it was great copy. People want treasure stories to be true and from the days of Jason and the Argonauts 'the Quest' has been an archetypal plot from folklore to Hollywood.

People also love a mystery, a 'whodunit?' or a 'why dunit?', and at a time when trust in our politicians and governments is at an all-time low, they also love a conspiracy theory.

The legend of the buried Spitfires contains all these elements.

'We would love to think that Lord Louis Mountbatten, one of the greatest self-publicists in military history, would have had a back channel to initiate a project burying Spitfires,' I suggest.

It would be a fabulous story if he had. But unfortunately, the team concludes that based on the evidence, he didn't.

'And this is where I have to step back and look at these stories as a generic part of the human experience.' I say, deflecting the thrust of the hypothesis away from a direct accusation that David Cundall misrepresented his 'evidence' deliberately.

'So I'm no longer talking about the Burma Spitfire project, I'm talking about the way that myths become a part of our daily lives, and come to be believed.'

I introduce the work of American psychologist Elizabeth Loftus, who is an expert in the generation of memory and how memory can be affected by external circumstances.

She observed, 'Misinformation can cause people to falsely believe that they saw details that were only suggested to them. Misinformation can even lead people to have very rich false memories. Once embraced, people can express these false memories with confidence and detail.'*

This is a deliberate allusion to the way Stanley Coombes' witness evidence was apparently enhanced by suggestions by David which were outside his actual experience.

Loftus continues: 'In the real world, misinformation comes in many forms. When witnesses to an event talk with one another, when they are interrogated with leading questions or suggestive techniques, when they see media coverage about an event, misinformation can enter consciousness and can cause contamination of memory.'

I show one more slide, with a quote from two more psychologists, Ross and Anderson, regarding the nature of belief.

'Beliefs can survive potent logical or empirical challenges,' Ross and Anderson state. 'They can survive and even be bolstered by evidence that most uncommitted observers would agree logically demands some weakening of such beliefs. They can even survive the total destruction of their original evidential bases.'**

The implications of this academic finding for the Burma Spitfires story is also clear and I push the point home, saying, 'Some people can find themselves in a psychological place where they are determined to believe not just in spite of all the evidence but because people are challenging their belief in the first place.'

From his posture it seems Peter Arnold is not convinced by the presentation.

As the team take questions, Peter holds up a scan from David's new geophysical survey, which he claims shows a massive electronic anomaly, just to the left of the runway lights.

'It is too wet to dig now but it will certainly be dug in January 2014,' he announces, stressing the word 'certainly'.***

He offers to share the report with us; however, Adam Booth takes the microphone and says, 'I have seen the data that you're referring to. I was sent them by Htoo Htoo Zaw of STP and they do indeed show one profile that has a very large anomaly.'

* 'Learning and Memory: Planting Misinformation in the human mind: a thirty-year investigation into the malleability of memory', Loftus, Elizabeth F., 2005.
** 'Shortcomings in the attribution process: On the origins and maintenance of erroneous social assessments', in Kahneman, Daniel; Slovic, Paul; Tversky, Amos. *Judgement under uncertainty: Heuristics and Biases*, Cambridge University Press, pp. 129–152.
*** The Q&A session is at www.youtube.com/watch?v=bsc33PkqWVk

Adam observes that there is an explanation that has nothing to do with buried aircraft. He points out that the anomaly is very close to the runway lights where the team also recorded large electromagnetic anomalies. Anomalies that are best explained by the high-voltage electrical cables and other infrastructure relating to the runway lights.

However, we soon discover that Peter's scepticism is shared by a vocal minority posting on the Key Historic Aviation Forum.

43

Tracy Spaight
Key Aviation Forum
Cyberspace
June 2013

Within hours of the presentation, the aviation forum lights up with heated debates about our findings. The arguments will continue for the next three years, with David's supporters waging a tireless campaign against the veracity of the research and the competency of the researchers to the extent that the most vocal seem to have taken on the mindset of a persecuted religious sect – while offering new and, to the more objective readers, increasingly complex and far-fetched explanations of how the Spitfires could have been transported to Mingaladon and buried secretly.

Eventually the thread racks up more than 5,000 posts and a million views before the moderators finally tire of the increasingly confrontational postings, and, like a pub landlord evicting the last few customers who are worse for wear and swearing eternal love and brotherhood before squaring off in the car park, close it down.

By now most of David's supporters (if not David himself) accept the fact that the Spitfires did not arrive through Yangon docks, as the original version of the legend maintained. They thus have to invent new mechanisms for the planes to have arrived, to keep the burial theory going. Soon after the

Hendon lecture, Peter suggests such a new hypothesis: that the planes were flown in, dismantled, loaded into spare crates, and then buried.*

In July 2013, he suggests a new variation on this theory: that the planes might have been sent to Mingaladon by rail from the sister airfield of Hwabi. However, once again there is no trace of such an operation in the documentary record.

Other theories are advanced. David's supporters argue that if the planes didn't arrive through Rangoon docks, then they could have been imported from India via a combination of rail, river and road transport.

No one in the pro-Cundall camp seems to care that, since aircraft can fly, one must immediately ask why would anyone in South East Asia Command authorise such a prodigious waste of scarce resources?

But nevertheless, our team have already examined the records of the Burma railway for 1945–46 held in the National Archives at Kew.

These show clearly that the railway network was in the process of recovery after extensive wartime damage caused by the initial demolition by retreating British forces in 1942, neglect by the Japanese, and particularly by the strategic bombing of transport infrastructure by the Allies during the Burma campaign. It is clear that even by January 1946, there remained gaps of hundreds of kilometres in the permanent way. This fact, combined with the shortage of rolling stock, makes such an operation improbable at best, particularly as there is once again no documentary evidence to support this theory.

If the transport method for the planes keeps changing, so too do the suggested burial locations.

In January 2013, after the T- and L-section announced as the burial location at the Imperial War Museum proves a bust, and the Myitkyina 'crate' proves to be old fencing material, David and Peter argue that the planes were actually buried in a gully just beyond the perimeter fence – and that post-war levelling had further buried the planes to a depth of 30ft.

By June 2013, this theory is discarded in favour of the brick vault burial theory, which is advanced *after* David uncovers a brick wall near the precision approach path indicator (PAPI) lights adjacent to the modern runway.

When this news breaks it is helpful that, as David reports it, Jim Pearce now remembers that he was told the planes were buried in a vault, with brick uprights for support and mahogany beams for protection.

---

*   Peter Arnold, Key Historic Aviation Forum, Burma Spitfire thread, post 2664, 22 June 2013.

Claiming to quote Pearce directly, Peter Arnold writes in the Key Historic Aviation Forum that Pearce told David, 'In response to your question I can advise that Tom [an American CB or Seabee] told me the Spitfires were buried quite deep. He also said the boxes were covered in shingle and that some had mahogany wood on top and sides for protection, as well as brick uprights for support.'*

Soon after, one of the forum readers asks, 'If you are burying some large objects with the intent of retrieving them later, why go to the considerable trouble of putting not just one but two concrete slabs over them. How on earth do you later get the objects out again?'**

The monsoons halt further digging in 2013, but the team (now with sponsorship from Claridon Group, a UK transport company that is developing a presence in Myanmar) returns to dig the same location in March 2014.***

JCB once again lend the expedition heavy earth-moving equipment.

On 15 March 2014, Peter Arnold announces on the Key forum that the concrete slab near the PAPI lights is a concrete bunker. However, after weeks of jackhammering and digging no Spitfires are found.**** However, Andy considers it is likely that this activity destroyed further significant archaeological evidence of the history of RAF Mingaladon.

Meanwhile, Peter Arnold has developed another thesis involving the use of the railway line. On 30 June 2014 he writes, 'I have a copy of the detailed sketch map reference runway 06/24 showing precisely to the foot where 12 crates were offloaded at the railhead at Mingaladon and buried end on end in a single trench straight off the train and into the trench.'*****

The records at Kew show that a railway was built by the British during colonial times and did indeed pass close to the airfield – but again there are no records of such a burial operation, and it is telling that Peter offers neither source nor date for his map. Neither does he offer any explanation as to why this version only emerges after the original explanation for how the aircraft arrived at Mingaladon is shown to be untenable.

*   Peter Arnold, Key Historic Aviation Forum, Burma Spitfires thread, post 2741.
**   Key Historic Aviation Forum, post 2649, 17 June 2013.
***   www.bbc.co.uk/news/uk-england-lincolnshire-26136291?fbclid=IwAR3blJeZ5voY
        hEtBvC7FrNGdY4TAQh_nZ5cDMttMcB5V9Tazjme5vs4atg4
****   w.birminghammail.co.uk/news/midlands-news/new-burma-dighidden-spit-
        fires-6776986
*****   Peter Arnold, Key Historic Aviation Forum, 30 June 2014.

This uncomfortable fact leaves an opening for a final explanation as to how the Spitfires come to be transported and buried without leaving a single trace in the documentary trail from Whitehall to Rangoon.

The theory that the burial is so secret that it never appeared in any of the official records!

As has been shown time and again, suggesting an activity was 'beyond top secret' is the last line of defence of conspiracy theorists faced with unassailable lines of mutually supporting conventional evidence that contradicts their fantastical construct.

Faced with this kind of assertion, there is nothing that a sane researcher can do except to resort once again to Occam's razor, that devastatingly simple test of logic that has done sterling service to scholars since the Middle Ages. That is, that the solution to a problem requiring the least number of assumptions is the most likely to be correct.

And if that fails, the only sensible remaining action is to pour a stiff drink.

44

The Spitfires of Rangoon

A Novel of the Secret War in Burma

by Major William Wills DSO OBE

London Airport
December 1949

On 15 January 1946, the Special Operations Executive was disbanded officially by the Labour Government as there was no longer any need to set Europe ablaze or to mobilise tribal armies in the Far East. Indeed, the amount of fire-arms and explosives in the hands of people such as the Karen was actually causing nightmares to some officials in the Foreign and Colonial Office, who were now concerned about the possibility of Communist insurgencies spreading across the Far East like a bushfire, fuelled by the political and economic bankruptcy of the old colonial powers like the British and the easy availability of military-grade weapons.

However, a number of former SOE officers were absorbed into the Secret Intelligence Service (MI6 to the novelists and journalists) and for one of the new intake, Major Bill Baron, the chance to spend Christmas in the bright lights of ration book-free Washington, rather than in the bone-chilling pea-souper fogs of a London still struggling with the economic austerity of Labour Chancellor of the Exchequer Sir Stafford Cripps was one of the principal bonuses of his new job. Indeed, it almost made up for the extra red tape and form filing that came with operating as a secretive extension of the British Civil Service.

The opportunity to travel in one of the brand new and luxurious British Overseas Airways Corporation (BOAC) Boeing 377 Stratocruisers was an another bonus, particularly to someone more used to the thrill a minute of clandestine short take-offs and landings squeezed into the gunner's seat of a Special Operations Squadron 'Lizzie' or the noise, freeze or fry heating, and stomach-hurling roller coaster ride ploughing through the worst of the weather in an RAF Dakota.

That said, as he boarded the aircraft Bill Baron could not help reflecting that the BOAC's shining new airliner was ugly as sin, looking exactly like a pregnant B-29 bomber. Which in fact was precisely what she was. The Boeing designers had taken the cutting edge, pressurised B-29, placed bunks and a cocktail bar where the bomb bay used to be, and added an upper deck to accommodate the passengers and flight crew, linking the two decks with a spiral staircase.

Now, instead of delivering of 5,000lb of ordnance, or a nuclear weapon, to a target 1,500 miles away, the Stratocruiser could deliver fifty passengers to New York's new Idlewild Airport in just under twenty hours non-stop, 150mph winds on the nose allowing.

Operating this service was considered so important that in a time of severe financial austerity and strict currency controls the national flag carrier, BOAC, had been given a special dispensation by the Treasury to buy ten of the American-built airliners at a cost of $1.5 million each.

The only drawback for the flight as far as Baron was concerned was that his reservation came too late to book one of the bunks, especially as they were large enough to easily accommodate two adults wishing to while away the long hours of the flight.

Nonetheless, this was as comfortable as air travel could get in 1949 and, settling into the wide window seat, he stowed his expensive leather attaché case discreetly in the footwell against the side of the cabin, so that only the most observant would spot the chain running through his sleeve that linked the handle of the case to the body belt that he wore under his civilian suit.

As BA Speedbird Sugar Able climbed into the night and headed west, driven by her four 28-cylinder 3,500hp Pratt & Whitney Wasp Major engines, Baron reflected on his mission and the briefing he received from no less than the Head of Service himself, Major General Sir Stewart Menzies, better known to the rest of Whitehall as 'C'.

In the case were briefing papers for a top-level meeting of intelligence officers regarding a matter of the highest importance for both the British and the Americans, because, since the summer of 1945, when Baron was still operating in the Far East, the Secret Intelligence Service had been trying to establish the identity of a Soviet MGB agent code-named 'Homer'.

Intercepted communications suggested Homer travelled from Washington to meet his Soviet handler in New York twice a week on average and it was now clear that the agent was almost certainly the Washington Embassy's former First Secretary, who was now the Head of Chancery in the Cairo Legation.

The meeting would assess the evidence of guilt, identify Homer's network of contacts and assess the damage his treachery might have done.

For Baron this was also something of a personal mission because Homer was alleged to be none other than one of his contemporaries at Trinity College Cambridge in the early 1930s; the high-flying diplomat, and youngest councillor in the British Foreign and Colonial service, Donald Maclean.

However, while one college alumnus was coming under suspicion as a traitor, he was also looking forward to catching up with the case officer who would be handling the investigation. This was another old friend from his time at Cambridge, who had been appointed recently to follow Maclean as First Secretary of the Embassy.

In the smoke and mirrors of the intelligence world the diplomatic title of 'First Secretary' hid the reality that the post holder was the SIS Head of Station and principal liaison officer with the American 'cousins' in the newly formed Central Intelligence Agency.

His name was Kim Philby.

However, in his head Baron carried another even more secret instruction that came from the highest level in the Government, from Prime Minister Clement Attlee himself.

```
The Terrace of the House of Commons
London
Spring 1950
```

Winston Churchill always denied that he had once joked, 'An empty taxi drove up to 10 Downing Street, and out of it stepped Clement Attlee,' saying instead that he found his wartime deputy '... a gallant and faithful servant of the Crown ...'

Now on a warm spring evening, the two men, the comfortable figure of wartime Prime Minister Churchill, cigar in hand, and the somewhat gangling, acetic frame of serving Prime Minister Attlee, were stealing a quiet moment in a quiet corner of the terrace of the House of Commons overlooking the rolling brown River Thames.

Across the river on the South Bank the new Festival Hall was taking shape and would soon be a part of the Government-inspired expression of confidence in a peaceful, outward-looking creative future, the Festival of Britain; while behind them in the House of Commons the builders and craftsmen were still hard at work salvaging the past as they undertook the final fit out of the chamber, which had been destroyed by the bombs of the Luftwaffe on 10 May 1941.

'Clem, we will disagree on many things,' Churchill ventured, 'but I will always be grateful for your unstinting support during the war.'

'The Labour Party did its duty,' Attlee replied. 'Although our political divisions were deep, our strength is that in time of need we were able to transcend them in the interests of the whole country. But,' Attlee added, 'that would have gone for nothing without your ability to turn emotion into action.'

Churchill smiled and drew on his cigar.

'So what is it that you wanted to tell, and which you could not communicate via a telephone call or a memorandum? Something of great sensitivity I venture, of which the Leader of the Opposition must be informed by a, um, "back channel"?'

'It is,' said Attlee. 'I have taken the decision to cancel Operation Merlin in Burma.' He paused for a moment for Churchill to take in the news.

'You are not disappointed?' Attlee asked.

'Of course not,' Churchill responded, 'Doubtless I would have taken the same decision had I gained the majority of five in the General Election and replaced you as Prime Minister.'

Churchill explained, 'It is clear to me that the strategic situation in the Far East has changed beyond recognition. Burma is no longer a part of the Empire and the aircraft, although beautiful airborne warriors, are obsolete.

'Of course, were the press to hear about the burial they might forget all the hundreds of other aircraft we broke up or pushed off aircraft carriers and label the Operation as another of their "Winston follies", which would be somewhat embarrassing.

'Although rather less of a catastrophe than the Dardanelles,' he added sardonically, referring to his disastrous plan to knock Turkey out of the First World War that had cost Churchill his place in the British War Cabinet and half a million British, ANZAC and Turkish servicemen their lives.

'That thought leads me to ask, who else knows about your decision?'

'In the Cabinet, just Bevin and Manny Shinwell,' said Attlee, indicating the Foreign Secretary and the Secretary of State for Defence, 'and of course Dickie Mountbatten had to be told as he oversaw the operation and he would probably try to write about it in his memoirs.'

'And what does Dickie think?' asked Churchill.

'Dickie ... understands,' Attlee smiled, his neutral bank manager's facade cracking a little. 'Besides, he is enjoying himself hugely charging around the Mediterranean with his cruiser squadron. Although,' Attlee added conspiratorially, 'I did hear that on an exercise he encircled the enemy and ordered his ships to train torpedo tubes to port. A braver man than I am on his staff had to point out that if he gave the order to launch, he would have sunk his own fleet.'

Churchill snorted with amusement, then said, 'Ah, but what about the Americans? They actually dug the ditches and my mother's people can be somewhat garrulous.'

'That too has been dealt with at the highest level,' confided Attlee 'I sent my personal emissary to talk to Harry Truman and to the Director of Central Intelligence.'

'Ah, so like the code breakers at Bletchley Park, these geese won't quack.'

'No,' said Attlee firmly. 'What is buried stays buried in all senses.'

'Thank you Clem, I am confident our reputations are safe in your hands,' Churchill concluded, adding as an afterthought, 'Besides, I think the gentlemen of the press will have enough on their plate chasing scandals closer to home emanating from Moscow and more imminently dangerous to our National Security than retired aircraft corroding in the jungle.'

45

Tracy Spaight
Nicosia, Cyprus
August 2013

The phone rings. It's Mark Mannucci, producer of our documentary film, which is now titled *Buried in Burma*. He's calling me from New York, his voice tinged with excitement. 'You're not going to believe this,' he says, after a quick greeting. 'Are you sitting down?' I tell him that I am, wondering what he's going to say. Mark drops a bombshell.

'We've just discovered that David has dug Mingaladon at least eight times from 1998 to 2000 and in 2004–05.' The revelation leaves me speechless for a moment.

'Eight times? Are you serious?' I ask incredulously. 'Yes,' Mark confirms. 'Deep trenches at multiple locations at Mingaladon.' He explains that this includes a huge area beyond the perimeter fence, where David was insisting we dig after the T- and L-section site proved a bust in January.

'Unbelievable,' I finally manage.

I'm angry at David but, after the events of January, not altogether surprised. I'm angrier at myself for not recognising the layers of misunderstanding shading into a fiction sooner. David led me, my colleagues, the archaeology team, the Leeds geophysicists, his Burmese partners, the British Prime Minister and the world press to believe that he had only done surveys and borehole tests on his early visits to Myanmar.

He told us that it was only in 2004 that he finally secured permission to dig at Mingaladon – and that his dig was halted by the Burmese almost as soon as it began, right at the cliffhanger moment when the excavator struck buried wood. An account which appeared to be backed up by Adam Booth's independent description of the same incident.

Although as our team dug into the archives in the autumn of 2012, we had come to doubt David's understanding and interpretation of the evidence, we continued to believe him when he said the 2013 excavation was his first real opportunity to dig at Mingaladon.

Mark and Anna uncovered David's duplicity by tracking down and interviewing David's former business partner Keith Win, who accompanied David in 1998–2000, and Malcom Weale, the geophysicist who worked with David in late 2004. Room 608's phone conversations with both men lead us to schedule one last shoot in the UK as the reality of the emerging story once again force the team to reconceptualise the film as a meditation on the nature of memory, the modern news cycle and the enduring fascination of wartime legends.

After I hang up the phone with Mark, I write an email to the archaeology and geophysics team, to tell them what Room 608 just discovered.

I also attach a screenshot of the Google Earth air photographs showing the extent of David's excavations in 1998–2000 and 2004–05.

While we had seen and discussed these images before in December 2012, Andy admits that, while they showed disturbed ground and not excavations in progress, he had dismissed them as airfield works, or perhaps the work of local excavators, or perhaps as the work of local excavators, or Ziv Brosh's Israeli consortium, which we knew had also undertaken excavations at the site.

Besides, it was clear that whoever had dug the site, nobody had found any Spitfires. If they had the world would have heard about it.

Of course, it turns out, the physical evidence of the excavation recorded in the Google images was indeed proven by the archaeology. However, nothing in the archaeology showed who had undertaken the digging. Indeed, following the confirmation from the Room 608 team that David was responsible, Andy tells me he regrets that, in what might be seen as a moment of post colonialist prejudice, his first suspects in creating the disturbance were the Burmese.

Of the wider research team, Dr Clark is the first to reply to the group.

'I have to say that a coffee cup got slammed hard on the desk when I saw the extent of activity out there that I never knew about.'

Dr Clarke adds bitterly, 'It feels somewhat of a betrayal.'

Martin Brown is still more outspoken, stating, 'Personally, I think it utterly stinks that we were deliberately directed to re-excavate some of his old workings. I also resent nearly being hurt because of the unstable trench edge, which was a direct result of the investigations that he had omitted to mention.'

Adam Booth, who accompanied David to Myanmar in 2004 and 2012, is the most surprised and shaken by the revelation.

In the relaxed setting of his London apartment he tells Mark on camera, 'I still would have liked there to be Spitfires there.' He adds ruefully, 'If I was a god I would go back to 1947 and I would put a Spitfire in the ground, because it would be fantastic to find that, wouldn't it?'

Then the unfairness of the situation catches him and he says, 'But I'm not a god and I can't do anything about it. And the fact that the geophysical data now cannot be explained is the biggest disappointment for me.'

'Here take a look at this,' Mark Mannucci says, and hands him a laptop.

'There are satellite images from November 2004.'

Adam studies the screen for a moment, and then looks up.

'This is David?' he asks, his voice incredulous. It turns out he has not yet seen my email.

'This is David's dig,' Mark confirms.

'Wow. That's going to explain a lot, isn't it,' Adam says.

Adam laughs, studies the screen, and laughs again.

It takes him a moment to recover his composure enough to speak.

'It's farcical, it's comedic,' he says. 'Blimey.'

Now to find out that he kept things from me. I'd want to sit him down and say, 'Why, why did you keep this stuff from me. I don't understand.'

'Why, why did it have to be that way?' Adam says, his voice breaking with emotion.

Faced with Room 608's August 2013 revelations, Andy and I wonder what else David has kept from us about his previous activities on Mingaladon.

We decide to find out.

46

In July 1993 a fax is sent pitching a TV documentary about the mystery of the buried Spitfires of Mingaladon with Jim Pearce featured as the heroic Spitfire hunter and access to the Burmese administration to be facilitated by an unnamed Burmese-born businessman and accountant.

That accountant we believe to be David Cundall's future business partner, Keith Win.

Born and raised in Myanmar, the son of a Burmese father and an English mother and as the product of two cultures, Keith has spent his working life trying to build bridges between the two countries and by the early 1990s he is living in London.

In 1995, after Aung San Suu Kyi is released from her first period of house arrest, Keith sets up a British–Myanmar trade association to help British businesses that want to invest in Myanmar – particularly in oil and gas, mining, agriculture, and telecoms. Similarly, he seeks to help Burmese companies that want to do business in the UK. As a result, he becomes known in the UK as someone who could navigate the corridors of power in Myanmar.

We believe this is how he comes to the attention of Jim Pearce, who recruits Keith to the cause of the missing Spitfires, initially as a consultant to advise on whether the Myanmar government could be persuaded to allow a group of Westerners to wander around what is effectively a military airfield, with a camera crew in tow, looking for 50-year-old buried aircraft.

At this time, Myanmar is ruled by the latest incarnation of its military government, the Orwellian-named State Peace and Development Council.

By August 1997, David Cundall, who was not mentioned at all in the 1993 fax, appears to have taken over running the Burma Spitfires project. We can state this with some certainly because Peter Arnold writes in a draft appendix to *Spitfire Survivors Volume 2* that on 13 August 1997 '… David Cundall rang me to discuss in confidence my views on a report he had of twelve Mk XIV Spitfires buried at or near Mingaladon airfield, the WWII base just north of Rangoon. That site is now Yangon International Airport.'

Jim Pearce clearly retained some involvement because in the same passage Arnold added, 'A telephone call to Jim Pearce on 2 December of that year alluded to the same story.'

Precisely why David had taken over what had hitherto been Jim Pearce's project is unclear, although it is the period when Jim was most active in getting warbirds out of Russia and so David may be right when he says that he did not have time to oversee the Burma adventure.

It is also the case that the passing of the Protection of Military Remains Act by the British Government in 1986 may have prompted warbird hunters such as David and Jim to search further afield, away from the new licence-based regime in the UK.

Also unclear is precisely how David was connected to the Burmese military government and what, if anything, was promised to whom. However, it has to be said that the members of Burma's successive military regimes have a reputation for not doing anything without an appropriate pay-off, or the promise of a pay off, as a library of US Department of State, European Union and United Nations documents and sanctions make clear.

Overall, as in 2013, it is reasonable to assume any business arrangement involved dividing up the ownership of any Spitfire airframes recovered.

However, we do know that the three existing partners have a falling out in early 1998, and David enters a new partnership with Keith Win to attempt to recover the Spitfires. Keith is able to negotiate access to Mingaladon via what he says is a chance encounter with General Khin Nyunt, Chief of Military Intelligence and first secretary of the SDPC.

Later in 2003–04 the general will become prime minister, before he is purged by the ultimate strong man of the regime, General Than Shwe, who opposes his proposed reforms..*

In 2013, Keith tells Peter Popham of the *Independent* newspaper that the general must have thought he had come with a message from the British Government

---

*   www.independent.co.uk/news/world/asia/some-of-our-spitfires-are-missing-doubts-over-existence-of-160-ww2-fighter-planes-in-burma-8458772.html

because present in his office for the meeting was the foreign minister and the Burmese ambassador to London, as well as a TV crew and photographers.

Keith leaves the meeting with the right to survey, excavate and repatriate any planes they might find, without any encumbrances or customs duties.*

Keith says the general receives a bottle of whisky and a book about the economy as a thank you for his trouble.

Following the agreement, between 1998 and 2000 Keith and David will make eight trips to Myanmar, not simply to undertake a reconnaissance survey, as David had told Wargaming, but in fact to undertake extensive excavations all over former RAF Mingaladon!

'In terms of survey and digs, we started the project really in full swing in 1998, so we had three years, two digs a year – we're talking about six, maybe seven max,' Keith explains to Room 608 in an interview recorded in London in autumn 2013.

Peter Arnold's account corroborates this, reporting that his diary for April 1998 records two mentions of a recent visit to Burma by David and that a further visit was planned for May.

Keith Winn described the nature of the work. 'We had to hire labourers, we had to hire excavators, and we had to bring these excavators on low-loaders. So this is quite serious stuff, it is not just a couple of people with spades digging around here and there.'

As a businessman and accountant, Keith's approach is more analytical than David's, and he recounts being troubled by what he perceived as the disordered state of David's research. He believes that if the story is correct then there must be records of the burial and he sets out to find them, delving into the archives at Kew and contacting surviving veterans of 273 Squadron.

When his research draws a blank, he raises the matter with David, who says simply, 'This was clandestine activity, this was top secret, of course there will be no records anywhere.'

Not satisfied that this is the whole answer, Keith decides to investigate further.

'I contacted a guy called Colonel Hoare, who was a famous commander during the British days fighting the Japanese. He had retired by then and was in the Star and Garter Homes. I went to see him,' he says.

This contact is Colonel Michael 'Mad Mike' Hoare, who served with the British Army in India and Burma during the Second World War, fighting at Kohima and in the Arakan, attaining the rank of major. He will later become famous, and then infamous, leading mercenary forces in the Congo in the

---

*   Room 608 interview with Keith Win.

early 1960s. In 1981 he leads an abortive, Washington-backed coup in the Seychelles, which results in his trial and imprisonment in South Africa.

Hoare, who is reputedly also the inspiration for the character Colonel Alan Faulkner, played by Richard Burton in the film *The Wild Geese*, tells Keith that there was no way this operation could have happened – and that if it had, he would have heard about it for certain.

However, despite this curt dismissal of the buried Spitfire thesis and the complete inability of anyone to find documentary evidence of the burial, Keith decides to press on with the project. He reaches this decision because he has discovered through his high-level contacts in Yangon that certain Burmese generals have heard similar rumours of aircraft buried at Mingaladon.

David has also told Keith that he knows exactly where the planes were buried, and that they just need to go to Mingaladon to dig them up – which is exactly what he also tells Wargaming fourteen years later in 2012.

In May 1998, Keith and David undertake their first dig at the south-east end of former runway 06/24, where there used to be a railway spur. They dig there because (according to Keith) this is where the alleged Seabees had told Jim Pearce the crates containing the aircraft had been buried.

However, 'We searched there. We found nothing,' Keith says.

Then the story changes to 'they were buried near a swampy area', where they then eventually sank. A search at that location again yields nothing.

For one of the subsequent excavations they fly in veteran Stanley Coombe, whom David has met recently. Stanley will visit Mingaladon for the first time since he passed through the airfield as a 21-year-old soldier in spring 1946.

'We went down the road to the site where he said it was. We surveyed. We found nothing,' says Keith.

Next they dig outside the perimeter fence (the same location David wanted to dig in 2013), after clearing a large area of vegetation. But they do not uncover anything here either.

Finally, they dig in the area of the famous 'T' section, which Adam Booth will survey in 2004. Again, nothing is found.

During these early digs, David undertakes the geophysical surveys himself, although he has no training or experience in the gathering and interpretation of geophysical data.

On one occasion, he claims to identify a series of rectangular features about 10ft underground, as Keith relates:

We hired a couple of labourers to dig because at that particular area it was fairly close to some hangars and we weren't allowed to use digging equipment. So we did a hole rather like digging a well. We got down to about 9, 10ft. Then we found these concrete blocks. Underneath we discovered there was an electric cable that supplied the whole airfield.

After this failure, which could easily have knocked out the power for the airport runway lights, Keith insists that they hire a professional geophysicist.

David agrees, so Keith hires Professor U Soe Thein, a Burmese geologist who is a lecturer at Yangon University. The professor surveys the whole area, from the runway to the perimeter fence and beyond.

At this time David is claiming that there were twelve buried planes and by a remarkable coincidence U Soe Thein produces a graph apparently showing twelve peaks.

Excited, Keith calls David, who is catching up with work back on his farm.

David flies out with the same documentary film crew that has covered previous excavation attempts. But when the team digs the new location at Mingaladon – reportedly to a depth of 20ft – they find no buried Spitfires but rather sheets of the same pierced steel plate which the military engineers used to build temporary all-weather roads and runways in the Second World War.

Keith confirms later that the team also excavated some discarded aircraft parts, although none can be identified as coming from Spitfires, but of some concern are the lumps of iron ore, "the size of a coffee table" which have also come up in the digger's bucket and which could skew the results of the magnetometry surveys.*

The film crew that accompanies David includes Gerrard Williams, a respected television journalist and filmmaker who has over the course of his thirty-year career worked for Sky, BBC and Reuters.**

Gerrard is a friend of Jim Pearce, which is how he meets David – and how he ends up travelling to Myanmar.

According to Keith, Gerrard travels to Burma twice, partly at his own expense, to shoot about thirty hours of video of the various excavations.

Gerrard's exact arrangement with David is unclear, but he may have had some form of financial interest in the results of the expedition, forming a company called Spitfire Hunters Ltd in January 2008.***

---

*   Room 608 interview with Keith Win.

**   Room 608 interview with Keith Win. Keith confirmed Gerrard Williams was present at the 1999–2000 digs.

***   Companies House: beta.companieshouse.gov.uk/company/06471945 retrieved 20/08/2019

Gerrard will eventually get tired of looking for the mythical Spitfires of Burma and decide instead to hunt for another quarry for which there is more documentary evidence than exists for the Spitfires, the alleged retirement home of Adolf Hitler and Eva Braun in the town of Bariloche in provincial Argentina.

The result is a name change for Spitfire Hunters Ltd, which becomes Greywolf Media in September 2011* and a book and documentary film, both titled provocatively *Greywolf: The Escape of Adolf Hitler.*

According to Gerrard's thesis, Hitler and Braun escaped the Führerbunker through a secret tunnel and made their way to a waiting aircraft, which flew them to General Franco's Spain. Then, as the people of Berlin suffered their Götterdämmerung in the pincers of the Soviet Army's 1st Belorussian Front led by Marshal Georgy Zhukov, and Ivan Koniev's 1st Ukrainian Front, the fugitives boarded a U-boat that brought them to the safety of fascist-influenced Argentina. There Hitler and Eva lived in a peaceful retirement, raising their two daughters and planning the Fourth Reich and revenge on the Allies, until Hitler died in 1962.

The book is greeted by scathing reviews from the world historical community. Respected UK historian Guy Walters dismisses the book as, '2,000% rubbish,' telling *The Guardian* subsequently that, in his opinion, 'It's an absolute disgrace. There's no substance to it at all. It appeals to the deluded fantasies of conspiracy theorists and has no place whatsoever in historical research.'**

Sergio Widder, Latin America director of the expert Nazi hunters at the Simon Wiesenthal Centre, also takes the trouble to condemn the premise of the book stating:

> Argentina was the main haven for Nazi war criminals. Men like Mengele and Eichmann were protected by the Argentine state.
>
> But there is no serious evidence Hitler survived the war, let alone came to Argentina. These stories should be for novels, not history.***

By now somewhat accident prone in his adventures in the nether regions of pseudohistory, Gerrard also finds himself of the wrong side of a lawsuit brought by Argentine author Abel Basti, who accuses him of plagiarising his

---

*   Companies House Note of Change of Name by Resolution, 14 September 2011.

**   www.theguardian.com/world/2013/oct/27/hitler-lived-1962-argentina-plagiarism

***   www.thesun.co.uk/archives/news/423353/did-hitler-live-to-old-age-here-in-argentina/

research into the Hitler in Argentina story – claims Gerrard denies*. While seperately his principal financial supporter, hedge fund manager Magnus Peterson, also runs aground on a legal rock and is sentenced to thirteen years in prison for fraud, forgery, false accounting and fraudulent trading in connection with the collapse of his Cayman Island Hedge Fund.**

The UK Serious Fraud Office issue a press release stating Peterson's investors have lost an estimated $536 million, while Peterson pays himself £5.8 million between 2005 and 2009, but at least Gerrard, who has no knowledge of, or role in, Peterson's criminality, has made his film, which is released in November 2012***.

But all that lies in the future; for now Gerrard is furious that the Mingaladon dig has once more proved a bust, since he had put up his own money to help fund the documentary.

He withdraws from the project.

In 2013, Room 608 contact Gerrard Williams to ask if he would be willing to talk with us or share the video footage. He replies helpfully that there was, 'not a snowball's chance in hell'.

Soon after Gerrard Williams' exit to pursue the location of Adolf's retirement home, David and Keith face a fresh disaster, losing the contract to search for the Mingaladon Spitfires to an Israeli team led by yet another friend of Jim Pearce from the small world of elite warbird hunters, former Israeli Special Forces operator, businessman and entrepreneur Ziv Brosh.

Ziv claims to be convinced that the planes are buried at Mingaladon, and he also claims to have documents to prove it.

A long-time aviation enthusiast and pilot, Ziv at one time even owned a de Havilland Tiger Moth, the basic trainer that introduced most future Spitfire pilots to the big blue in the late 1930s. But that is not the only personal and cultural connection between Myanmar, the State of Israel and the Spitfire. R.J. Mitchell's fighter also holds a special place in the hearts of Israelis.

During the Israeli War of Independence, sixty-two aging Mark IX Spitfires purchased from Czechoslovakia are among the first aircraft to be flown by the fledgling Kheil HaAvir (Israeli Air Force), while the architect of Operation Focus, the pre-emptive strikes that destroyed the Egyptian Air Force on the ground on the first day of the Six-Day War in 1967, and later seventh President

*   www.theguardian.com/world/2013/oct/27/hitler-lived-1962-argentina-plagiarism
**   Serious Fraud Office press release. 23 January 2015, www.sfo.gov.uk/2015/01/23/mag-
       nus-peterson-sentenced-13-years-prison, retrieved 20 August 2019.
***   www.imdb.com/title/tt2493402/

of Israel, Ezer Weizman, earlier flew a personal black-painted Spitfire with a rakish red-painted prop spinner.

In another twist of the plot, worthy of author and former RAF pilot Roald Dahl, the Israeli military and arms industry develop a long-term relationship with Burma's military, with the result that these same Spitfires will be sold to Burma in 1954; while adding yet another layer of irony, the first air-to-air kill made by the Kheil HaAvir is an Egyptian Air Force Spitfire shot down by Gideon Lichtaman on 8 June 1948.

Between 2000 and 2003, Ziv travels to Myanmar several times[*] and excavates four times at Mingaladon.[**] Nothing is found to corroborate the burial story and no report of the excavations are ever published, although Peter Arnold reports that the Israeli team concluded that they were in the right area but not digging deep enough.[***]

We later find out that Ziv might have been playing with loaded dice. Interviewed again by Room 608 Productions in autumn 2013, David claims to have fed the Israeli team false information on the burial location to throw him off the track – though typical of the shifting alliances in the warbird world, the two also appear to have been working together on other occasions.[****]

---

[*]   In July 2002 Brosh met with the Minister for Communications, Posts and Telegraphs Brig. Gen. Thein Zaw. At the time the Israeli was a Director of the Rural Telephone Communication (RT Com: Investment) Co. of Israel. www.burmalibrary. org/NLM/ archives/2002-07/msg00021.html
[**] Communication with Tracy Spaight, 20 August 2013.
[***] 'And finally those buried Burmese Spitfires!' Peter Arnold, draft appendix to *Spitfire Survivors Vol. 2.*
[****] Room 608 interview.

47

Lincolnshire and Myanmar
2004

In 2004, David manages to wrestle back control of the contract from Ziv Brosh's Israeli group and is back in Myanmar by the autumn, ready to undertake yet more surveys and excavations.

David has also broken with Keith Win, with Keith claiming in an interview with the *Independent* newspaper that in 2000 he was left stranded in Myanmar with a bill for £5,500 to pay for their rented apartment after David told him he had run out of money and would return to the UK to obtain more.[*]

However, Keith claims it was he who introduced David his next business partner, an English-born, Australian-based marine salvage skipper called Michael Hatcher.

Keith tells Room 608 Productions that Mike Hatcher became involved through another deal Keith was brokering with the Myanmar Government, to locate the famous Dhammazedi Bell, stolen from the Shwedagon Pagoda by Portuguese colonialists in 1612 and lost in the Rangoon river.[**]

What is certain is that in the autumn of 2004 Hatcher and his Singaporean partner, businessman Edward Wong are on the ground at Yangon Airport along with David, geophysicist Adam Booth and an Australian TV crew who have worked with Hatcher on previous projects.

---

[*] 'Some of our Spitfires are missing: Doubts over existence of 160 Second World War fighter planes in Burma', Peter Popham, the *Independent*, Sunday, 20 January 2013.

[**] Keith Win, interview with Room 608 Productions.

Hatcher and Wong appear to be facilitating the project through their own high-level contacts within the Burmese government and business elite.*

As Adam Booth recalls, David was also in for an abrupt lesson in control, not least because, in contrast with the Lincolnshire farmer, and not least according to his own legend constructed through biographies and TV documentaries, Mike Hatcher is one of the most successful treasure hunters in the world, and he is conscious of maintaining that image on camera.

What seems like a single-minded desire to achieve status and control is perhaps no surprise because, born in 1940, Yorkshireman Mike Hatcher had the toughest and most unstable of of childhoods. After his parents' marriage breaks up in 1942 the 2-year-old Mike, along with his older brother David and younger sister Jessie, enter the Hollins Hall children's home. It will be the first of a series of such homes. Eventually, like many poor British children with difficult family backgrounds, Hatcher becomes a Dr Barnardo's boy and is sent to Australia to make a new life, arriving at Sydney's Circular Quay in 1954 as part of the Australian Government's effort to increase the new nation's population by at least 1 per cent per year.

As a 'New Australian', Mike Hatcher gets his start in marine salvage in 1970, when he sets up a salvage company to recover scrap metal, tin and rubber from Second World War merchant ships, and by 'cracking' lost submarines for scrap and their clandestine cargos, regardless of the fact they are the maritime military graves of their crews.

In the 1980s he switches focus to the cargos of export porcelain that are available on the shallow and treacherous reefs of the South China Sea around Cambodia, Vietnam and Indonesia. The switch is lucrative, as Mike Hatcher becomes a multi-millionaire when, after years as a jobbing salvage operator, he strikes pay dirt in 1985 with the discovery of the wreck of the 1,150-ton Verenigde Oost-Indische Compagnie (VOC), or Dutch East India Company, ship *Geldermalsen*, and her cargo of 150,000 pieces of export porcelain made in the Jingdezhen region of Jiangxi province, the 'porcelain capital of China'.

The so-called 'Nanking Cargo' is sold over five days in April and May 1985 by Christie's, who take over two floors of the Amsterdam Hilton for the auction. The auctioneers print a record 12,000 catalogues for the sale, which attracts 125,000 absentee bidders and 5,000 bidders who plan to bid in person at the auction.

---

*   David Cundall, interview with Room 608 Productions, Dr Adam Booth, interview with Andy Brockman.

Come the auction itself, eight auctioneers work in a relay to bring the hammer down on the 2,800 lots.

However, in spite of being given the No. 1 paddle at the auction as a courtesy, two Chinese ceramics experts, who are sent from Beijing to bid for what the Chinese Government regard as their stolen cultural heritage, leave empty-handed. Their budget of $30,000 does not even cover the opening price of the lots they wish to bid for. This does not concern Michael Hatcher, who leaves the auction richer by more than $20 million.

Then in 1999 he hits a second, even greater, commercial and publicity jackpot when he discovers the wreck of the ocean-going junk *Tek Sing* in the Gaspar Strait in Indonesia.

Known popularly as China's *Titanic* on account of the more than 1,500 souls who were lost with the ship on the night of 6 February 1822, at modern prices the cargo of classical Chinese porcelain *Tek Sing* has taken to the seabed is worth an estimated £100 million at auction. It is this mother lode of porcelain that Mike Hatcher intends to mine.

However, in addition to attracting the ire of archaeologists, Hatcher's activities have also led him into legal squalls. In the case of the *Tek Sing*, Hatcher's Australian company claims to be working under a permit held by an Indonesian company, but this is later revealed to be a shell company and the alleged beneficial owner is an Indonesian general who has forged signatures for the permit.[*]

As a result, seven containers of artefacts that Hatcher has quietly shipped out of the country are seized in Australia, under the Protection of Movable Cultural Heritage Act 1986, and in 2001 some 71,939 pieces of porcelain from the *Tek Sing* cargo are returned to Indonesia,[**] however, the bulk of the cargo has already been sent to auction in Europe, netting almost $410 million.

Captain Hatcher will later find himself on the run from the Indonesian police on suspicion of illegal recovery operations in Indonesian waters and attempting to smuggle antiquities out of the country. It is reported in *The Times* that he faces a five-year prison sentence if captured.[***]

In 2004, however, still flush from his success lifting and selling the Tek Sing cargo, Hatcher partners with David Cundall to dig for the potentially

---

[*]   Hauser-Schaublin, Bridget and V. Prott, Lyndel (eds), *Cultural Property and Contested Ownership: The Trafficking of Artefacts and the Quest for Restitution*, p. 97.

[**]   www.unesco.org/new/fileadmin/MULTIMEDIA/HQ/CLT/pdf/Report_from_Australia_anne.pdf

[***] www.thetimes.co.uk/article/treasure-hunter-michael-hatcher-becomes-prey-for-deep-sea-looting-t56vhdqqb78

equally valuable buried Spitfires of Mingaladon and, while Adam Booth recalls that Hatcher ensured that he, not David would be depicted as the finder in the event Spitfires were discovered, at a fundamental level the project remains a partnership of like minds. The published records of both men suggest neither has much time for the methods, and ethics, of mainstream archaeology. The feeling is mutual.

Many archaeologists regard the approach taken by Mike Hatcher and David Cundall as unethical treasure hunting leading to the illegitimate commercial exploitation of cultural heritage.

In his review of Christiaan J.A. Jorg's book, *The Geldermalsen History and Porcelain*,* which details the sale of the *Geldermalsen* cargo, archaeologist George L. Miller quotes the catalogue description of Hatcher's work provided by Christie's in 1986, 'The Nanking Cargo is the result of exhaustive professionalism which is the hallmark of Captain Hatcher and team.'

Miller then comments acidly, 'As the Christie's copywriters did not name the profession involved, perhaps they are right; however, they certainly were not talking about archaeology.'**

The Chinese Government are equally scathing. As reported in a 2007 article carried on the Chinese Government news website China.org.cn, Mike Hatcher is the treasure-hunting 'disaster' who forced the Chinese to set up their own maritime archaeology unit.

Precise details of the partnership between David and Mike Hatcher are unclear, however, Adam Booth recalls Hatcher was the financial backer and figurehead of the 2004–05 excavations with the result that, in August 2004, David is able to fly the young geophysicist from Leeds University to Yangon. Adam is tasked with undertaking a survey of the latest alleged Spitfire burial site at former RAF Mingaladon to professional standards.***

Discussing the events of 2004 with Andy Brockman, Adam recalls that there was also a local business partner present at the survey site. A man who appeared important enough to inspire fear among some of the Burmese members of the team.

In an interview with Room 608 Productions David confirms that this was his Burmese agent, a 40-year-old Burmese business tycoon named Tay Za.

---

*   Jorg, Christiaan J.A., *The Geldermalsen History and Porcelain*, Groningen, Netherlands: Kemper Publisher, 1986.

**   Miller, George L., 'The Second Destruction of the Geldermalsen', *The American Neptune*, 1987, 47(4): pp. 275–81.

*** Adam says that they only did a small test dig in August 2004 before it was halted. He was unaware of the November excavations, as he had already returned to the UK.

Like Mike Hatcher, Tay Za has a very interesting back story, at least according to a leaked profile forwarded to the US State Department from the embassy in Yangon, which describes him as the Burmese military regime's 'Number One Crony' and a man with close business links to Singapore.

In the early 1990s, Tay Za begins his relationship with the ruling Burmese military, and in particular with Brigadier General Win Hlaing, the Director of the Ministry of Defence Directorate of Procurement. The general helps Tay Za and three other young businessmen to establish the Myanmar Billion Group. The new venture becomes Burma's leading business conglomerate.

Tay Za himself maintains his connections with the Tatmadaw's Defence Procurement Department and developing a good relationship with the Russian ambassador to Burma, he obtains sales posts representing various Russian companies in the defence sector, including the Military Industrial Group (MAPO), Aviaexport, and the helicopter company Rostvertol. He also forms Myanmar Avia Export and reportedly earns substantial commissions from sales to the Burmese military of arms, ammunition, Mi-17 transport helicopters, and MiG-29s jet fighters. In short, although he denies it, many, including the United States Government Treasury Department, believe Tay Za is now one of Burma's leading arms dealers.*

By 2004, when David states he was his agent in Burma, Tay Za's business empire has grown to include land and marine transport, plantations, an airline, telecommunications, oil exploration, rice mills, and vehicle imports, while his construction arm undertakes projects ranging from building service apartments to golf clubs and high-end shopping malls. Yet there are reports that behind the flashy cars, a private gambling resort, and a string of multi-million dollar houses in Yangon and Singapore, the tycoon has cash flow problems.

A subsequent leaked US Embassy email describes how Tay Za is reported to owe a fellow high roller $10 million as a result of bets laid on English Premier League football matches.**

Seen in that light, Tay Za's involvement with David and Mike Hatcher in the search for the mythical Spitfires of Mingaladon may be just another punt for a compulsive gambler. Or it may be that, like David, Tay Za sees himself basking in the international spotlight if the punt succeeds and the Spitfires fly. He certainly seems to enjoy the limelight.

Another leaked US Embassy intelligence report drops the usual epithet of regime 'crony', instead describing the businessman as 'Tay Za the Rock

---

*   US Treasury Department Press release 2/5/2008 www.treasury.gov/press-center/press-releases/Pages/hp807.aspx.
**   Leaked US Embassy Intelligence Report, 15 December 2008.

Star' and adding that several sources have claimed the tycoon always wanted to be the centre of attention, to the extent that at an anniversary party for his airline, Air Bagan, he climbed on stage and sang several songs to an adoring audience of 1,500.*

However, in October 2004, even as the fieldwork at Yangon airport is in full swing, with the apparent support of both one of the regime's leading fixers and the Prime Minister, a power struggle at the top of the State Peace and Development Council (SPDC) renders these high level contacts suddenly useless, perhaps even dangerous.

On 18 October 2004 a terse one-line announcement over the signature of SPDC Chairman General Than Shwe, confirms that Prime Minister, and early facilitator of the search for the buried Spitfires, Khin Nyunt has been permitted to retire on health grounds. That is the kind of 'ill health' which requires the now former Prime Minister to be placed under house arrest with an armed guard and to be sentenced later to forty-four years in prison on corruption charges (he was released in 2012).

These are the events which lie behind Adam Booth's recollection of soldiers arriving at the dig site on Yangon airport to close down the excavations without warning.

With David's highest-ranking patron in Burma suddenly rendered a non-person, and facing accusations of corruption, it is no surprise that this latest phase in the search for the buried Spitfires is facing imminent collapse.

David claims later to Room 608 that Than Shwe was particularly angry because he had been kept out of the loop regarding the search for the Spitfires and that, on account of the General's displeasure, he spent five weeks confined in his hotel, before he was allowed to leave for the UK.

However, some sort of accommodation with Than Shwe and the Generals appears to have been patched up by late November 2004, because further geophysical surveys, undertaken by yet another surveyor, take place at Mingaladon extending into the early months of 2005.

This train of events leads to one final conclusion to be drawn from the series of abortive surveys and digs at Mingaladon between 1997 and 2005. That is, that when it came to contacts at the highest levels of the Burmese military regime, David Cundall and his various associates during this period, were swimming in those murky waters, taking the role of the guileless pilot fish picking advantageous titbits from the teeth of at least two of the largest sharks in the pool.

---

*   Leaked US Embassy Report, 6 November 2007.

48

Tracy Spaight
East Anglia
Summer 2012

The interview takes place in a parked car on a suburban street and has something of the feel of a clandestine rendezvous between a spy and their controller during the Cold War. In fact, far from being a long-term deep penetration agent, Malcolm Weale is an East Anglian archaeology enthusiast with a passion for his version of archaeological geophysics.

A youthful forty-something, Malcolm has been metal detecting since he was 7 years old. He even lives in an underground house and at this time he operates a company, Geofizz Ltd, which acts as an agent for metal detecting equipment marketed by German company OKM GmbH. On his website he claims to have helped to find a Roman villa in Norfolk, a Viking ship buried under a car park, and First World War trenches in Ypres.*

However, as Andy had already warned Wargaming, Malcolm's work is controversial in archaeological circles because he does not produce written reports and his equipment supplier does not produce detailed technical specifications, which would allow the data from the equipment to be peer reviewed. This is a core requirement of academic acceptance and, as a result, fairly or not, most mainstream geophysicists, including the Wargaming team of Adam Booth and Roger Clark, dismiss his work as, at best, crude metal detecting.

However, this no academic frills approach has found a ready market in amateur-led projects that do not follow the same professional working

---

*   news.bbc.co.uk/2/hi/uk/6386991.stm

models as academic archaeology and one such ready and unregulated market lies among the groups who search for crashed military aircraft.

It is this work that brings Malcolm and Geofizz Ltd to the attention of David Cundall via a television programme called *Fighter Dig* on the British television network Channel 5. In the broadcast Malcolm claims to use state-of-the-art ground-penetrating radar to locate the famous Hurricane fighter which crashed near Buckingham Palace during the Battle of Britain after colliding with a Dornier Do 17 bomber of the Luftwaffe's KG76 that had been lining up to attack the Royal residence.[*]

When the programme airs in late May 2004 Malcolm appears to pinpoint the site, allowing the excavators to find the aircraft, live on television, in the presence of the pilot of the Hurricane, Flight Sergeant Ray Holmes RAFVR of 504 Squadron. This no doubt impresses David, so he gets in touch with Malcolm in the autumn and convinces him to embark on the long flight to Myanmar.

Malcolm is sceptical of David's story, but he is a practical businessman with a living to earn and, as he says it in an interview with Room 608 Productions, 'If someone's going to pay me and I've got the equipment, I will go and look.'

And go he does, arriving in Yangon in late November.

While the mainstream of archaeological geophysics discounts his work, Malcolm is conscientious in his own way and wants to undertake a systematic survey of the area. However, he finds David's approach is less focused.

As Malcolm describes it in an interview with Room 608 Productions (imitating David's voice):

> *'Try over here. Try here. Try here. Try here.'*
>
> And I was, like, 'David, we need to scan the whole area to see the make-up and the build-up of the land. And then, try and pick out somewhere that's different that's got anomalies in the same sizes and shapes that you're looking for.'
>
> But David keeps moving from one place to another, to another, to another, to another. We couldn't build up a decent picture of the area.

Malcolm also recalls looking at his data and telling David, 'We've got an anomaly here, let's investigate this further.'

Malcolm continues, again mimicking David's voice:

[*]   Broadcast on 30 May 2004.

'No, no, no, no, get the digger over, get the digger over.' And within minutes, they ripped it all open, there was water gushing everywhere and broken drains and you know, big old corrugated metal pipes.

There was no archaeological method in it at all. It was just totally, as quick as he can dig it out, find out what it was and then no, never mind, fill it in, move on. Nothing recorded, nothing apart from me taking the photographs.

As soon as he realised it wasn't what he was looking for, the crated Spitfires, he just turns around, scratches his head and, says, 'Right, try over here Malcolm.'

And I was just like, this is madness.*

On their last day on the airfield, David asks Malcolm to scan the perimeter road. 'Just go out there and do a long scan of the red road, just a quick one.'

'So that's what I did,' Malcolm says, adding, 'And the results were quite interesting, to be fair. And he saw them, and he said, "That's it. You found them. That's the Spitfires!"'

Malcolm tries to explain that it could be anything, but David is convinced he has found his aircraft. He even tells Malcolm that he has ten transport aircraft on standby to fly out the Spitfires and that American collector Jerry Yagen, owner of the famous Military Aviation Museum and Fighter Factory restoration workshop at Virginia Beach, is in line to buy some of the aircraft.

However, this will be a parting of ways. Malcolm has had enough and returns to the UK. He will later tell the *Independent* newspaper and Room 608 Productions that he was never paid for his work. However, later still he tells Room 608 that Gerrard Williams actually paid him 'several thousand pounds' for the data from Mingaladon.

When in 2012 the BBC reports that David has discovered thirty-six Spitfires at Mingaladon, Malcom can only laugh. 'If David is out there telling the world that these [the scans] are buried Spitfires and that I told him they were, then that's not true.'

Malcolm attempts to rationalise the irrational, 'No, he's elaborated that in his head. You know, I never said that. They're just anomalies on the side of an airfield.'

Malcolm looks at the screen of the Mac that displays his scan from 2004. 'They do look a bit aircraft shapey,' he says, adding quickly, 'if you use your imagination.'

---

*   Room 608 interview with Malcom Weale.

The impression he leaves is that he believes David Cundall possesses just that kind of imagination. The imagination of a born storyteller, or a born salesman.

Malcolm is curious also as to where our team had dug in January 2013 – he is shown the location on a shot taken from Google Earth. Malcolm studies the image. 'Exactly the same place,' he exclaims. 'It's exactly the same spot, exactly the same place where he already knows that there was nothing there because he's already dug it!

'And presumably the archaeologists knew that it had been disturbed already, it wasn't virgin ground?' he asks.

'They realised that in the middle,' Mark confirms.

Malcolm laughs. 'You could see from the ground that a lot of it had been disturbed where he had been digging before and he was putting in trenches everywhere. I mean, as deep as possible until the sides were falling in and they were filling up with water.'

The excavation begun in November 2004 continues into the early spring of 2005, at which point, with nothing to show for their effort and expenditure except a series of collapsing water-filled holes, Mike Hatcher and the Singapore based investors back out. Once again David has run out of money and is forced to shut down the dig.

He returns to Myanmar in 2007 to try to secure a new contract from his contacts in the government, but by then the State Peace and Development Council has other, more pressing, concerns.

49

On 25 May 2007 the ruling SPDC lays down an unmistakable warning to dissidents as Daw Aung San Suu Kyi's term of house arrest is extended for a further year.

However, the act of political repression aimed at the one person who has enough respect both within Burma and internationally to achieve a peaceful transition of power to a civilian government does nothing to stave off the inevitable social explosion, because, distorted as it is by the incompetence and corruption of the generals and their civilian hangers-on, the Burmese economy is a basket case.

On 15 August 2007 the state-owned Myanmar Oil and Gas enterprise abruptly removes all fuel subsidies, raising the price of diesel oil overnight from $1.40 to $2.80 a gallon, and the price of natural gas by 500 per cent, which has the effect of raising other prices, principally the price of food.

This is critical because the average family in Myanmar spends 70 per cent of its income on food and this level of price increase is unsustainable by the bulk of the population. The situation is not tenable because, in the name of liberalising the national economy, as suggested by the International Monetary Fund, the government has lit a fuse of resentment within its own population.

In less than a week the fuse burns down and, led by Buddhist Monks, the streets of Yangon explode with righteous, but non-violent, anger. On 19 August 2007, the citizens of Yangon take to the streets in protest.

The regime responds by well-practised reflex and a wave of arrests is instigated in an attempt to decapitate the growing movement. However, for now it is too little, too late to prevent the human streams of hope and anger from spreading across the country and coalescing into a tide.

Worse still for the regime, on 28 August Buddhist monks in the oil town of Sittwe, in the Rakhine State in the remote north-west of Myanmar, join the protest.

By September the demonstrations have spread to more or less every city and division of the Union of Myanmar and, in spite of fierce censorship and a limited telecommunications infrastructure outside Yangon, witness reports and video begins to appear on the internet via independent news websites and blogs, raising the profile of the growing insurrection in the outside world to the embarrassment of the SPDC.

The regime can only respond in its, by now customary, thick-eared manner, by upping the level of violence, and on 5 September a peaceful demonstration led by monks in Pakkoku, close to Mandalay, is broken up by riot squads using tear gas, warning shots and the liberal employment of bamboo riot sticks.

In reaction to this latest provocation, a new umbrella group, the All Burma Monk's Alliance, demands an apology from the regime, an end to the violence, the release of all political detainees and action to mitigate the price rises that kicked off the whole protest movement. The regime is given until 17 September to respond.

Of course, the SPDC has no intention of responding positively to the demands. Although President Than Shwe seems to want to bring about reforms, the army cannot afford to be seen to buckle under duress, especially when the opposition is armed with nothing more lethal than a begging bowl. But for now it seems to sit frozen in the face of the rearing cobra upon which it has placed its boot.

The failure of the regime to take any positive action to halt the growing protest movement results in a further wave of protests which shows all the signs of growing into a fully fledged insurrection as people from all walks of life begin to sense that this time, maybe, just maybe, there are simply too many of them for the regime's conscripts to face down at the barrel of an assault rifle.

The authorities in Nay Pyi Taw now decide enough is enough and send out the army and paramilitary thugs of the Swan Ahr Shin to reclaim the streets.

Ngway Kyar Yan Monastery
South Okkalapa township, Rangoon
27 September 2007

After a twenty-minute stand-off and an exchange of bricks and stones, the two-star general in charge of the search and arrest operation runs out of patience and orders one of his Chinese-built trucks to ram the gates of the monastery.

With an entry forced, the soldiers gather together any monks and civilians they can find, regardless of age or sex, beating them up with fists and bamboo riot sticks and making free with their assault boots. The general berates and strikes out at any of his men who appear to hesitate in dishing out the punishment. Then the soldiers ransack the place.

After around an hour and a half witnesses report it is all over. The courtyard of the monastery is an ugly mess of broken glass, torn saffron robes, and blood.

Around 70 people, lay persons and monks, have been thrown into the back of army trucks and driven off to an unknown destination.[*]

In response to this and other brutalities, the United Nations, United States and European Union impose stringent economic sanctions on Myanmar, which make it impossible for David Cundall to resume digging until the political and economic thaw following the elections of March 2012.

---

[*]   *Bullets in the Alms Bowl: An Analysis of the Brutal SPDC Suppression of the September 2007 Saffron Revolution*, p.83

50

On his return to Great Britain from Jerusalem, Captain Montagu Parker tells *The Times of London* that his team's scientific work was of extraordinary interest, the publication of Père Vincent's report 'Underground Jerusalem-Discoveries on the Hill of Ophel' demonstrates that. However, unfortunately the team has failed to find any new Hebrew documents.

Questioned by the reporter, Captain Parker also regrets that, 'I cannot say anything about the rumours in connection with the Mosque of Omar until the Turkish commission of inquiry has presented its report.' The captain adds that he has 'definitely' arranged with Turkish officials to resume work on 1 August.

This news is reported all over the world, including in the *New York Times*, and on 26 October Clarence Wilson's yacht once again enters the Palestinian port of Jaffa with Captain Parker on board. However, before he can continue his scientific work a message is communicated that it would be 'unwise' for Parker's team to go ashore. The message is heeded and the *Water Lily* steams away, heading for Port Said.

During the First World War, Captain Montagu Brownlow Parker will serve once again in the British Army, being mentioned in dispatches for brave and meritorious service five times and winning the French Croix de Guerre.

On 10 October 1951, he succeeds to the title of Earl of Morley. He dies on 28 April 1962 at the age of 83, unmarried. Archaeologist Père Louis-Hugues Vincent dies in Jerusalem aged 88 on 30 December 1960.

Their excavations in Jerusalem are never resumed.

Meanwhile some $125,000 of investors' money has been spent on the adventure and no one quite knows how. That is approximately $2.9 million at 2012 values.

Yet that lesson, just one of many in the shadow economy of treasure hunting, has still not stopped the fools, charlatans, true believers and commissioning editors on digital TV channels, who are still searching for the Ark of the Covenant, or for their own Holy Grail, and who are prepared to bet the farm on finding it.

Meanwhile, even a century later, Père Louis-Hugues Vincent's academic report, describing the archaeological evidence excavated by the Parker expedition, remains one of the core texts in the archaeological literature of Jerusalem.

51

```
Goldeneye
Oracabessa Bay, Jamaica
March 1955
```

To Willy Wills the piano keys seem to dance as Nöel Coward, that unmistakable voice rich as a fruit cake, his wit stiletto sharp, regales his audience with a performance of one of his most famous songs, 'Mad Dogs and Englishmen'.

As well as Nöel's boyfriend, Graham Payn, gathered around the piano on this balmy evening in Jamaica are Willy's host, Ian Fleming, Fleming's muse and sometimes girlfriend, Blanche Blackwell, and Nöel's house guests, David Niven and his new Swedish wife, Hjördis, who are here for drinks and supper.

'Niv' is still looking somewhat rough after a dose of chickenpox, but that had not stopped him sitting up late last night with Willy and Ian as the three men reminisced about the war in the shadows that had brought all three of them together; Wills at the Special Operations Executive, Fleming with the Naval Intelligence Division's specialist 30 Assault Unit, which hunted down secret Nazi and Japanese technology and scientists, and Niven with the elite Phantom GHQ Signals Regiment, where he ended the war outranking them all as a lieutenant colonel.

As the drinks flowed, and helped by the convivial company and the perspective given by the ten years that had passed since the war ended, Willy Wills has an idea. He will write a spy thriller about a secret British operation designed to prevent a communist takeover in Burma, like the disaster the French are facing in Vietnam.

He is inspired for certain by the news that *Moonraker*, Fleming's third book about Commander James Bond, is about to be published in London by Jonathan

Cape, and Ian is living very nicely on the proceeds of the first two; but he is also annoyed.

Duff Cooper, a minister of the Crown no less, has played fast and loose with the Official Secrets Act and published his spy novel, *Operation Heartbreak*, which drew on secret briefings about Operation Mincemeat, 'the man who never was', while Wills and the rest of Ewan Montagu's team have done their duty and stayed silent.

Given Cooper's arrogance in thinking himself above the law, why shouldn't a major from SOE with knowledge of another deception operation in Burma write his own novel based on that experience and make a few pounds in Grub Street or even Hollywood?

In the end he thinks simply, 'Why not?'

And it will be fun.

Stepping into the study, Wills goes to the drinks cabinet and pours himself another tumbler of Canadian Club rye with ice and soda and, lighting a cigarette, sits down at the writing desk.

Installing two sheets of paper sandwiching a carbon, he stares at the blank page for a moment, then begins to type …

The Spitfires of Rangoon
A Novel of the Secret War in Burma
by Major William Wills DSO OBE

```
RAF Mingaladon Burma
17 August 1945
1830 hours
```

It was 1830 hours on 17 August 1945 and as the setting sun exploded on the great golden stupa of the Shwedagon Pagoda, Squadron Leader Sylvester of 273 Squadron, Royal Air Force, reached into the breast pocket of his crumpled cotton drill tunic and withdrew a battered packet of cigarettes.

As the keys of the typewriter clack and thump against the roller, in the background, Nöel has reached the verse about the Burmese shunning the noon day sun.

So many coincidences. Nöel is also a close friend of the man who had run Operation Merlin at Mingaladon, Dickie Mountbatten, who is now personal Aide de Camp to the Queen and about to take up his father's old post as First Sea Lord and Chief of the Naval Staff.

Wills smiles to himself.

Just as Fleming has drawn on his wartime career in describing the exploits of Commander Bond, he will work thinly disguised portraits of his own friends, enemies and acquaintances into his cast of characters as a way of paying tribute, or of settling scores.

Then Willie Wills has another thought.

Perhaps, in the same way Fleming wants the actor to play Bond, Niv could play his hero, who he will call Bill Baron, in the film?

52

Tracy Spaight
Nicosia, Cyprus
July 2014

'Obviously, they've never heard of the Burma Spitfire project,' jokes Wargaming's CEO, Victor Kislyi, as he tells me about reports that the search to find Malaysian flight MH370, which vanished somewhere in the Indian Ocean, is now the most expensive aviation recovery operation in history.[*]

I share the joke – not about the tragedy of the lost airliner and the 239 souls on board, of course, but at the unlikely comparison between our adventure and the greatest mystery in modern aviation history.

In truth, Wargaming is down less than half a day's revenue on the project, most of which went into financing the documentary film, but Victor's good-natured reproach still bothers me.

After all, I am a historian by training. I've worked in archives, and published meticulously researched articles.

I even debunked an iconic story about life in virtual worlds.[**]

Which makes me wonder why I believed David Cundall's story for so long? Indeed, why had I carried on believing even as the counter-evidence mounted in autumn 2012?

The fact that the British Prime Minister publicly backed David's version of history, and even negotiated an agreement to recover the planes, certainly loomed large in my initial acceptance of the story. So too did the extensive

[*]   'New missing Malaysian plane MH370 search area announced', BBC News, 26 June 2014.
      The search for the missing airliner is already among most expensive in aviation history.
[**] www.salon.com/2003/04/14/who_killed_miss_norway

coverage and support given to the legend by the BBC and many of the UK's leading newspapers.

Even so, I pride myself on being a level-headed fellow and I've seen enough churnalism and spin to know journalists and politicians can get things completely and disastrously wrong, most infamously in the case of the 'dodgy dossier' containing claims, later debunked, about the presence of weapons of mass destruction in Iraq, published by the British and American governments in the lead-up to the 2003 Gulf War.

In the end, I think that, like so many other people, I believed David because a part of me wanted his story to be true and by the time our team had uncovered sufficient evidence that it couldn't be true in the way David believed, we were already speeding down the runway with the project approaching take-off speed.

Of course, I could have stood on the brakes and applied full reverse thrust, even if we skidded off the end of the runway, but our team believed then, and still believe, that the fieldwork at the former RAF airfield would prove valuable, whatever we found.

Moreover, had we not undertaken the surveys and excavation work at Yangon critics of the conclusions of our desktop study would still be saying, 'Ah, but how can you say there are no Spitfires when you did not dig?'

We owed it to the story, to the public who heard it, and above all to the veterans and the Burmese people whose actual history was being drowned in the white noise generated by the legendary Spitfires, to reveal the whole truth as we saw it, including the ground truth.

I still believed, up until the moment we dug on the locations David chose for us, that there might be a kernel of truth to David's story and that we might very well uncover discarded airframes from the post-war clean-up of the airfield. After all, there was hard evidence that hundreds of planes had been broken up and recycled by RAF repair and salvage units in Burma, including on RAF Mingaladon.

More than that, Keith Win revealed later that David had found unidentified parts of aircraft, including an air intake, but had not told us, and there is photographic evidence that there was at least one partially buried aircraft under the runway extension at Mingaladon. On 1 October 1945 RAF Dakota KN594 suffered an engine failure on take off and crash landed, ending up in the chung next to the runway. The aircraft was stripped of anything useful and her carcass left to be swallowed up by the runway works which were then in progress.

In business and in life, you don't always arrive at the place you'd hoped at the start of the journey. We didn't find buried or discarded planes. What we uncovered instead are truths about the modern news media, about the nature of memory and belief, and about the enduring power of legend in the modern world – and in those truths are lessons for us all.

PART FIVE
FAKE HISTORY

A man with a conviction is a hard man to change. Tell him you disagree and he turns away. Show him facts or figures and he questions your sources. Appeal to logic and he fails to see your point.

Festinger, Riecken and Schachter, *When Prophecy Fails*

53

Andy Brockman and Tracy Spaight
London and Cyprus
Spring 2019

In his 1997 book *The Demon-Haunted World: Science as a Candle in the Dark*, the great American astronomer, communicator and philosopher of science Carl Sagan foresaw a time in one or two generations when the centralisation of technological power in the hands of a few would see anyone trying to act in the public interest, such as politicians and journalists, unable to grasp even the most important issues and ordinary people unable to set an agenda or question those in authority over them. Then, Sagan argued, we would be unable to tell the difference between what was 'true' and what simply 'felt good', and such a moment would mark the decline of our critical faculties and the start of a retreat into what Sagan termed, 'superstition and darkness'.*

Just over two decades later, with all but unaccountable transnational corporations such as Google and Facebook alleged to be facilitating the 'Post-Truth' ecosystem of Big Data, fake news and bot farms, it can be argued Sagan's dystopia has arrived slightly ahead of schedule.

In the same book, Sagan also sought to balance the demands of science for sceptical enquiry with the need to be open to new ideas, arguing that 'an openness to new ideas, no matter how bizarre or counter-intuitive they may be, and the most ruthless sceptical scrutiny of all ideas, old and new. This is how deep truths are winnowed from deep nonsense.'

---

*   *The Demon-Haunted World: Science as a Candle in the Dark*, Chapter Two, Science as Hope (1995).

In spite of many aspects of the story seeming bizarre and counter-intuitive, in 2012 and 2013 Wargaming.net's research team examined objectively the evidence for David Cundall's theory that Spitfires were buried in Burma by the Royal Air Force and our conclusion, based on the evidence we were able to gather from multiple sources, shows that the deep truth of the legend is that, as David tells it, the story is indeed deep nonsense.

Central to our thesis is the fact that David, and his various partners, have undertaken significant excavations at Mingaladon airport a dozen or more times over three periods; between 1998 and 2000, again from 2004 to 2005, and finally between 2013 and 2015 without even the smallest part of a Spitfire being recovered.

Supporting this view, the abundant documentary evidence from the UK National Archive and elsewhere shows that the legend of Mingaladon could not have happened in the manner David Cundall describes.*

Nevertheless, David and his supporters remain undeterred. In June 2016, after months of petitioning the British Government, and a letter to the Myanmar Government asking that he is not allowed to dig any further because of the potential danger to himself, his workforce and the heritage of Myanmar, signed by the entire Wargaming research team, David is finally granted another licence to dig for Spitfires at Yangon airport.

We are not surprised.

Half a world away, off the coast of Nova Scotia, an excavation based on a theory that is similarly bizarre, counter-intuitive and possessed of much deep nonsense has been proceeding for more than 200 years.

Like Mingaladon airfield, Oak Island is rumoured to be the site of a lost treasure, this time the plunder of the notorious pirate Captain William Kidd who, according to local legend, buried his treasure somewhere on the 600-acre island.

Since the late eighteenth century, fourteen major excavations have taken place on Oak Island at vast cost to enthusiasts and unfortunate investors. Treasure hunters have pockmarked the landscape with dozens of shafts, created a causeway to the mainland to bring in heavy equipment for digging and pumping, and even built cofferdams in an attempt to keep the tidal water from flooding the 'booby-trapped' pits.

In the course of these efforts at least six treasure hunters have lost their lives to cave-ins and other misadventures.

---

*   www.heritagedaily.com/2015/03/assumed-missing-reported-buried-the-search-for-the-lost-spitfires-of-burma/107095

And there too the digging continues to this day to the extent that, in 2014, the History Channel puts another nail in the coffin of its reputation as a serious platform for historical documentary when it begins airing a reality TV strand called *The Curse of Oak Island*, which follows the 'excavation' undertaken by brothers Rick and Marty Lagina.

As at Mingaladon, after six seasons and eighty-four episodes, nothing of significance pertaining to the veracity of the legend has ever been found on Oak Island. Indeed, while the timescale is longer, the parallels between the legends of Oak Island and Mingaladon are striking.

The Oak Island legend appears to have its origins in the eighteenth century when, it is said, local people living on the mainland report seeing 'strange lights' on the island at night. This folklore becomes connected with the uncheckable alleged deathbed confession of a sailor who, it is said, claims to have been a member of Captain Kidd's crew.

In 1803 an excavation team claims to be in possession of a treasure map (also conveniently since lost) showing the location of the treasure.

David's story of buried Spitfires rests on similar evidence: an uncheckable story allegedly told to Jim Pearce in Florida and the reported reminiscences of aging members of the British armed forces, none of whom actually saw the crates being buried, let alone set eyes on what they are alleged to have contained.

This stew of hearsay and shaggy dog stories became coupled with rumours that documents describing the burials had been found in the National Archive, fuelling suspicions of a conspiracy at the top of the British Government to keep the burial secret.

However, there are differences between the two narratives.

Whereas proponents of the Mingaladon burial have seldom questioned what was buried, only why the burial was undertaken and who did the digging (British Royal Engineers or American Seabees), the same unanimity is not present among Oak Island treasure hunters, where theories about what the treasure is, and who buried it, have evolved over time.

For example, the pirate theory falls into disfavour in the nineteenth century, though it is revived briefly in the 1930s, before being discarded again. This is because the problem with the pirate thesis is that, while Captain Kidd's treasure has been variously reported at hundreds of islands along the Atlantic coast, various locations in the Caribbean, and on the remote Île Sainte-Marie off Madagascar, D'Arcy O'Connor, a serious scholar of William Kidd's life, argues that the pirate never once set foot on Oak Island, nor indeed even knew of its existence.*

More to the point, nobody applied Occam's razor to ask, if an eighteenth-century pirate crew intended to bury and then recover their treasure in reasonable time, why on earth would they bury it at the bottom of a 100ft shaft that would have required skilled engineers and an immense investment in time and material to construct?

A similar question hangs over David and his proponents' argument (which they unveiled in the summer of 2013) that the Spitfires are buried in underground vaults protected by a reinforced concrete roof. Nobody on David Cundall's side of the argument thinks it necessary to explain why the British would take so much trouble to bury aircraft under the water table at Mingaladon in 1945 to help the Karen in an uprising, which won't take place for another three years.

Another difference is that while the current version of the Legend of Mingaladon remains relatively close to its origin myth, the Legend of Oak Island has departed along a number of pseudohistorical byways.

Many of the early Oak Island treasure hunters were Freemasons, so it is perhaps not surprising that some came to believe the 'Money Pit' is a depositary for the fabled lost treasure of the medieval order of the Poor Fellow-Soldiers of Christ and of the Temple of Solomon, better known as the Knights Templar. The Templars are, of course, the alleged ancestors of modern Freemasonry.

Another treasure hunter, Gilbert Hedden, becomes convinced the legendary vault contains the original manuscript of the works of Shakespeare (or rather the works of Sir Francis Bacon. Hedden subscribes to another conspiracy theory that the Elizabethan polymath wrote Shakespeare's back catalogue).

Others believe that the island hides treasure smuggled out of England during Cromwell's Protectorate, Marie Antoinette's jewels, or hides a secret repository built by British engineers to hold the Crown's military payroll during the American War of Independence.

One of the more colourful theories is advanced by amateur historian Eric Hamblin, who maintains the Aztecs built the Money Pit to hide their wealth from the Spanish conquerors.**

Needless to say, there is not a single thread of verifiable evidence for any of these theories.

---

* O'Connor, D'Arcy, *The Secret Treasure of Oak Island* (Guildford, Connecticut, 2004), pp. 40–41.
** Ibid., pp. 77–90.

The same phenomenon will play out among proponents of the Spitfire burial when the Wargaming team prove that there are no records of crated Spitfires being delivered through the Yangon docks in 1945–46.

Given the lack of documentary evidence for either burial, both David Cundall in Burma and the Lagina brothers at Oak Island turn to apparently objective science and telegenic hi-tech gadgetry to advance their cause.

David works first with the University of Leeds, and later with private companies including Malcolm Weale's Geofizz and local Yangon company Suntec, to map the site using EM, resistivity and ground-penetrating radar. The 2004 surveys certainly produce interesting anomalies indicating subsurface features, as does Malcolm's scan along the Red Road.

The geophysicists who undertook the surveys say that the brightly coloured computer images they produced are consistent with buried metal – but that they do not prove the presence of buried aircraft and could simply be the result of a high iron content in the soil.

David, on the other hand, concludes that the scans show exactly that and, unable or unwilling to address nuances of interpretation, the media largely quote David's conclusions uncritically.

He will continue to show these images to potential backers and Myanmar officials as final proof of his discovery.

And in the waterfront bars along the Florida coast, treasure hunters in search of investors will take a seat next to a likely mark, offer to buy them a beer, and then, slapping down a battered silver Spanish piece of eight on the counter, they will say, 'How would you like to see more of these?'

In the final episode of series three of *The Curse of Oak Island*, which airs in February 2016, Rick and Marty Lagina lower radar equipment down a 6in borehole. The audience is told that the resulting images appear to show a chamber (or natural cavern?) some 235ft below the surface and it is speculated that rectangular features in the radar image might be treasure chests ... Or they might be rocks ... Or they might have been created by the decisions made by software engineers programming the means by which the computer programme turns the electrical returns from the signal emitter into coloured pixels on the screen of a laptop computer.

In the end, until proven by facts in the ground, this is all speculation based on a fallible human interpretation of an electronic image and the desire of the media story tellers for a cliffhanging ending inviting the series to be recommissioned.

Like the Lagina brothers, in 2004 David's team at Mingaladon also sink a borehole and put down a camera.

Following this he claims repeatedly that the camera shows the inside of a crate with a Merlin engine visible. But despite the hi-tech images of purported treasure chests and aircraft, no pirate/Templar/Aztec gold, and no crated Spitfires, have come to light.

Putting all this contradictory speculation in its place, Irish archaeological geophysicist Kevin Barton once explained the dark art of interpreting geophysics plots to Andy Brockman in this way.

'There are objects, then there are one pint of Guinness objects, two pints objects and so on.'

In other words, once the plain as a pikestaff, visible from the moon, obvious walls, pits and buried objects have been recognised, the interpretation of archaeological geophysics becomes increasingly a matter of experience, instinct and ultimately an almost metaphysical truth you can only see if you have drunk enough of the means to see it.

David, meanwhile, embodies an unquestioning faith in his personal processing and visualisation of the data.

Back in Lincolnshire, after the extent of his previous unacknowledged work emerges in 2013, Mark Mannucci of Room 608 Productions asks David why he returned again and again to the same spot he had dug between 1998 and 2004 and found nothing. David responds, 'Because, because we didn't go deep enough. If you haven't found anything there is only one way you're going to go and that's deeper.'

Adding that he had never said there was a 100 per cent certainty there were buried Spitfires and that Tracy and the team were free to talk to the eyewitnesses and read the letters, blinking heavily, he asserts, 'I haven't done anything wrong. It was a risk that Tracy took. Nothing to do with me.'

David concludes with what might be his creed in his search for the secular relics of Britain's winged saviour in the Second World War, 'I believe Spitfires are worth every ounce of energy. I have to find them and I am not going to give up until I die.' he says defiantly, adding 'I'm not obsessed with this Burma Project. I just do not quit. End of story.'

One reason he is able to hold onto his faith must be that tales of buried treasure exert a powerful hold on the human mind. In Carl Sagan's words, they make us 'feel good'.

Human beings have always told stories about the quest for treasure and in a world increasingly divorced from such things, such tales conjure up images of swashbuckling pirates or outlaws in the Wild West, burying their ill-gotten gains to keep them safe from the law. Pirates and outlaws who always plan to return later, when things cool down, to recover their loot – often with the assistance of that indispensable aide-memoire, the treasure map.

Lost treasure also looms large in many tales about the Second World War, from Rommel's gold, allegedly lost in the Mediterranean, through the famous Amber Room looted by Hitler's art thieves from the Tsar of Russia's Summer Palace outside St Petersburg (Leningrad), to the fortune in gold reputed to have been buried by General Yamashita's retreating Japanese troops in the Philippines and the 'Nazi gold train' alleged to have been found in a tunnel in Poland.

In more recent years the plot of the satirical Hollywood thriller *Three Kings* (1999) is predicated on the hunt for gold missing in Iraq following the 1992 Iraq War.

The legend of the Nazi gold train, in particular, shares many of the characteristics of the legend of the Burma Spitfires.

According to the legend, it is late spring 1945 and the Second World War in Europe is drawing to its bloody and chaotic conclusion. As the Soviet armies drive all before them, in Nazi-occupied Poland a heavily laden steam train pulls into a remote siding away from prying eyes and screeches to a stop alongside a new maximum security excavation that is part of the top secret SS Project Riese (Giant). What happens next and how the precious contents of that train appears to vanish into thin air has become the stuff of the folklore of the Second World War.

Leap forward more than sixty years and the deathbed confession of a military veteran and other tantalising, half-remembered stories of previous abortive searches during the Cold War, told by former soldiers and local people, lead Pole Piotr Koper and German Andreas Richter, who happen to be co-owners of mining company XYZ S.C., to search for the contents of the lost train in the archives and then at the alleged burial site.

For many years the searches have proven fruitless, but now advances in technology give Koper and Richter's quest new hope and impetus. In particular, the wider availability of ground-penetrating radar offers archaeologists and treasure hunters the ability to locate and define structures deep underground and imparts those results with an apparently objective scientific credibility.

Intriguing images are produced at a press conference that appear to show structures of the right shape in the right place and these, coupled with the testimony of the veterans, are so convincing that Polish Deputy Culture Minister Piotr Żuchowski announces the images recorded by Koper and Richter show with a 99 per cent probability that a buried train 100m long has been located at kilometre 65 of the Polish State Railways' Wrocław–Wałbrzych line.

Speculation mounts that it could contain anything from secret Nazi weapons technology to stolen art treasures, or gold destined for the Reichbank or the Swiss bank accounts of leading Nazis.

While many geophysicists and scholars of the Second World War treat these claims with scepticism, negotiations with the state government results in a permit for an excavation, the agreement stating that if the mysterious lost cargo of the train is recovered, the discoverer and their sponsors, who have funded the dig to the tune of a reported €116,000, will be rewarded.

With the deal in place, excavations begin on 15 August 2016 under the watchful eye of the Polish military. The work is halted seven days later because the anomalies on the geophysics plots turn out to be natural geology created during the Ice Age 15,000 years ago.

In the meantime, the *New York Times* reports Barbara Nowak-Obelinda, the curator of historic monuments in Lower Silesia, as saying that a number of archaeological sites, including cemeteries and a Napoleonic battlefield, have been damaged by treasure hunters inspired by the farce taking place at Kilometer 65.

But it is an ill wind …

Arkadiusz Grudzien, the head of the city promotion office at the nearby town of Walbrzych, tells the media in an interview that tourism rose by 44 per cent for the year the gold train was in the news (he does not say how much of the rise can be accounted for by the 120 documentary and news crews who descend on the region), and he claims 'the publicity the town has gotten in the global media is worth roughly around $200 million.'

Putting the windfall in perspective, Mr Grudzien explains, 'Our annual budget for promotion is $380,000, so think about that. Whether the explorers find anything or not, that gold train has already arrived.'

In truth, these Indiana Jones–style stories appeal to our love of adventure, our desire for riches and, to some, the love of stories of conspiracy by the so-called 'Deep State'.

For example, according to one version of the tale, set out by Sterling Seagrave and Peggy Seagrave in their 2003 book *Gold Warriors: America's Secret Recovery of Yamashita's Gold*, the fabled treasure, looted on an industrial scale by the Japanese, bankrolls the Marcos dictatorship in the Philippines and forms a slush fund to pay for the early activities of the CIA.

Meanwhile, as recounted in any number of films and novels from Ira Levin's best-selling airport thriller *The Boys from Brazil* to supposedly factual television series such as *Hunting Hitler*, hidden Nazi gold and Swiss bank accounts fund the shadowy and almost certainly fictional Odessa organisation of former Nazis and their alleged attempts to create a Fourth Reich in South America.

Stories of lost treasure also offer an escape from the mundane by putting fame and riches in reach of anyone who can identify a mystery in even the best-known history, interpret the information in the right way and is possessed of the grit, determination and perhaps a commission from a digital TV channel in need of clickbait content, to find it.

The conclusion of this story is that, while the wreck of Dakota KN594 was at least partially buried by runway works where she crashed in October 1945, this means of disposal appears to have been a matter of convenience, not RAF policy and no buried Spitfires have been found at Mingaladon. Indeed, our documentary research (published fully in 2015*) proves beyond a reasonable doubt that no crated Spitfire aircraft were delivered to Mingaladon or Myitkyina in 1945/46, let alone deliberately buried in crates at either site.

That said, we are unable to state definitively whether warbird dealer Jim Pearce was spinning his own shaggy dog story about the Spitfires to David Cundall and Peter Arnold; whether he too was deliberately hoaxed about the legend of Mingaladon by others, or whether he simply heard what he wanted to hear and passed his version of the story on.

However, the evidence from modern psychological studies, pioneered by Elizabeth Loftus and reinforced most recently by Dr Julia Shaw of University College London and Dr Stephen Porter of the University of British Columbia, is that in telling their version of the legend of Mingaladon the three men connected most closely with the story, Jim Pearce, Peter Arnold and David Cundall, may have been instrumental unwittingly in writing the script for their own 'eyewitnesses'.

As a measure of the fragility of this so-called eyewitness evidence, a peer-reviewed academic study conducted by Dr Shaw and Dr Porter, published in the January 2015 edition of the journal *Psychological Science*, found that 70 per cent of participants in the experiment recalled committing a fictitious crime when they were adolescents and even went on to describe a subsequent encounter with the police which never took place.**

However, this evidence-based, if disappointing, conclusion turns out to have a silver lining. We believe that the legend of the buried Spitfires of

---

*   www.heritagedaily.com/2015/03/assumed-missing-reported-buried-the-search-for-the-lost-spitfires-of-burma/107095

**   'Constructing Rich False Memories of Committing Crime', Shaw, Julia; Porter, Stephen, *Psychological Science*, Vol. 26, Iss. 3, pp. 291–301.

Burma is the first such piece of Second World War folklore to have been
investigated objectively and scientifically – both in the archives of paper
and those of human memory – tested in the field archaeologically and then
published openly.

The conclusions from that work are that, although sadly there will not be a
newly discovered squadron of vintage aircraft gracing our skies, Wargaming's
team uncovered the fascinating genesis and evolution of a wartime legend,
born in the mud, chaos and boredom of RAF Mingaladon in 1945, in a
world that now lies at the fragile and fraying edge of living memory.

When that last thread of contact with the human reality of Rangoon in
1945 is severed the buried Spitfires of Burma will belong completely to the
world of legend. The world that, in truth, they have always inhabited.

THE GROUND TRUTH

'In reading the history of nations, we find that, like individuals, they have their whims and their peculiarities; their seasons of excitement and recklessness, when they care not what they do. We find that whole communities suddenly fix their minds upon one object, and go mad in its pursuit; that millions of people become simultaneously impressed with one delusion, and run after it, till their attention is caught by some new folly more captivating than the first.'

Preface to *The Memoirs of Extraordinary Popular Delusions and the Madness of Crowds*, Charles Mackay

Mingaladon Airport
Yangon, Myanmar
15 January 2012
1330 hours

To the eyes of an experienced archaeologist such as Martin Brown the tip
lines left by a machine backfilling an excavation visible in the sides of the
machine trench, the random collection of broken structural timbers that
already appear to have been excavated at least once before, and the water
slowly seeping in to cover the pristine natural blue grey clay at the base of the
trench are a ground truth that is about as clear and incontrovertible as you
can ask for on an archaeological site.

This patch of ground has been disturbed by a modern industrial excavator down
to the level of the natural geology more than once, and it is highly likely that at
least one large, strongly built wooden structure has been destroyed in the process.

However, the natural clay found at a depth of just over 2m and the ground-
water that rapidly fills the trenches at Mingaladon, even in the dry season,
represent two strands of the final proof that no Spitfires in crates could ever
have been buried here.

However, there is one further piece of evidence that another party has dug
here and dug here recently. Martin holds up a plastic carrier bag that he has
picked out from the spoil lifted out by Manny's JCB.

It is clear that the team was mistaken in believing the claims that there have
been no previous excavations on this spot at Yangon.

Meanwhile, David Cundall has wandered away down the red road, already
dreaming of digging somewhere else.

Already turning his thoughts to finding new sponsors to enthuse with his
dream to dig once again in Burma. Because, as he will tell Room 608, if you
don't find what you are looking for, dig deeper.

Meanwhile, when the jets are all on the ground at Yangon International
Airport, the Hintha bird owns the blue dome of the sky above the golden
Shwedagon Zedi Daw, looping and rolling in the ecstasy of freedom in time
and space, Burma's only genuine flying legend.

While if you listen hard enough, deep beneath the sun-beaten earth of the
Mingaladon plateau, below the modern runway and taxiways; deeper than
the backfilled trenches, buried roads and the wrecked ruins of air raid shelters; deeper even than the sodden blue clay that has lain there for millennia;
you can hear the uproarious laughter of the Nāga.

AFTERWORD

Anyone who has followed this international expedition into the world of historical spin and what happens when fake history meets the modern rolling news cycle is entitled to ask the authors, 'How much of the story of David Cundall and the buried Spitfires of Burma is true?'

The short answer is, it is all true. But not necessarily all true at the same time, or in the same universe.

To understand how this could be so, one needs to look to an idea developed over the past four decades that has become central to modern cosmology debates: the multiverse or parallel universe theory.

This theory maintains that 'eternal chaotic inflation' means there are an infinite number of universes, with multiple copies of Earth and of each of us, with new universes spun off every second, ad infinitum.

If the theory is correct, then David Cundall is right in at least one universe. In our case he just happens to be digging in the wrong one!

In our universe this narrative is grounded on verifiable records from public and private sources, as well as interviews with key players and last, but not least, our own records and photographs. These include a detailed journal and notes kept by Tracy Spaight throughout the Burma Spitfires project and extensive email records and photographs and documentary records obtained and kept by Andy Brockman.

This evidence suggests, beyond reasonable doubt, that there are no squadrons of crated Spitfires buried at Mingaladon International Airport, nor anywhere else in Myanmar.

The fieldwork in 2012 and 2013 was financed by international computer gaming company Wargaming.net. Wargaming, and especially its Chief Executive Victor Kislyi, had the courage to stay with the project even when Andy Brockman and the archaeology team concluded that it was almost certain that there were no Spitfires buried in crates at Mingaladon, but that it was perfectly possible that evidence of the dumping and even of the burial of surplus or decommissioned aircraft parts, existed on the former RAF airfield.

The archaeological fieldwork that ground-truthed this theory was carried out in unique and often physically and mentally demanding conditions by Field Director Martin Brown FSA MCIfA, and field archaeologist and ammunition technical officer (ATO) Rod Scott BA hons. Martin and Rod worked closely with our survey team; geophysicists Dr Roger Clark of the University of Leeds; Dr Adam Booth, then of Imperial College London; and Dr Andy Merritt, then a postgraduate research student at the University of Leeds; and with our expert plant operator, the late Manny Machado.

It has not been necessary for us to fictionalise, or otherwise embroider in any way, the good humour, skill and professionalism that these colleagues brought to the project.

We have also played a straight bat in describing the support given to the project by the Shwe Taung Por (STP) group of companies under their chair, Htoo Htoo Zaw. In particular we thank STP's project manager, U Pe Win, and our indefatigable translator, Daw Tin Ma Latt ('Auntie Latt') for translating, literally, our plans and ideas into facts on the ground at Mingaladon.

The fact that the project ended in a very public disappointment for them was not of their making.

And the fact that you are reading about it at all is thanks to the patience, professionalism and good advice of our literary agent Peter Buckman of the Ampersand Agency and the editorial team at The History Press, in particular Amy Rigg and Alex Waite.

We must add, of course, that all the opinions regarding the people and events about which you have just read are those of the authors alone. We also apologise for any mistakes of fact, or failures of attribution, which we will endeavour to remedy in any future editions of *The Buried Spitfires of Burma*.

When it comes to outside resources, our first thanks must go to the staff of the National Archives in London. The simple existence of this unparalleled repository of British Government papers (those at least that have survived generations of fire, water and the Whitehall shredder) and the assistance of its always helpful staff, made it possible to reconstruct what is most likely to have happened to Spitfires that passed through RAF Mingaladon between 1945 and 1947.

Records, including the individual aircraft recorded on the Air Ministry Form 78 record cards, held in the RAF Museum library in Hendon and at the documentary and film archives of the Imperial War Museum in Lambeth were also invaluable in our research and we thank also the librarians and archivists of those two organisations.

Equal thanks go to archivists in the United States who were consulted by Room 608 Productions and confirmed that there is no record there either that CBs, or Seabees, ever buried crated Spitfires at RAF Mingaladon, or anywhere else for that matter.

Other independent researchers who have looked at the legend of Mingaladon have also been generous and helpful even when, in some cases, they disagree profoundly with the conclusions we have reached. They know who they are and we thank them.

Of the human witnesses (and recognising that 'eyewitness' is a much-abused term in this story), the late Stanley Coombe, the late Group Captain Maurice Short RAF, and the late Major Roger Browning Royal Engineers in particular gave generously of their time and memories of being stationed in Rangoon in 1945 and 1946.

Major Browning also gave valuable information about the operational capabilities of the Indian Royal Engineers who did work at RAF Mingaladon in the autumn of 1945, based on his first-hand experience serving with the unit, backed up by his collection of original documents, photographs and cine film.

Other memoirs and accounts of the human background to the legend of the buried Spitfires that we consulted are listed in the bibliography, but the late Professor Martin Gilbert's magisterial biography of Winston Churchill and Philip Ziegler's edition of the wartime diaries of SEAC's commander, Lord Louis Mountbatten, deserve a special mention.

Those publications enabled us to see which members in the chain of command between Rangoon and London were where and when during late 1945 and early 1946, and they support the operational documents in suggesting strongly that one item that was not on the agenda at SEAC, or in Whitehall, was the burial of Spitfires to aid the Karen people in any future ethnic conflict in Burma, or for any other reason.

Crop duster turned aircraft recovery entrepreneur, the late Jim Pearce, gave an extended interview to Mark Mannucci and Anna Bowers of Room 608 Productions, the unedited recording and transcripts of which form the basis of our interpretation of the origins of the legend of the buried Spitfires of Mingaladon.

Overall, the work of Director Mark Mannucci and Producer Anna Bowers and their team from Room 608 Productions in recording the events of January 2013, as they happened, made it possible to reconstruct events on the ground, even as the archaeological team attempted to recover facts from that ground. Room 608 generously shared with us the entire archive of unedited video and audio files of these events.

Room 608's researcher, Meghan Horvath, also shared the results of her work at the National Archives and RAF Museum archive, without hesitation, becoming part of the wider research team and we thank her, too.

In the mainstream historic aviation press, aviation historian Andy Saunders, then editor of *Britain at War* magazine, has been an invaluable sounding board. While Rob Pritchard, the principled and long-suffering moderator of the Key Publications Historic Aviation Forum, deserves the cyber equivalent of the DFC, or at least a hat tip, for remaining a pillar of balance and sanity throughout the online discussions of the Burma mystery; at least until it all became too much and the Burma Spitfires thread was banished to the outermost circles of cyber purgatory.

Given that outcome it is fortunate we obeyed the first commandment of modern investigative journalism: 'If thou doth see an interesting or incriminating fact online, screenshot the page in case the subject deleteth it.'

Talking of journalists, over tea at the Imperial War Museum, Nick Springate of the BBC gave Andy Brockman valuable advice regarding how the contemporary successors of Rudyard Kipling, Noël Coward and George Orwell should approach working in modern Myanmar.

Other journalists from all parts of our modern, multi-lingual, multi-platform world listened, commented on and questioned our story on and off the record. Of these, Adam Lusher, then of *The Telegraph*, merits a special mention for his generosity in sharing ideas and his own research as he followed the story for his paper in Britain and on the ground in Yangon in early 2013.

In Yangon the staff of the British Embassy, including then ambassador to Burma Andrew Heyn and then Third Secretary Fergus Eckersley, behaved with all the courtesy, tact, professionalism and impartiality we would hope of the British Foreign Office.

However, the Cabinet Office, which acts as gatekeeper to UK prime ministers, has refused our Freedom of Information Requests aimed at discovering just what then Prime Minister David Cameron was told about the Burma Spitfires in April 2012, and just what was the nature of discussions, if any, between his staff, the Foreign Office and millionaire Oxfordshire-based Spitfire enthusiast Steve Brooks. We cannot imagine why.

However, we would be happy to include any information on these subjects that the Cabinet Office, or a principled whistle-blower, might care to send us, in any future editions of this story.

Finally a word on form.

We chose to use that literary hybrid, the documentary novel, because it seemed to us that to do full justice to the full, self-satirising madness of the legend of the Burma Spitfires we needed a form that could not only range freely across time and multi-dimensional space but one that would also enable us to write the internal monologues, dialogues and soliloquies the narrative seemed to call for.

If there is one moment when this solution presented itself to us, it lay in the inspired comments made by Wargaming executive Gavin Longhurst when introducing a private screening of an early cut of *Buried in Burma*, the Room 608 documentary about the Burma Spitfires project.

As the audience enjoyed bottles of Shepherd Neame Spitfire beer, Gavin took to the stage and pointed out the similarities between our quest for buried Spitfires and the collision of religious mysticism, archaeology and investors' money when Walter Juvelius persuaded Captain Montagu Parker to ignore the febrile political and religious climate of Ottoman Jerusalem and to look for the lost treasures of Solomon's Temple beneath the Haram al-Sharif.

In those few minutes Gavin gave us our framing device.

Of course, in another universe the adventure in Yangon has been a political and personal triumph and, as you read this, David Cundall is standing on the balcony of Buckingham Palace alongside a beaming David Cameron, who is still Prime Minister, and the Royal Family, a member of which, Princess Eugenie, has astonishingly for the British ruling class, recently married a divorced mixed-race actor from the United States.

All of them bask in the warmth of tabloid headlines under a bright September sun and blue skies on Battle of Britain Day, while the brand new squadron of twelve Spitfires, factory fresh from the Virgin Atlantic Airways-sponsored restoration workshop in Castle Bromwich, flies down the mall; the shadows of those classically elegant elliptical wings falling across the cheering, flag-waving crowd.

As the aircraft turn on red, white and blue smoke and perform a starburst above Buckingham Palace itself, the techno music of twelve Merlin engines segues with, and then smothers, the sound of the Central Band of the Royal Air Force playing Sir William Walton's majestic 'Spitfire Prelude' on the parade ground below.

Meanwhile, in another universe still, the vision of artist, photographer and author, the late Patrick Ryoichi Nagatani, has been realised and fifteen of the Spitfires recovered by the reimagined team of RAF widow Mary Cundall and archaeologist Ruta Brickman have been converted into state-of-the-art floatplanes and flown across the Pacific by fifteen women pilots.

As they reach up into the big blue and traverse featureless ocean between Tokyo Bay and San Francisco, the fictional successors of Amy Johnson, Amelia Earhart and Jean Batten respond to the famous credo that, 'The ultimate responsibility of the pilot is to fulfil the dreams of the countless millions of earthbound ancestors who could only stare skyward and wish.'*

They accomplish this by reflecting on culture, gender, morality and the state of the planet, all informed by Nagatani's own mysticism.

In Nagatani's vision, coming as it does from an accomplished artist, in touch with a sensibility founded on the same Buddhism that also underlies Burmese culture, the buried Spitfires of Mingaladon have completed their journey that never was from Castle Bromwich and evidence-led history, to the soil of Yangon airport and legend.

In making that journey they have transcended any attempt we might make to reduce the story to a factual airframe of documents and psychology by becoming a work of art.

We are very happy with that conclusion because, for us, art, which employs our boundless capacity as human beings for invention and imagination in exploring the human condition, and our place on this planet, and in this universe, is infinitely preferable to unquestioning, exploitative, fake history every time.

Andy Brockman and Tracy Spaight
London and Nicosia
January 2020

* Ryoichi Nagatani, Patrick, *The Race: Tales in Flight*, 2017.

BIBLIOGRAPHY

The backcloth to this story is the bitterly fought air campaign in Burma. These events are described in as much detail as anyone could ask for in the monumental *Bloody Shambles* trilogy by Christopher Shores and his co-authors for the first two volumes, Brian Cull and Yasuho Izawa (*Bloody Shambles Volume One*, 1992, *Volume Two*, 1993, and *Volume Three*, 2005, Grub Street).

This is also a story about the frailties of human psychology and memory, and the methods of psychological warfare used to exploit and manipulate these by our agent 'Bill Baron' and his colleagues at the Special Operations Executive have been published as *SOE Syllabus: Lessons in Ungentlemanly Warfare, World War II* by the UK National Archive (2001).

When it came to understanding the growth of legends, we began with the seminal study of crowd psychology *The Memoirs of Extraordinary Popular Delusions and the Madness of Crowds*, by Scottish journalist Charles Mackay, published in 1841.

The work of Professor Elizabeth Loftus, including her book *Eyewitness Testimony – Psychological Perspectives*, provided the academic bedrock upon which we built the suggestion that the Legend of the Burma Spitfires is largely the result of the over-interpretation of alleged and unreliable eyewitness evidence by interrogators wanting to confirm their own pre-existing biases.

The work of Dr Julia Shaw and Dr Stephen Porter, which demonstrated mechanism for the imparting of false memories of significant life events, was published too late to form a part of our primary research, which was conducted between 2012 and 2014, but we cite it here as further support for our conclusion.

As we have seen, early in the project Andy Brockman introduced Tracy Spaight to Robert Harris's necessary and hilarious deconstruction of the infamous Hitler Diaries fiasco, *Selling Hitler* (1986), with its astonishing cast of characters ranging from Fleet Street's finest and a world-class academic expert on Hitler, through a Holocaust-denying jobbing historian with an agenda to a German forger and con man, and not forgetting Rupert Murdoch.

In exchange Tracy introduced Andy to the pioneering study of the cognitive dissonance which is so much a part of our own story, *When Prophecy Fails* (1956) by Leon Festinger, Henry W. Riecken and Stanley Schachter.

In just those two titles clear warnings about the probable veracity of the Burma Spitfires story were hiding in plain sight before the world's media.

Indeed, even before the phenomenon of 'post truth' became a mainstream concern in the wake of the 2016 cultural double whammy of the Brexit vote in Britain and the election of Donald Trump as President of the United States, several authors had already surveyed the landscape of modern culture that enables conspiracy theory and pseudohistory to thrive. Of these, David Aaronovitch's study of the role of conspiracy theory in shaping the perceptions of modern history, *Voodoo Histories* (2009), and Michael Shermer's 1997 study *Why People Believe Weird Things*, proved particularly valuable.

Like weeds choking a flowerbed, such 'alternative facts' also require a nourishing medium in which to grow and in *Flat Earth News*, Nick Davies, then of *The Guardian*, described the new media landscape in which the need to cut costs, shift copies and drive clicks has led to the uncritical recycling of press releases as news and a media ecosystem in which an unsupported legend like that of the Burma Spitfires can indeed thrive and multiply like Japanese knotweed.

Of course, 'churnalism', 'fake news', and its bastard cousin 'fake history', rely for their successful promulgation on an uncritical acceptance of assertions as fact and an unwillingness, or downright refusal, to ask those beautifully simple, but essential, questions 'Who? What? When? Where? Why? And who benefits?

For anyone who wishes to follow in our footsteps and ask those questions these are the principal sources consulted in the course of researching the *Buried Spitfires of Burma*.

Primary Sources

(All held at the UK National Archive at Kew unless stated)
Cabinet Records relating to Burma 1945–47 including:
CAB/66/65/40 White Paper on Burma Policy
CAB/129/4 Political Situation in Burma Telegrams
CAB/129/3 Developments in Burma
(available on line at www.nationalarchives.gov.uk/cabinetpapers)
Air 2/5498: Spitfires for India
Air 23/457 Target Maps, Reports and Photographs, Myitkina Burma
Air 23/2334: Loose Minute LM/JP/114 24 August 1945
Air 23/2334: 13 February 1946 AMC266 Confidential Message HQ ACSEA from
    AHQ Burma
Air 23.2350: Operations Zipper Mailfist Malaya
Air 23.2351: Operations Zipper Mailfist Malaya
Air 23.2352: Operations Zipper Mailfist
Air 23/3869: Interpretations and Bomb Damage Reports Mingaladon
Air 23/3870: Interpretations and Bomb damage Assessment Reports Mingaladon
    Military Area
Air 23/3914: Interpretation and Bomb Damage Assessment Reports Myitkyina
Air 26/4351: Reports on the Defence of RAF Mingaladon 1942
Air 23/4375: Operations in support of Force 136
Avia 15/2139: Disposal of surplus aircraft situated outside UK
Avia 15/3660: Arrangements for handling surpluses overseas, machinery for disposal in
    India
FO371: Rebuilding of Rangoon Airport Terminal
FO643/18: Administration Governor's Office Railway Board
FO/643/66/4: The future of the Karens Part I
FO/643/66/5: The future of the Karens Part II
FO643/78: Arms in possession of the Karens Ex Force 136
FO643/78: Outstanding claims for payments of arrears & compensation to personnel
    employed by Force 136
HSI/212: SOE Far East India/General
Prem 3 150/7: Spitfires for Australia
Prem 8 417: Military Settlement of Independent Burma
Research Aircraft 7231/01: Condition of aircraft on receipt by SE Asia Command
WO203/1760: Engnrs priorities after D+31
WO172/7903 123 Independent Mechanical Equipment Company Royal
    Engineers October–December 1945.
WO203/1352: Planned RAF build up at Mingaladon

Operations Record Books in the UK National Archive

Air 24/359: AHQ BURMA ORB November 1945
No. 2 Forward Equipment Unit
No. 41 Embarkation Unit
No. 56 Forward Repair Unit

No. 101 Repair and Salvage Unit
No. 132 Repair and Salvage Unit (Mobile)
273 Squadron, 1945
357 Special Duties Squadron 1945
607 Squadron 1945
902 Wing SEAAF 1944–1945

Miscellaneous Files

Burma Railways Evaluation Report August 1946

Period Manuals

Royal Engineers Training Memorandum No. 17 Far Eastern Warfare, The War Office
     August 1945
US Bureau of Ordnance, 14 June 1946, Japanese Explosive Ordnance

Political Documents

Unpublished diplomatic communications originating from the UK
Government, the US Department of State, and Leeds University were sourced
from requests under the UK Freedom of Information Act and WikiLeaks.

Secondary Sources

Aaronovitch, David, *Voodoo Histories: The Role of the Conspiracy Theory in Shaping Modern
     History*, Jonathan Cape, 2009.
Aldrich, Richard K. and Rawnsley, Ming-Yeh, *The Clandestine Cold War in Asia,
     1945–65: Western Intelligence, Propaganda and Special Operations*, Routledge, 2013.
Allen, Louis, *The Longest War 1941–1945*, Dent, 1984.
Bayly, Christopher and Harper, Tim, *Forgotten Wars: The End of Britain's Asian Empire*,
     Penguin, 2008.
Benzinger, Dr Emmanual, *Palestine and Syria with the Chief Routes through Mesopotamia
     and Babylonia*; handbook for travellers; 4th English Edition, Baedecker, 1906.
Brayley, Martin J. and Ingram, Richard, *Khaki Drill and Jungle Green: British Tropical
     Uniforms 1939 to 1945*, Crowood Press, 2000.
Brown, Martin and Osgood, Richard, *Digging Up Plugstreet: the Archaeology of a First
     World War Battlefield*, Haynes, 2009.
Browning, Roger, *Rangoon to Great Tey*, self-published memoir, 2002.
Clark, A., *Seeing Beneath the Soil: Prospecting Methods in Archaeology*, 2nd edition, Taylor
     & Francis, 2017.
Cruickshank, Charles, *SOE In The Far East*, Oxford, 1993.

Duckett Richard, *The Special Operations Executive (SOE) in Burma: Jungle Warfare and Intelligence Gathering in WW2*, Bloomsbury Publishing, 2017.

Gentleman Amelia, *The Windrush Betrayal, Guardian/Faber, 2019.*

Gillings Murray, *The Shiny Ninth: the Ninth Battalion the Royal Sussex Regiment 1940–1946*, Pinwe Club, 1986.

Hickey, Col Michael, *The Unforgettable Army: Slim's XIV Army in Burma*, Spellmount Ltd, Tonbridge Wells, 1992.

Hauser, Kitty, *Bloody Old Britain: O.G.S. Crawford and the Archaeology of Modern Life*, Granta, 2008.

Hauser-Schaublin, Bridget and Prott, Lyndel V. (Eds), *Cultural Property and Contested Ownership: The Trafficking of Artefacts and the Quest for Restitution*, Routledge, 2016.

Holmes Richard, *Tommy: The British Soldier on the Western Front 1914–1918*, Harper Collins, 2004.

Holyoak, B. and Schofield, J., *Military Aircraft Crash Sites: Archaeological Guidance on their Significance and Future Management*, English Heritage, 2002.

Human Rights Documentation Unit, *Bullets in the Alms Bowl: An Analysis of the Brutal SPDC Suppression of the September 2007 Saffron Revolution*, National Coalition Government of the Union of Burma, 2008.

Institute for Archaeologists: *Code of Conduct*, 2010, and *Standard and Guidance for an Archaeological Watching Brief*, 2008.

Jorg, Christiaan, J.A., *The Geldermalsen History and Porcelain*, Kemper, Groningen, Netherlands, 1986.

Kaye, G.W.C. and Laby, T.H., *Tables of Physical and Chemical Constants*. 14th Edition. Longman, 1973.

Keane, Fergal, *Letter to Daniel*, Penguin Books, 1996.

Keane, Fergal, *Road of Bones*, Harper Press, 2011.

Lawyer, L.C., Bates, C.C., and Rice, R.B., *Geophysics in the Affairs of Mankind*, 2nd edition. SEG publications, Society of Exploration Geophysicists, Tulsa, OK 74170-2740, USA, 2001.

Loftus, Elizabeth F., *Eye Witness Testimony*, Harvard University Press, 1979.

Mackintyre, Ben, *Operation Mincemeat*, Bloomsbury, 2010.

Maslen-Jones, E.W., *Fire By Order: Recollections of Service with 656 Air Observation Squadron in Burma*, 1997.

McHenery, John H., *Epilogue In Burma*, Spellmount Ltd, Tonbridge Wells, 1990.

McNeill, J.D., *Technical Note TN-8: EM34-3 Survey Interpretation Techniques*, Geonics Limited, 1745 Merseyside Dr., Unit 8, Mississauga, Ontario, Canada, L5T 1C5, 1983.

Milbrooke, Anne et al, *Guidelines for Evaluating and Documenting Historic Aviation Properties*, US Department of the Interior, National Parks Service and National Register of Historic Places, 1998.

Montoriol, Thierry, *Spitfire En Birmanie: la Quête de l'Escadrille Rerdue*, 100001 Mots, 2014.

Morgan, Eric B. and Shacklady, Edward, *Spitfire the History*, Guild Publishing London, 1989.

Mosse, George L., Fallen Soldiers: Reshaping the Memory of the World Wars, Oxford University Press, 1880.

Mussett, A.E., and Khan, M.A., *Looking into the Earth: An Introduction to Geological Geophysics*, Cambridge University Press, 2000.

O'Connor, D'Arcy, *The Secret Treasure of Oak Island*, The Lyons Press, 2004.

Orwell, George, *Shooting an Elephant and Other Essays*, Secker and Warburg, 1950.

Orwell George, *Burmese Days*, Harper and Brothers, 1934.

Orwell, George, *Nineteen Eighty-Four*, Secker and Warburg, 1949.

Owen, Lt Col Frank OBE, *The Campaign in Burma*, HMSO, 1946.

Park, Sir Keith, 'Air Operations in South East Asia 3 May 1945 to 12 September 1945', *London Gazette*, 13 April 1951.

Reynolds, J.M., *An Introduction to Applied and Environmental Geophysics*, 2nd Edition, Wiley-Blackwell, 2011.

Riley, Gordon, Trant Graham and Arnold Peter, *Spitfire Survivors: Then and Now: Vol. 2: Spitfire XIV – F24 Seafire L11 to FR47*, A-Eleven Publications, 2013.

Roberts, Andrew, *Eminent Churchillians*, Weidenfeld and Nicolson, 1994.

Saunders, Andy, *Spitfire Mark 1 P3974*, Grub Street, 2012.

Saunders, Nicholas J., *Killing Time – Archaeology and the First World War*, Sutton, 2007.

Saunders, N., 'Matter and memory in the landscapes of conflict: The Western Front 1914', In Bender, B. and Winer, M. (eds), *Contested Landscapes: Movement, Exile and Place*, pp. 37–53. Oxford: Berg, 1999.

Scott, R., 2009, 'Dangerous artefacts', in Brown, M. and Osgood, R., *Digging Up Plugstreet*, Haynes, 2009.

Schofield, John et al, *Modern Military Matters*, Council for British Archaeology, 2004.

Service Personnel and Veterans Agency (Joint Casualty and Compassionate Centre), *Crashed Military Aircraft of Historical Interest – Licensing of excavations in the UK: Notes for Guidance of Recovery Groups*, Online publication, 2009.

Shaws, Christopher, *Air War for Burma*, Grub Street, 2005.

Shaws, Christopher and Cull, Brian, with Yasuho, Izawa, *Bloody Shambles Vol. 1*, Grub Street, 1992.

Shaws Christopher and Cull, Brian, with Yasuho, Izawa, *Bloody Shambles Vol. 2*, Grub Street, 1993.

Shermer, M., *Why People Believe Weird Things*, Souvenir Press, 1997.

Sliberman, N., *Digging for God and Country*, Random House, 1982.

Slim, Field Marshall Sir William, *Defeat Into Victory*, Cassell and Company, 1956.

Sommerville, Christopher, *Our War: How the British Commonwealth Fought the Second World War*, Weidenfeld and Nicolson, 1998.

Stevenson, AVM D.F., 1948, 'Air Operations in Burma and Bay of Bengal January 1st to May 22nd 1942', *London Gazette*, 1948.

Stichelbaut, B., Bourgeois, J., Saunders, N. and Chielens, P. (Eds), *Images of Conflict: Military Aerial Photography and Archaeology*, Cambridge Scholars Publishing, 2009.

Suntac Technologies, *Geophysical Investigation on Buried Spitfire Aircraft Project in Mingaladon Airport*, Suntac Technologies, 2004.

Tanner, R.E.S. and Tanner, D.A., *Burma 1942: Memories of a Retreat*, History Press, 2009.

Tuchman, Barbara W., *Sand Against the Wind: Stilwell and the American Experience in China 1911–1945*, Papermac, 1970.

Watkinson, D. and Neal V., First Aid For Finds, RESCUE/Museum of London, 2001.

Wong, Hong Suen, *Wartime Kitchen: Food and Eating in Singapore 1942–1950*, Editions Didier Miller/National Museum of Singapore, 2009.

Zeigler, Philip, *Mountbatten*, Book Club Associates/William Collins and Co. Ltd, 1985.

Zeigler, Philip (Ed.), *Personal Diary of Admiral the Lord Louis Mountbatten 1943–1946*, Collins, 1988.

Oral Histories

Room 608 Productions provided transcripts and recordings of interviews with
Dr Adam Booth, Andy Brockman, Martin Brown, Dr Roger Clarke, Stanley
Coombe, David Cundall, Jonathan Glancy, the late Jim Pearce, Rod Scott,
the late Group Captain Maurice Short, Malcolm Weale and Keith Win. Andy
Brockman interviewed the late Major Roger Browning RE Retd.

Academic Articles

Hansen, R.O., Racic, L. and Grauch, V.J.S., 'Magnetic Methods in Near-Surface
    Geophysics', in *Near-Surface Geophysics* (Editor: D.K. Butler), Chapter 6, SEG
    publications, Society of Exploration Geophysicists, Tulsa, OK 74170-2740, USA,
    2005.
Loftus, Elizabeth F., 2005, 'Learning and Memory: Planting Misinformation
    in the human mind: a thirty-year investigation into the malleability of
    memory', Coldspring Harbour Press online publication, learnmem.cshlp.org/
    content/12/4/361.full
Miller, George L., 'The Second Destruction of the Geldermalsen', *The American
    Neptune*, 1987, 47(4):275–281. R.
Shaw, Julia, Porter, Stephen, 'Constructing Rich False Memories of Committing
    Crime', Psychological Science Vol. 26, Iss. 3, January 2015.
'Shortcomings in the attribution process: On the origins and maintenance of erroneous
    social assessments', in Kahneman, Daniel; Slovic, Paul; Tversky, Amos, *Judgment under
    uncertainty: Heuristics and Biases*, Cambridge University Press, pp. 129–152, ISBN
    978-0-521-28414-1, OCLC 7578020.

Digital Media Archives

The Daily Mail
Flight Magazine
Flypast Magazine
Fox News
The Guardian
The Independent
The Irrawaddy
National Public Radio
Sky News
The Straits Times
The Daily Telegraph
The Sunday Telegraph
The Times

Television

BBC World
Forces TV
BBC *Timewatch*, 'Forgotten Allies: The Search for Burma's Lost Heroes', 1997.
BBC, *Who Really Killed Aung San?* 1997.
BBC 1, *The One Show*, segment with Steve Boultbee Brooks, broadcast 16 April 2012.

Film Sources

Buried In Burma (working title) Room 608 Productions, in progress cut and unedited digital video and audio files.
Imperial War Museum film ID: JIN 62, The first large merchant ship is piloted into Rangoon's devastated docks.
Imperial War Museum Film ID: RMY 132-2-17: Special Erection Party assembling Spitfires on Gibraltar in mid-1942.
Imperial War Museum Film ID JIN 89: 15 August 1945: A delegation of Japanese senior officers arrives at Mingaladon airfield to discuss surrender.
Imperial War Museum Film ABY 123: Air Vice Marshal Cecil Bouchier addresses airmen on the occasion of the disbandment of RAF 607 (County of Durham) Squadron at Mingaladon airfield.
Imperial War Museum Film JFU 316: Lord Louis Mountbatten, Supreme Allied Commander of South East Asia Command (SEAC), arrives by air in Rangoon.
Imperial War Museum Film JFU 298: Japanese emissaries arrive at Mingaladon airfield to begin preliminary surrender negotiations.
Forgotten Allies, BBC Timewatch 1997,

Photographic and Visual Art Sources

Gavin Longhurst
Documentary photography of the 2013 Wargaming/STP Spitfire excavations.

RAF Museum Collections

Grounded Dakotas: From reception tent, Mingaladon Burma: Artist Thomas Barclay Hennell: PAINTING FA03107.
Hoppers clearing and levelling for extension to airfield Mingaladon: Artist Mr Thomas Barclay Hennell PAINTING FA03108.
Fighter dispersal at Mingaladon, Artist Mr Thomas Barclay Hennell PAINTING FA03106.
Liberators and Dakotas, Pioneers Relaying the airstrip at Mingaladon June 7th 1945, Artist Mr Thomas Barclay Hennell PAINTING FAO3110.
Mingaladon aerodrome, Burma 1945; Artist Frank Anthony Albert Wootton PAINTING FA03182.
Rangoon: Aircraft taking-off from waterlogged runway: Artist Frank Anthony Albert Wootton; PAINTING FA03179.

Wrecked bamboo hangars built by Burmese for Japanese, Mingaladon, June, 1945; Artist Thomas Barclay Hennell; PAINTING FA03120.

Control tower, Mingaladon, Burma; Artist Frank Anthony Albert Wootton; PAINTING FA03181.

Dispersal, Mingaladon, Burma: Artist- Frank Anthony Albert Wootton: PAINTING FA03178.

Fires burning in Rangoon during bombing raid by 356 Squadron Liberators, 1 February, 1945: MONOCHROME PRINT PC71/19/1669.

SAW Marshal Schen and wife with Sqdn Ldr Turner and pilot, Mingaladon: MONOCHROME PRINT PC71/19/1867.

Officer in charge of Force 136 and his assistant, Mingaladon: MONOCHROME PRINT PC71/19/1869

Sqdn Ldr Turner and Lysander pilots in front of one of their aircraft, Mingladon, 1945: MONOCHROME PRINT PC71/19/1854.

Sqdn Ldr Turner (right) conferring with members of the Military Administration prior to their take-off for Bolo: MONOCHROME PRINT PC71/19/1859.

Loading supplies into a S.D. Lysander 'C', No 357 Squadron, Mingladon 1945: MONOCHROME PRINT PC71/19/1861.

Flying Officer Hallett, Adjutant of No. 357 Squadron Detachment, Mingladon c.1945: MONOCHROME PRINT PC71/19/1855.

Long-range fuel tank fitted to S.D. Lysander, No. 357 Squadron? 1945: MONOCHROME PRINT PC71/19/1862

Ground crew remove wheel from undercarriage of a S.D. Lysander, 1945: MONOCHROME PRINT PC71/19/1863.

Group of Burmese and Chinese personnel of 136 Force, Mingladon, 1945: MONOCHROME PRINT PC71/19/1874.

Unloading a jeep from a S.D. Dakota at Mingaladon, 1945: MONOCHROME PRINT PC71/19/1907.

Imperial War Museum Collection

Art.IWM ART LD 5181: a view from a ship towards the quay side where civilians are gathering to welcome the troops.

Art.IWM ART LD 5529 image: a view of a merchant ship unloading her cargo onto a bomb-damaged jetty.

CF660 Royal Air Force Operations: Airmen prepare a Supermarine Spitfire Mark VIII of 607 Squadron during monsoon conditions at Mingaladon, Burma.

CI1567 A Supermarine Spitfire Mark VIII of No. 607 Squadron RAF being serviced at Mingaladon, Burma.

CF663 Pilots of No. 607 Squadron RAF walk past their Supermarine Spitfire Mark VIIIs at the monsoon-flooded airfield at Mingaladon, Burma.

CI1458 Pilots of No. 607 Squadron RAF, leave their Supermarine Spitfire Mark VIIIs to cross the rain-soaked airfield at Mingaladon, Burma.

CI1565 Air Vice-Marshal C.A. Bouchier greets Flight-Lieutenant D E Nicholson of Harrow, Middlesex, on completing the last operational sortie by No. 607 Squadron RAF prior to its disbandment at Mingaladon, Burma.

Australian War Memorial

SUK14323 and SUK14339: The famous 'Japs Gone' message on the roof of Rangoon
    Prison.
SUK14336: Bomb damage to Rangoon Central Station.
SUK14337: Bomb damage to the Rangoon waterfront.
SUK14338: An abandoned Japanese Anti-Aircraft position in Rangoon.
P02284.010: Tents on RAF Mingaladon.
SUK14673: Japanese surrender negotiators arrive at Mingladon. Commentary by 'All
    India Radio'.
SUK14683: POWs Arrive Mingaladon on a DC-3.
P02284.014: Japanese liaison officers ferried by the RAF to get remote groups of
    Japanese soldiers to surrender. The caption misidentifies the aircraft behind – it is an
    Auster.
P02284.015: Japanese and British officers. Note the large blast pen. These were built
    around the dispersal areas of the airfield including where the 2013 team were
    digging.
P02284.012 and P02284.019: An SD Squadron Lysander, its crew and the Japanese.
SUK14674: The control tower at Mingaladon with interpreter Flight Lieutenant
    W.W. Hassall, RAF.
SUK14608: Indian engineers laying PSP on the Cocos Islands during the advance on
    Burma, a Spitfire in the background.
SUK14609: Crated Spitfire on a low-loader.
P02284.023: Squadron Leader George Turner of 357 SD Squadron,
P02284.021: Karen villagers who have just been supplied by 357 SD Squadron
    Lysanders.
P02284.017 and P02284.018: 357 SD Sqd Lysander at a Karen-controlled airstrip with
    villagers and members of Force 136 in the field.

Online Sources

forum.keypublishing.com/showthread.php?116104-Burma-Spitfires-Abandon-hope-
    all-ye-who-enter-here%E2%80%A6 (Forum thread since removed from public view
    by publisher)
www.spitfires.ukf.net/p014.htm
www.spitfiresociety.com/content/Airworthy_Spitfires/default.html
www.hse.gov.uk/radiation/rpnews/rpa21.htm#a12
fkf.net/RonWyatt/liitonarkki/juvelius.html

INDEX

Akhenaten 82

al-Aqsa Mosque 91, 211

Allied Command South East Asia (ACSEA) 28, 101

American Volunteer Group (AVG) aka the Flying Tigers, on RAF Mingaladon 234

Ark of the Covenant 48, 50, 95, 226–7, 296

Arnold, Peter
  on the Key Publications Historic Aviation Forum 25, 264
  Spitfire collector and dealer in Spitfire parts 25
  involvement with David Cundall 26
  at 2013 Yangon excavations 218, 229, 247–9
  at CWGC Cemetery Taukkyan 197–200
  plan to retrofit Yangon Spitfires to Mark VIII standard 199
  with David Cundall and *Telegraph* reporter in Yangon 216
  alleged to be briefing on behalf of David Cundall in Yangon 221
  at Hendon public lecture 254, 260–1
  first mention of involvement in buried Spitfires project 275–6
  comments on Ziv Brosh excavations 281
  unwitting part in perpetuating buried Spitfires legend 312

Attlee, Clement 74, 268–70

Auguste, Victoria Empress 91

Aung San General 29, 56, 73, 224

Aung San Suu Ky 32–4, 55–6, 80, 105, 176, 274, 292

Azmey Bey Pasha 50, 91, 227, 250

Bader, Douglas 21, 35, 117

Bennett, very Reverend Reginald 84

Binyon, Laurence, author of 'For the Fallen' 133

Birtles, Sergeant RE 210, 212–13

Bogyoke Market 62–3

Booth, Dr Adam 41, 43, 68, 82, 102, 105, 115, 141, 146, 193, 206, 240, 257, 260, 272–3, 277, 282, 285, 288

Bowers, Anna 70, 94

British Army
  652 Mechanical Equipment Company Indian RE 134
  Berkshire Regiment 122
  Royal Sussex Regiment 122

British Broadcasting Corporation (BBC) 25, 33, 46, 140, 146–7, 149, 171, 187, 219, 223–4, 228, 278, 290

Brief Encounter (film) 145

Brockman, Andy 46, 93, 97, 102, 104, 113, 135–7, 141–3, 145–6, 148–53, 158–65, 170, 175, 177, 180–2, 185–8, 192, 195, 204–05, 217–18, 220–1, 223, 228, 230,

232, 235, 238–9, 248, 253–4,
    264, 272–3, 285, 288, 304, 309
Brosh, Ziv, Israeli Spitfire enthusiast
    280–2
Brown, Martin, WYG, Archaeological
    Field Director Yangon Airport
    18, 149, 152, 158–60, 162–3,
    177, 180, 189–90, 192, 195,
    197, 203–07, 217, 220, 225, 230,
    232–3, 235, 257–9, 272, 315
    Excavating Shorncliffe redoubt for
    Time Team 98
Browning, Major Roger RE, at 2012
    November 11 commemoration
    134–5
    company commander 652 MEC
    Indian Engineers, RAF
    Mingaladon 134
Burma Railway 75, 177, 196
    suggestion crated Spitfires delivered
    by train 159, 264, 277
    damage assessment in 1945 263

Cameron, David (British Prime Minister)
    32, 38, 47, 59, 101, 137, 188,
    241, 254
Castle Bromwich 27, 165
CB's (US Army Construction Battalions)
    92, 139, 193, 237, 256, 318
Chartered Institute for Archaeologists
    (CIfA) 152
Chiang Kai-Shek 92
Churchill, Sir Winston British Prime
    Minister 118
    at the Potsdam Conference 71–3
    instructions for the burial of RAF
    Spitfires in Burma 72–3
    consulted by Clement Atlee
    regarding the Burma Spitfires
    268–70
Clark, Dr Roger 41, 68, 105–08, 110,
    147, 158, 163, 165, 180, 192,
    203, 205, 231, 257, 288
Claude, Grahame-White Flying School 51
Collins Foundation B17 Flying Fortress 45
Conspiracy Theory, Amber Room 310
    Atlantis 98
    Knights Templar 307

Nazi Gold Train 310–11
Oak Island Money Pit 305–08
Rommel's Gold 310
Yamashita's Gold 310–11
Coombe, Stanley, principal witness
    112–13, 122–3, 126–8, 141, 163,
    178–9, 183, 186–91, 195, 197,
    200, 204, 208, 229, 231, 233,
    253, 257–8, 260, 277
Coward, Sir Noel 155, 173, 298
Cox, Sebastian 38, 117, 159, 239
Cribbins, Bernard 201
Cundall, David 18, 22, 26, 34–47, 53, 59,
    62, 68–70, 77–9, 82–5, 92, 94,
    99, 101–05, 107–08, 110–13,
    115–17, 122–3, 129–31, 133–8,
    140–4, 146–53, 158–65, 170,
    178–9, 181, 183–93, 197–200,
    203–05, 207–09, 216, 218–22,
    225–6, 228–32, 235–42, 245,
    247–50, 253–60, 262–3, 271–8,
    280–7, 289–91, 294, 300–01,
    305, 307–09, 312, 315

Dhammazedi Bell 282
Dome of the Rock 91, 227

Eckersley, Fergus, 2nd Secretary British
    Embassy Yangon 59–60, 129
England, Mr E.C. pioneer aviator in
    Burma 51–3

First of the Few (film) 21
Fleming, Ian 156–7, 297–9
Flight (magazine) 51
FlyPast (magazine) 25, 41, 112, 123

Galland, Adolf Luftwaffe general 118
Geofizz Ltd 288–9, 308
George VI, King 74, 245
Greater-Asian Co-Prosperity Sphere 55
Grey Wolf: The Escape of Adolf Hitler (book
    and film) 279

Hall, Robert 171
Haram al-Sharif 91, 211–12
Hatcher, Michael, Treasure hunter
    282–91

Introduced to David Cundall by
        Keith Win 282
    childhood 283
    Tek Sing porcelain 284
    Geldermalsen controversy 285
Hawker Hurricane 22, 24, 36, 86, 118,
        289
Hedges, Matthew, deputy British
        Ambassador to Myanmar 2013
        129–30
Hennell, Thomas 255
Heritage Daily 47, 93
Herzog, Werner 229
Heyn, Andrew, British Ambassador to
        Myanmar 2013 133
Hirohito, Japanese Emperor 169
History Channel 93
    Curse of Oak Island 306
    Hunting Hitler 165
HMS *Victory* 1744 146, 171
Hoare, Colonel Michael 'Mad Mike'
        276–7
Holly Bush Public House 121
Hovath, Meghan 98, 105, 110–13
Htoo Htoo Zaw 56, 67, 130, 235, 239,
        260
Hunt, Isabel 59, 68, 145–6, 149–53
Hunting Hitler (TV Series) 165, 311

Imperial War Museum, Duxford 117
Imperial War Museum, Lambeth 139,
        145–6, 171, 189, 193, 223, 263
Indian Air Force, 8 Squadron IAF 115
Institute for Archaeologists (IfA),
        see Chartered Institute for
        Archaeologists

JCB Ltd 17–18, 35, 93, 180, 189, 203–05,
        207, 209, 217, 264, 315
Juvelius, Walter Henrik, Finnish librarian
        and mystic 49–50, 96
    side-lined by Captain Parker 226
    contracts malaria 226

Karen, ethnic group in Burma/Myanmar
        29, 43,
    theory Spitfires were buried as
        payment to 72, 74, 115, 117,

        121, 140–1, 156, 160, 170,
        238–9, 266
Keane, Fergal 140, 223–5
Kennedy, Maeve, Culture Correspondent
        for the *Guardian* 170
Key Publishing Historic Aviation Forum
        25, 197, 219, 226, 249, 261–2,
        264
Khin Nyunt Brigadier-General 42,
    meets Keith Win 275
    arrested and imprisoned for
        corruption 287
Kidd, Captain William 305–06
Kipling, Rudyard 27, 67, 132, 155
Kohima Epitaph 133, 197, 200
Kislyi, Victor, CEO of Wargaming.net 146,
        148, 300
Ko Ko, Lieutenant General, Home Affairs
        Minister 235–6

Lapu Lapu, Chief 53
Leeds University 41, 59, 68, 78, 105, 111,
        145–8, 271, 285, 308
Lend-Lease, wartime US/UK supply
        agreement 24, 75, 165
Loftus, Professor Elizabeth 259–60, 312
Longhurst, Gavin 216, 219–22, 224, 230
Lusher, Adam, journalist at *The Telegraph*
        37, 68

MacArthur, General Douglas 34
Machado, Manny 18, 130, 180, 258
Magellan, Ferdinand 53
Main, Lieutenant Colonel Tony 245
Mallory, Thomas, author of *Morte d'Arthur*
        103
Mannucci, Mark, Room 608 Productions
        70, 101, 105, 164, 178, 183,
        198, 230, 271, 273, 309
Merritt, Andy 192, 257
Mile115 Café 61
Moore, Noel Temple, British consul
        Jerusalem 211–12
Mountbatten, Lord Louis, 1st Earl
        Mountbatten of Burma 30, 71,
        73–6, 88, 115, 140, 156, 167,
        170, 175–6, 257, 259, 269, 298

Myitkyina 100, 114, 130–1, 185–7, 228,
    238, 241, 245, 247–9, 263, 312

Nagatani, Patrick Ryoichi 320–1
Nang Phyu Phyu Aye 61
Nash, Frazer 136–7, 144–5, 170, 185,
    187, 218, 220–1, 224
National League for Democracy 33, 105
Nay Pyi Taw (City of the Kings) 32, 57–9,
    61, 80–2, 85, 129, 141, 147, 216,
    293
Nennius, British chronicler and monk 103
Ngway Kyar Yan Monastery 294
Niven, Lt Col David 21, 297

Obama, Barack 33
Operation Merlin 169, 269, 298
Operation Zipper 42, 75, 126, 156, 189
Orwell, George (Eric Blair) 55, 97, 224,
    246

Park Royal Hotel 84, 177, 180, 185, 188,
    192, 209, 215, 217, 220, 223,
    228
Park, Sir Keith 30, 73–76, 101, 256
Parker, Captain Montagu Brownlow
    49–50, 91–2, 95–6, 210, 214,
    226–7, 250, 295–6
Pearce, Jim, warbird finder and importer
    22–4, 26, 41, 110, 123, 144, 151,
    193, 247, 249, 263–4, 274–5,
    277–8, 280, 306, 312
Peterson, Magnus 280
Pe Win 180
Pilot (magazine) 152
Plug Street Project 149, 195, 233
Poe Poe, STP family monk 57, 194, 204
Prome Road 27, 31, 90, 134, 138, 181–2,
    193, 229, 233, 245, 249, 257–8
Protection of Military Remains Act 35,
    94, 146, 275

Raffles Hotel 155
Room 608 Productions 17, 69–70, 92, 94,
    98, 102, 104, 129, 158, 165, 183,
    189–90, 200, 215–17, 236–7,
    239, 272–3, 276, 280–2, 285,
    289–90, 315

Royal Air Force (RAF)
    Burma Communications Squadron
        88
    41 Embarkation Unit 139, 189
    67 Squadron 235
    82 Squadron 87
    110 (Hyderabad) Squadron 87
    133 Eagle Squadron 133
    194 (Transport) Squadron 139
    211 Squadron 196
    267 Squadron 124
    273 Squadron 27–8, 84, 116, 189,
        276, 298
    355 Squadron 88
    357 Special Duties Squadron 89
    603 Squadron 23
    607 County of Durham Squadron
        115
    608 Squadron 140
    610 Squadron 196
    RAF Bentley Priory 118
    RAF Mingaladon (aka Mingladon)
        26–7, 37, 87–9, 99, 103, 113,
        115–16, 138, 181, 190–3, 203,
        207, 229, 232, 234–5, 237, 245,
        254, 259, 264, 276, 285, 298,
        301, 313

Sagan, Carl 304
Saunders, Andy 219, 248
Scott, Rod 46, 137, 139, 149, 158, 163,
    165, 177–80, 187–90, 192, 195,
    200, 203–06, 217, 220, 225,
    232–3, 235, 238, 257
Seabees, US Navy Engineers 18, 92, 139,
    144, 179, 193, 237, 277, 306
Serviço Aéreo S.A. (SonAir) 33
Shwedagon Pagoda 27, 32, 52, 57–8, 81,
    282, 298, 315
Shwe Taung Por (STP) 18, 56, 59, 129,
    130–1, 177–8, 180–1, 186–8, 203,
    207, 216, 230, 237–41, 257, 260
Shwe Win, translator and former political
    prisoner 242–4
Singapore 54, 68, 78–9, 85, 123, 126,
    154–6, 166, 178, 180, 189, 286
Singapore Cricket Club 154–5
Soe Maung 61–2, 69, 82–3, 85

South East Asia Command (SEAC) 31, 65, 72, 74–5, 88, 90, 101, 156, 161, 168, 175–6, 209, 255, 263

Spaight, Tracy 34, 53, 67, 77, 92, 101–02, 104–05, 111, 117, 122, 124, 129–30, 133, 139, 145, 158, 176, 180, 185, 203, 207, 215, 220, 228, 235, 237, 242, 247, 262, 271, 288, 300, 304

Special Operations Executive (SOE) 72, 154–5, 157, 166, 255, 266, 297–8

Springate, Nicholas, BBC producer/Far East specialist 222, 224–5

State Peace and Development Council (SPDC)
    internal coup against Prime Minister Khin Nyunt 287
    2007 crackdown 291–3

Tatmadaw 134, 181, 183, 235, 286

Taukkyan CWGC Cemetery 131–3, 195–7

Tay Za, David Cundle's agent in Burma 285–6

Than Shwe 80, 275, 287, 293

Thein Sein 32, 37, 39, 59,

Tin Ma (Auntie) Latt 56–7, 62, 82–3, 85, 200, 209, 217, 221, 230, 236, 238–9, 240, 245

Verne, Jules 54

Vincent, Louis-Hugues 95–6, 226, 295–6

Waikzawtayon Monastery 244

Walton, Sir William (composer of Spitfire Prelude) 21

Wargaming.net 37–8, 40, 44, 70, 98, 100–01, 104, 131, 136–7, 141–2, 146, 148–9, 152–3, 177, 180, 188, 216, 218, 220–1, 225, 228, 238–40, 248, 253–4, 257, 276–7, 288, 300, 305, 308, 313

Warren, General Sir Charles 210–14

Watt, Nicholas 32

Weale, Malcolm 43, 99, 272, 288–91, 308

Wilhelm II, Kaiser 91

Williams, Gerrard 278–80

Wills, Willie, SOE Operator, SIS Liaison Officer (author) 27, 64, 71, 89, 154, 166, 266, 297–9

Windrush Scandal 97

Win, Keith 68, 123, 272, 274–6, 282, 301

Wong, Edward 'Ed', Singaporean businessman 282–3